GLOBAL CATHOLICISM

Portrait of a World Church

The Catholic Church Today

A three volume profile and reflection on the contemporary reality of the Catholic Church in the United States and around the world.

Bryan T. Froehle, Series Director
Mary L. Gautier, Series Editor

Center for Applied Research in the Apostolate
Georgetown University

I: CATHOLICISM USA
A Portrait of the Catholic Church in the United States

II: GLOBAL CATHOLICISM
Portrait of a World Church

III: CHALLENGES AND OPPORTUNITIES
Catholicism in the Twenty-First Century

GLOBAL CATHOLICISM

Portrait of a World Church

Center for Applied Research in the Apostolate
Georgetown University

Bryan T. Froehle
Mary L. Gautier

ORBIS BOOKS

Maryknoll, New York 10545

Copyright © 2003 by the Center for Applied Research in the Apostolate (CARA) at Georgetown University.

Published by Orbis Books, Maryknoll, New York, U.S.A.

Manufactured in the United States of America.

Library of Congress Cataloging-in-Publication Data

Froehle, Bryan.
   Global Catholicism: portrait of a world church / Bryan T. Froehle, Mary L. Gautier.
      p.   cm.
"Center for Applied Research in the Apostolate, Georgetown University."

Includes bibliographical references and index.
   ISBN 1-57075-375-X (pbk.)
   1. Catholic Church–Statistics. 2. Ecclesiastical
geography–Statistics. I. Gautier, Mary, 1952- II. Center for Applied
Research in the Apostolate (U.S.) III. Title.
   BX946 .F76 2003
                                                            2002155092

In pastoral care, sufficient use must be made not only of theological principles, but also the findings of the secular sciences, especially of psychology and sociology, so that the faithful may be brought to a more accurate and mature life of faith.

—*Gaudium et Spes*, n.62
(Decree of the Second Vatican Council on the Pastoral Constitution of the Church in the Modern World)

Contents

List of Tables and Figures xi

Foreword xv

TRENDS

1: Catholic Population Worldwide **1**
    World Population Growth 1
    Catholic Population Growth 4
    Current Catholic Population Dynamics 7
    A Composite Global Portrait 9
2: Catholic Institutions **13**
    Catholic Institutional Structures 13
    Institutional Distribution and Growth 21
    Contrasting Relative "Installed Capacity" 22
    Composite Regional Portraits 24
3: Church Personnel **27**
    New Patterns 27
    Bishops 29
    Growth and Distribution of Priests Worldwide 31
    Seminarians and Priestly Ordinations 35
    Permanent Deacons 38
    Men Religious 41
    Women Religious 42
    A Composite Global Portrait 43

REGIONS

4: Africa **45**
    Overview 45
    Population 46
    Institutions 47
    Personnel 49
    Regions of Africa 50
    North Africa 52
    West Africa 53
    Central Africa 56
    Southern Africa 58

The Indian Ocean 60
East Africa 61

5: America **67**
Overview 67
Population 71
Institutions 72
Personnel 73
Regions 74
North America 75
Caribbean 78
Mesoamerica 80
South America 81

6: Asia **85**
Overview 85
Population 86
Institutions 87
Personnel 88
Regions 89
Western Asia 90
South Asia 93
Southeast Asia 94
Northeast Asia 96

7: Europe **101**
Overview 101
Population 102
Institutions 103
Personnel 104
Regions 105
Northwestern Europe 107
Southwestern Europe 109
Eastern Europe 111

8: Oceania **115**
Overview 115
Population 116
Institutions 117
Personnel 118
A Diverse Region 120

9: Looking to the Future **127**
    Contrasts by Continent 127
    The Church and the World Economic Divide 129
    From Christendom to Pluralism 131
    A Look Back to Look Forward 133

APPENDICES

I: Statistical Sources and Chapter Notes **137**
II: Definitions of Selected Terms **145**
III: Country and Territory Listings **151**
IV: Country and Territory Profiles **157**

Bibliography **273**

Index **281**

List of Tables and Figures

1: Catholic Population Worldwide
Table 1.1   World Population: 1900, 1950, and 2000 1
Figure 1.1 World Population: 1900-2000 2
Table 1.2   Land Mass and Population Distribution:
            1900, 1950, and 2000 3
Table 1.3   Countries of the World: 1950-2000 4
Table 1.4   Catholic Population: 1900, 1950, and 2000 5
Figure 1.2 Catholic Population Change through 20th Century 5
Table 1.5   Catholic and Total Christian Population: 1900 and 2000 . 6
Table 1.6   Number of Countries by Proportion Catholic: 2000 7
Table 1.7   Population Distribution and Sacramental Dynamics: 2000   9
Table 1.8   Distribution of Catholic Population, by Region: 2000 . . . 10

2: Catholic Institutions
Table 2.1   Selected Catholic Institutions: 1950, 1975, and 2000 . . . 14
Table 2.2   Selected Ecclesiastical Territories: 1975 and 2000 16
Table 2.3   Pastoral Centers: 1975 and 2000 17
Table 2.4   Selected Catholic Educational Institutions:
            1975 and 2000 18
Table 2.5   Catholic Universities: 2000 18
Table 2.6   Selected Catholic Charitable Institutions: 2000 20
Table 2.7   Catholic and Institutional Distribution:
            1975 and 2000 21
Table 2.8   Selected Church Institutions: 2000 22
Table 2.9   Ecclesiastical Territories and Parishes:
            1975 and 2000 23
Figure 2.1 Catholics per Parish: 1950-2000 24
Table 2.10 Distribution of Selected Church Institutions,
            by Region: 2000 25

3: Church Personnel
Table 3.1   Bishops, Archbishops, and Cardinals: 2000 30
Table 3.2   Catholic Clergy: 1950, 1975, and 2000 31
Table 3.3   Diocesan and Religious Priests: 1950, 1975, and 2000 . . 32
Table 3.4   Catholics per Priest, by Region: 1950, 1975, and 2000 . . 33
Figure 3.1 Shifting Distribution of Priests Worldwide:
            1950-2000 34
Table 3.5   Diocesan and Religious Seminarians: 1950, 1975,
            and 2000 35

Table 3.6   Diocesan Priests and Diocesan Seminarians: 1975
and 2000 36

Table 3.7   Diocesan Priestly Ordinations: 1975 and 2000 37

Table 3.8   Distribution of Diocesan Priests, Seminarians, and
Ordinations: 2000 38

Table 3.9   Permanent Deacons, by Region: 1975 and 2000 39

Figure 3.2   Worldwide Distribution of Deacons: 2000 40

Table 3.10   Men Religious: 2000 41

Figure 3.3   Selected Church Personnel Worldwide: 2000 42

Table 3.11   Women Religious: 2000 43

Table 3.12   Distributions of Selected Church Personnel,
by Region: 2000 44

4: Africa

Table 4.1   Selected Church Population Statistics, Africa:
1975 and 2000 46

Table 4.2   Selected Church Institution Statistics, Africa:
1975 and 2000 48

Table 4.3   Selected Church Personnel Statistics, Africa:
1975 and 2000 50

Table 4.4   Selected Church Statistics, North Africa: 1975 and 2000   52

Table 4.5   Selected Church Statistics, West Africa: 1975 and 2000 . 54

Table 4.6   Five Most Populous Countries in Africa: 2000 55

Table 4.7   Top Fifteen African Countries, by Percent
Catholic: 2000 56

Table 4.8   Selected Church Statistics, Central Africa:
1975 and 2000 57

Table 4.9   Selected Church Statistics, Southern Africa:
1975 and 2000 59

Table 4.10   Selected Church Statistics, Indian Ocean:
1975 and 2000 61

Table 4.11   Selected Church Statistics, East Africa: 1975 and 2000 . 62

Table 4.12   The Catholic Church in Africa, by Region: 2000 65

5: America

Table 5.1   Countries with Populations over 75 Percent Catholic:
2000 68

Table 5.2   The Changing Face of Christianity in Latin America:
2000 70

Table 5.3   Selected Church Population Statistics, America:
1975 and 2000 71

Table 5.4 Selected Church Institution Statistics, America:
1975 and 2000 72
Table 5.5 Selected Church Personnel Statistics, America:
1975 and 2000 74
Table 5.6 Selected Church Statistics, North America:
1975 and 2000 76
Table 5.7 Selected Church Statistics, Caribbean Basin:
1975 and 2000 79
Table 5.8 Selected Church Statistics, Mesoamerica:
1975 and 2000 81
Table 5.9 Selected Church Statistics, South America:
1975 and 2000 82
Table 5.10 The Catholic Church in the Americas, by Region: 2000 . 83

6: Asia
Table 6.1 Selected Church Population Statistics, Asia:
1975 and 2000 86
Table 6.2 Selected Church Institution Statistics, Asia:
1975 and 2000 88
Table 6.3 Selected Church Personnel Statistics, Asia:
1975 and 2000 89
Table 6.4 Selected Church Statistics, Western Asia:
1975 and 2000 91
Table 6.5 Selected Church Statistics, South Asia: 1975 and 2000 .. 93
Table 6.6 Selected Church Statistics, Southeast Asia:
1975 and 2000 95
Table 6.7 Selected Church Statistics, Northeast Asia:
1975 and 2000 97
Table 6.8 The Catholic Church in Asia, by Region: 2000 99

7: Europe
Table 7.1 Selected Church Population Statistics, Europe:
1975 and 2000 103
Table 7.2 Selected Church Institution Statistics, Europe:
1975 and 2000 104
Table 7.3 Selected Church Personnel Statistics, Europe:
1975 and 2000 105
Table 7.4 European Religious Divisions, by Region: 2000 106
Table 7.5 Selected Church Statistics, Northwestern Europe:
1975 and 2000 107
Table 7.6 Selected Church Statistics, Southwestern Europe:
1975 and 2000 110

Table 7.7   Selected Church Statistics, Eastern Europe:
1975 and 2000 112
Table 7.8   The Catholic Church in Europe, by Region: 2000 113

8: Oceania
Table 8.1   Catholic Presence in the Countries of Oceania: 2000 .. 116
Table 8.2   Selected Church Population Statistics, Oceania:
1975 and 2000 116
Table 8.3   Selected Church Institution Statistics, Oceania:
1975 and 2000 118
Table 8.4   Selected Church Personnel Statistics, Oceania:
1975 and 2000 120
Table 8.5   The Catholic Church in Oceania: 1975 and 2000 125

9: Looking to the Future
Table 9.1   The Economic Divide: 2000 130
Figure 9.1   World Distribution of Priests, Seminarians, and
Catholics: 1950 134
Figure 9.2   World Distribution of Priests, Seminarians, and
Catholics: 2000 135

Appendix I: Statistical Sources and Chapter Notes
Table A.1   Number of Countries by Proportion Catholic: 2000 ... 144

Appendix III: Country and Territory Listings
Table A.2   Dioceses (and Other Ecclesiastical Territories),
Parishes, and Priests by Catholic Population 151

Appendix IV: Country and Territory Profiles
Table A.3   Count of Countries and Territories 157
Table A.4   Territories of the World 158

Foreword

CARA was founded following the Second Vatican Council to serve the needs of the Catholic Church by providing high quality social science research. CARA's mission as a national Catholic research center is to conduct quality social science research rather than advocate any particular interpretation or agenda. Thus, this book is specifically a portrait of the Catholic Church worldwide using available statistics along with a context to help readers make sense of those statistics.

In this we follow the path first forged by Rev. Karl Streit, SVD, who prepared the groundbreaking *Atlas Hierarchicus*, published in its most definitive version in 1929. Streit's work is perhaps the most significant inspiration for this work. Over a decade ago, one of us first saw Streit's *magnum opus* in a forgotten corner of a far-away library and dreamed of providing similar information in a more contemporary and accessible form.

Our statistical sources include the official Vatican publications *Annuarium Statisticum Ecclesiae* and *Annuario Pontificio,* both based on the reports sent by the some 2,846 dioceses or similar Church units around the world. We have also utilized statistical summaries published by individual countries, the United Nations, and other international agencies. And we have reviewed and carefully studied a variety of additional statistical and historical sources.

Since 1998 we have computerized international Church statistics going back to 1950, as well as additional material predating that, including Streit's work. Our databases were designed by CARA researchers, programmers, and assistants who diligently entered and cross-checked the data from published sources. Much of this work was created under the leadership of Kristina A. Boylan, D.Phil., for which we are most grateful. Programmers have included Prakit Hirankarn and Guy Angouma.

Cristina L. Aquino helped to coordinate the massive effort required to direct those who assisted in the project. Together with Margaret M. Howard, Ph.D., she also provided key support in personally cross-checking data and preparing some early drafts. William Bole also prepared an initial chapter draft. During the beginning stages, much of the data entry was done by Silvia and Sandra Lara, as well as by Prakit Hirankarn. Toward the end of the process, Georgetown University students Maria Moser and Pat Hurley, recent graduate Adam Dufault, and Rosemary Dirita, JoEllen Windau, and Erin Branch were most helpful in final data entry and fact checking. We would be remiss if we did not mention in particular the role of Jacqueline Baselice as fact checker, a graduate of Boston College and second year student at Georgetown University's Medical School. Her care and enthusiasm will serve her well in her medical career.

Ultimately, acknowledgments go to all our CARA colleagues and collaborators, who have helped us conceptualize our work and have provided vital personal and organizational support from the start.

Finally, we want to acknowledge the leadership, encouragement, and vision of Bishop William B. Friend, the current Chair of CARA's Board of Directors, along with all of CARA's Board Members and Research Advisors. We also acknowledge the patient, yet persistent, guidance and support of our editor at Orbis, Bill Burrows.

We dedicate this book to the Rev. Louis Luzbetak, SVD, CARA's first executive director and an internationally renowned missiologist. We hope the clarity of presentation we have sought will help advance his, and CARA's, vision.

Bryan T. Froehle and Mary L. Gautier
Center for Applied Research in the Apostolate
Georgetown University, August 2002

CHAPTER 1

Catholic Population Worldwide

This book is designed to "paint by numbers" a global portrait of the Catholic Church at the very beginning of the twenty-first century. Any examination of the Catholic Church in a global context at this period in world history must begin with consideration of population change that has so marked recent global history, and this book is no exception. The first chapter introduces Catholic and worldwide population growth on a comparative basis. It presents comparisons by continent and regions within each continent or continental area that will be at the heart of this book.

WORLD POPULATION GROWTH

Perhaps the most distinguishing demographic feature of the twentieth century is the sheer scale of population change. That century saw the greatest increase in global population in human history. Numerous demographic estimates suggest that more people were alive at the end of the twentieth century than the total number of people who had ever previously lived on the planet.

	1900	1950	2000	1900-2000 Change	1950-2000 Change
Africa	107,808,100	191,173,488	789,455,000	632%	313%
America	146,767,800	326,978,316	826,554,000	463%	153%
Asia	956,196,200	1,809,610,197	3,698,043,000	287%	104%
Europe	402,607,550	444,676,076	702,661,000	75%	58%
Oceania	6,246,350	9,892,967	30,566,000	389%	209%
World	1,619,626,000	2,782,331,044	6,047,279,000	273%	117%

Table 1.1 World Population: 1900, 1950, and 2000

During the twentieth century, world population increased at a spectacular rate and its distribution fundamentally shifted away from Europe. In addition, the number of independent countries also grew dramatically. New centers of political power and economic vitality emerged around the globe and developed in increasingly interdependent ways.

Represented graphically, one can observe how the overall growth patterns have shifted between the continents, as well as the scale of human population growth during the twentieth century in general. By the beginning of the twenty-first century, world population exceeded six billion–more than double what it had been 50 years earlier and over three times what it had been a hundred years earlier. The most dramatic growth took place in Africa. The total population of Africa exceeded that of Europe in 2000. Only 50 years before, Europe's population had been more than twice as large as Africa's.

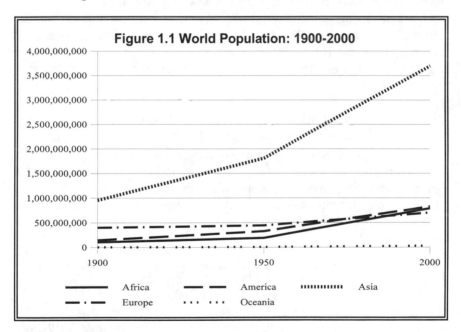

Comparing the relative size of the different continental areas as used in this book offers a sense of scale that is useful in considering population growth on a continental basis. This also allows for contextualizing relative population distribution in terms of the size of a particular continental land mass. Thus, Asia occupies 30 percent of the world's land mass, yet contains 60 percent of the world's population. Compared between the beginning of the twentieth century and its closing, Asia's share of world population changed relatively little. Europe's share of world population, however, dropped by half.

Table 1.2 Land Mass and Population Distribution: 1900, 1950, and 2000				
			Population	
	Land Mass*	**1900**	**1950**	**2000**
Africa	20%	7%	7%	13%
America	28%	9%	12%	14%
Asia	30%	59%	65%	61%
Europe	7%	25%	16%	12%
Oceania	5%	<1%	<1%	1%
World	100%	1,618,897	2,782,331	6,047,279

*Figures for the world land mass exclude Antarctica and Greenland, which comprise 10% and 1% of the world's entire land mass, respectively.

Rapid increases in human population during the twentieth century are matched by the growth in political institutions and sovereign states recognized on a worldwide basis. In 1945, at the conclusion of the Second World War and the beginning of the United Nations, fifty-one countries belonged to this global body, representing almost every sovereign territory then existing. In 2000, the U.N. had 189 member states, and East Timor was set to join the body after a brief transition to independence. The two sovereign states that do not belong to this world body–Switzerland and Vatican City–have permanent observer status.

In short, the second half of the twentieth century saw a rapid expansion of the international system as more than 140 new countries emerged out of Western European and Russian colonialism and a variety of local contexts in Africa, Asia, Oceania, and elsewhere. Africa has the highest percentage of newly independent countries established between 1950 and 2000 as well as the greatest absolute number of new countries. Every continent, however, saw considerable change by the end of the twentieth century.

Of the 192 countries listed in the appendix of this book, just 80, or 42 percent, would have been listed in 1950. These changes in people and in sovereign states are important aspects of demographic change in the twentieth century. They have created a new global environment that likely will define the context for the Church's existence over the twenty-first century.

Table 1.3 Countries of the World: 1950-2000			
	Countries in 1950	Countries Established 1951-2000	World Territories in 2000*	Countries and Territories 2000**
Africa	4	48	5	57
America	22	13	15	50
Asia	25	25	4	54
Europe	28	13	4	45
Oceania	2	13	9	24
World	80	112	27	219

*The 27 territories are those identified for the purposes of this book. They are not the only such territories that could be so identified. Although East Timor was not yet fully independent in 2000, it is grouped among the countries here and in the appendix.
**Selected demographic and Church-related statistics are provided for these countries and territories in the appendix of this book.

CATHOLIC POPULATION GROWTH

During the last half of the twentieth century, increases in Catholic population outpaced the rate of growth in the total worldwide population. Global population increased by 117 percent and Catholic population rose by 139 percent. In general, however, Catholic growth patterns mimic world population growth patterns. That is, Africa leads Catholic population growth and Europe lags behind, just as is the case with world population growth overall. What varies is the pace of growth.

Catholic population in Africa grew 708 percent while the total African population increased 313 percent. In Asia, Catholic population rose 278 percent, compared to overall population growth of 104 percent. The only region where Catholic population growth rates lagged behind total population growth rates was in Europe, where the population increased by a relatively modest 58 percent while Catholics increased by just 32 percent.

Growth rates are only part of the picture of Catholic population shifts during the last 50 years of the twentieth century. While the growth in Africa and Asia is steep, the total number of Catholics in those countries started small and remains a relatively small proportion in spite of the large percentage increases. By the beginning of the twenty-first century, Europe still had 27 percent of the world's Catholics, a higher proportion than in Africa and Asia combined. As a result, although Catholic population growth

Table 1.4 Catholic Population: 1900, 1950, and 2000				
	1900	1950	2000	1900-2000 Change	1950-2000 Change
Africa	1,909,812	16,085,541	130,018,400	6,708%	708%
America	71,700,770	180,763,515	519,391,300	624%	187%
Asia	11,162,799	28,420,359	107,302,000	861%	278%
Europe	180,722,280	211,826,147	280,144,200	55%	32%
Oceania	1,052,096	219,083	8,202,200	680%	3,644%
World	266,547,757	437,314,645	1,045,058,100	292%	139%

rates for Europe are much smaller than those for Asia (32 percent compared to 278 percent), the overall magnitude of growth in absolute numbers is relatively small. Relatively low percentage increases of Catholics in Europe between 1950 and 2000 represent an increase of nearly 70 million Catholics. The absolute increase in Catholic population in Asia during the same period was approximately 80 million.

As the graph below suggests, perhaps the greatest shift in Catholic population over the twentieth century occurred between the two most Christian continental areas, the Americas and Europe. In the Americas, the Catholic growth rate over the last half of the twentieth century was 187 percent, well above the world average of 139 percent. In 1950, however, the Americas had 41 percent of the world's Catholics, more than the combined

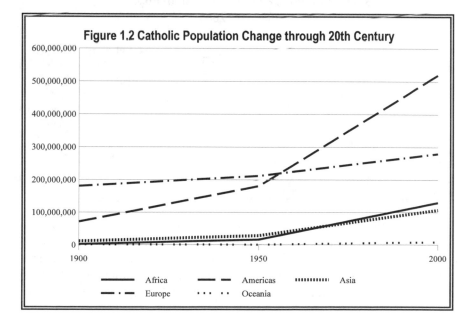

Figure 1.2 Catholic Population Change through 20th Century

proportion for Africa, Asia, and Oceania. By 2000, that proportion had become even larger, and the Americas contained half of all Catholics in the world. In 1950, half of the world's Catholics were in Europe.

Europe's relative decline as a center of Catholic population in the last half of the twentieth century has been swift and decisive. In 1900, Europe had 68 percent of the world's Catholics. The Americas contained 27 percent of the world's Catholics. A hundred years later, Europe had effectively changed positions with the Americas and contained the same proportion of the world's Catholics, 27 percent, that had been in the Americas at the beginning of the twentieth century.

Taken together, Europe and the Americas have much in common in terms of Catholic presence. Europe and the Americas have a preponderant proportion of the world's Catholic population. Put another way, Catholicism is a dominant religion in both continental areas. Church statistics for the year 2000 indicate that the Americas are 63 percent Catholic and Europe is 41 percent Catholic.

Unlike the situation in Africa, Asia, or Oceania, Catholics also make up the majority of Christians in Europe and the Americas. Available estimates of the numbers of Catholics and Christians overall suggest that approximately 60 percent of Christian Europeans are Catholic and perhaps as many as 72 percent of all Christians in the Americas are Catholic.

Table 1.5 Catholic and Total Christian Population: 1900 and 2000*

	Catholics		All Christians		Christians Who Are Catholic	
	1900	2000	1900	2000	1900	2000
Africa	1,889	120,281	9,917	360,006	19%	33%
America	71,701	534,736	140,810	745,805	51%	72%
Asia	11,407	111,981	83,422	397,071	14%	28%
Europe	180,460	284,448	318,976	474,885	57%	60%
Oceania	1,052	8,080	1,793	24,647	22%	33%
World	266,509	1,059,526	557,918	2,002,414	48%	53%

*Population figures are given in thousands.

The situation is different elsewhere. Catholics comprise about 16 percent of all Africans and 33 percent of all Christian Africans. Only 3 percent of all Asians are Catholic, and just 28 percent of Asian Christians are Catholic. In sparsely populated Oceania, Catholics make up about 26 percent of the population. However, this represents only about 1 percent of the world's Catholics. As in Africa, about one in three Christians in Oceania are Catholic.

Another way to consider the presence of Catholicism throughout the world is by reviewing the proportion of the Catholic population on a country by country basis. While it may be difficult to define a "Catholic country," it is a relatively straightforward matter to calculate what proportion of countries in each continent have a population more than four-fifths Catholic. A total of 33 countries, 17 percent of all countries, have populations with such large Catholic majorities. They may be contrasted to the 58 countries, about 30 percent, that have a Catholic population of less than 3 percent, and indeed often less than 1 percent. A similar proportion of countries have a population of between 3 and 20 percent Catholic.

Not surprisingly, more than half of the countries in the Americas (60 percent) and well more than a third of countries in Europe (42 percent) have populations more than three-fifths Catholic. In contrast, well over half of all Asian countries (64 percent) have populations less than 3 percent Catholic. Outside of Europe and the Americas, the typical situation in which the Church finds itself is not one where Catholics are a dominant or majority presence but rather one where Catholics are a significant minority.

Table 1.6 Number of Countries by Proportion Catholic: 2000						
	< 3%	3-20%	21-40%	41-60%	61-80%	81-100%	Total
Africa	15	16	10	7	1	4	53
America	0	7	3	4	5	16	35
Asia	29	13	0	1	0	2	45
Europe	13	9	2	2	8	11	45
Oceania	1	7	3	3	0	0	14
World	58	52	18	17	14	33	192

CURRENT CATHOLIC POPULATION DYNAMICS

General human population dynamics are the result of changing proportions and frequencies of births and deaths and, for particular subpopulations, of migration patterns. For Catholic population dynamics, the event most analogous to birth is baptism, since that single event permanently marks membership in the Church.

Church statistics distinguish "infant" baptisms, defined as those under age seven, from baptisms of those age seven or over. Because baptism and birth are each a single event, and because most infant baptisms tend to occur within the first year of birth, comparing the worldwide distribution of infant baptism with the worldwide distribution of births offers some insight into the likely longer-term dynamics of Catholic population distribution.

Baptisms of those that are age seven or over may be more likely to be a result of conversion rather than births to Catholic parents. While this is not always the case, it is useful to note that these baptisms are much more likely to occur in some parts of the world than others. Almost half of all these baptisms, for example, take place in Africa, even though this continent has only an eighth of the world Catholic population. About 85 percent of all baptisms are of infants. However, only 63 percent of baptisms in Africa are infant baptisms. Not surprisingly, the Americas and Europe, with a large and well-established Catholic Church, show the highest percentage of infant baptisms, 91 and 96 percent, respectively.

In general, the distribution of all baptisms–that is, those who joined the Church in the year 2000–as compared to all Catholics is higher in some continents and lower in others. These figures suggest that the proportion of Catholics who live in America, Asia, and Africa is likely to continue to increase while the proportion in Europe is likely to continue to decline.

Patterns in the reception of another sacrament of initiation, confirmation, offer additional analytical value. Those who are confirmed may be more likely than those who are baptized, but not confirmed, to be tied to a regular practice of the faith. They may also be more likely to see to it that whatever children they may have are baptized within the Catholic Church. Statistics from Africa show that the proportion of confirmations relative to baptisms is lower, while figures from Europe show the reverse. As a result, one may conclude that baptized Europeans are probably more likely than those in other continents to also be confirmed. However, because most Catholics who are confirmed receive the sacrament well after baptism, figures for confirmations in 2000 cannot be compared directly to baptisms for the same year since they refer to different people. Significant differences in the relative reception of the sacrament worldwide may also reflect contrasting levels of the Church's institutional presence or even access to a bishop, since bishops are the ordinary ministers of this sacrament.

Finally, the celebration of marriage within the Catholic Church may also signify a greater level of practice and commitment. In addition, the proportion of marriages celebrated between a Catholic and a non-Catholic within the Church may say something about the relationship of the Catholic community to the larger population as well as a measure of "practical ecumenism" that Catholics experience in their family life. Interestingly, such mixed marriages are less likely to take place in continents where the

Catholic presence is weakest, such as Africa or Asia. They are most likely to take place in North America.

Here as elsewhere, considerable caution is warranted. Proportions of those who are married within the Church do not represent the same people who were baptized or confirmed in the year 2000–these sacraments typically take place at other times in a person's life. Further, the average age of marriage may be very different in various parts of the world, reflecting contrasting demographic and ecclesiastical realities–and often cultural, economic, and legal ones as well. Nonetheless, patterns in Catholic sacramental receptions help nuance interpretation of the figures representing the worldwide distribution of Catholics.

Table 1.7 Population Distribution and Sacramental Dynamics: 2000						
	Africa	**America**	**Asia**	**Europe**	**Oceania**	**Total**
World Population	13%	14%	61%	12%	1%	100%
Catholic Population	12%	50%	10%	27%	1%	100%
World Births that year	23%	12%	61%	4%	<1%	100%
Catholic Baptisms under 7 years old	14%	55%	14%	16%	1%	100%
Catholic Baptisms over 7 years old	48%	31%	16%	4%	1%	100%
All Baptisms	19%	51%	15%	14%	<1%	100%
Confirmations	16%	48%	13%	22%	1%	100%
All Marriages	10%	43%	19%	28%	1%	100%
Catholic-non-Catholic Marriages	14%	37%	20%	24%	4%	100%

A COMPOSITE GLOBAL PORTRAIT

The Catholic experience on each continent presents a composite picture of often quite complex local situations that may well be more dissimilar than similar compared to other regions within the same continent. The regional chapters that follow the first three chapters of this book therefore enter into considerable depth for each of the world regions identified in this book. These regions were chosen because they are relatively homogeneous from a cultural point of view and represent commonly grouped countries and territories. They were not selected to represent similarly sized groupings of land mass or population. For country-specific information beyond the text, the appendix provides a statistical profile for each country or territory identified in this book.

Table 1.8 Distribution of Catholic Population, by Region: 2000					
	World Population	% of World Catholic Population	% Catholic in Each Region	% of World Catholic Baptisms*	Infants Baptized Catholic**
Africa Total	13%	12%	16%	19%	7%
Central	2%	4%	45%	5%	10%
East	4%	4%	17%	6%	8%
Indian Ocean	<1%	<1%	27%	1%	18%
North	2%	<1%	<1%	<1%	<1%
Southern	2%	2%	18%	2%	5%
West	4%	3%	12%	5%	5%
America Total	14%	50%	63%	51%	54%
Caribbean	1%	2%	67%	2%	43%
Mesoamerica	2%	11%	90%	16%	75%
North	5%	7%	25%	7%	27%
South	6%	28%	87%	27%	60%
Asia Total	61%	10%	3%	15%	3%
Northeast	26%	1%	<1%	1%	<1%
South	22%	2%	1%	2%	1%
Southeast	9%	7%	15%	11%	14%
Western	5%	<1%	1%	0%	<1%
Europe Total	12%	27%	40%	14%	44%
Eastern	5%	7%	23%	4%	34%
Northwestern	4%	10%	40%	5%	35%
Southwestern	2%	10%	96%	5%	88%
Oceania Total	1%	1%	27%	1%	23%

*Refers to all baptisms, both infants and adults.
**An estimate calculated by dividing the number of infant baptisms by the estimated total number of births for the year 2000.

With the exception of Africa and Asia, most continents have a proportion of Catholics much larger or much smaller than the overall proportion of Catholics within the world's population. In most regions, Catholics are neither a majority nor a statistically insignificant minority. In fact, of the regions listed above, counting the continental area of Oceania as a single region, four have populations more than 50 percent Catholic, and four have populations with 1 percent or fewer Catholics. Five regions have populations between 10 percent Catholic and under 25 percent Catholic. Five other regions vary from 25 percent Catholic to near Catholic majorities.

The pages that follow will further present this composite global portrait of Catholic life around the world, in both continental and regional perspectives, and particularly in terms of the Catholic Church's internal institutional and personnel dynamics. Given the uniqueness of regions within each continent, as well as among specific countries, the picture presented in the continent-specific chapters distinguishes the broad characteristics and experiences of each region in terms of the same three perspectives of Catholic people, institutions, and personnel.

CHAPTER 2

Catholic Institutions

As noted in Chapter 1, the Catholic population in the world more than doubled between 1950 and 2000, and in fact grew faster than world population during the same period. This chapter explores how Church institutions shifted and changed alongside the Catholic population. It will consider institutional structures within Catholicism overall, with particular attention to the distinctions between the Eastern Churches and the Western Church, dioceses and structures similar to dioceses, parishes and structures similar to parishes, educational institutions and charitable institutions. It will also present information on the changing distribution and growth patterns of Catholic institutional life around the world, as well as the distribution of these institutions relative to the numbers of Catholics or relative to other institutions. Finally, the chapter will give a composite picture of Catholic institutional life on a worldwide regional basis.

CATHOLIC INSTITUTIONAL STRUCTURES

The key institution in Catholic life worldwide is the diocese. The diocese, or similiar ecclesiastical entities such as the eparchy in the Eastern Catholic Church, is the basis for organizing local Church life. It is, in fact, the "local Church" in the sense that it is organized under a bishop who serves as a successor to the apostles who governed the early Church.

Parishes pertain to a diocese, or an analogous level of Church life in exceptional or mission contexts, and are not in themselves independent entities. Consistent with the role of the bishop (who is sometimes referred to by other titles, such as eparch in the case of the Eastern Catholic Churches), the parishes and other pastoral centers or worship sites are ultimately expressions of the entire local Church and are therefore under the authority of the bishop.

Each local church–that is, each diocese or equivalent ecclesiastical territory–typically contains a number of educational and charitable institutions founded and operated under Catholic auspices in communion with the diocesan bishop and as a response to local needs and circumstances. However, these educational and charitable institutions are often themselves founded and operated outside formal diocesan structures, frequently by separate institutes of men and women religious.

The table below lists the numbers of ecclesiastical territories, parishes, educational and charitable institutions in 1950, 1975, and 2000, along with a number of other measures that help contextualize those figures. The table also distinguishes dioceses from apostolic vicariates, prefectures, administrations, and territorial prelatures. While the histories of these non-diocesan designations are different, they share many things in common. In each case, the term "apostolic" implies that the area is under the direct care of the successor to Peter, and therefore administered through the Vatican Congregation *Propaganda Fide* (Latin for "growing the faith"). And in most cases, they are established in mission areas as an antecedent to formal diocesan structures.

Table 2.1 Selected Catholic Institutions: 1950, 1975, and 2000			
	1950	**1975**	**2000**
Catholic Population	439,292,000	709,558,000	1,045,058,000
Ecclesiastical Territories	1,900	2,342	2,846
% Arch/dioceses or Arch/eparchies	75%	88%	91%
% Apostolic Vicariates	12%	3%	3%
% Apostolic Prefectures	7%	2%	<1%
% Apostolic Administrations	<1%	<1%	<1%
% Territorial Prelatures	na	4%	2%
Parishes	178,233	200,116	218,196
Parishes per Territory	94	85	77
Educational Institutions	112,910	106,966	125,010
Charitable Institutions	na	na	103,417

Since 1950, the number of ecclesiastical territories has grown by a little over 50 percent. Perhaps most interesting, however, only 75 percent of all ecclesiastical territories worldwide in 1950 were dioceses or at the stage of Church life to which the term "diocese" refers. By 2000, that percentage had increased to 91 percent, a result of the sheer growth in the number of dioceses coupled with absolute declines in the number of vicariates and the other forms of ecclesiastical territories generally first planted when a local Catholic community is young or just beginning to lay roots.

Dioceses are ordinarily part of an ecclesiastical province which is headed by an archdiocese, or "chief" diocese of the province. This is therefore termed a "metropolitan archdiocese" and the dioceses in its province "suffragan" dioceses. Exceptions are chiefly in those areas where such a structure cannot function due to the stage of development of the local Church, historical circumstances, or the current state of Church-state relations. For example, many of the Catholic dioceses in Scandinavia are established as immediately subject to the Bishop of Rome. Because those dioceses were re-established centuries after the Reformation, they are quite small and re-establishment of the full provincial system impractical.

Eparchies and Dioceses

Most of the 2,846 ecclesiastical territories of the Catholic Church in 2000 pertain to the Western Church. However, the Western Church is simply one among many different Churches that comprise the Catholic Church worldwide. In this case, it celebrates the Eucharist following the Latin Rite and follows a distinct set of practices and norms, including a code of Church laws (Canon Law) uniquely designed for it. A total of 12 distinct Churches are separately organized and follow one of the Eastern Rites in worship, as well as the Code of Canons for the Eastern Churches. Each of these Churches is headed by a patriarch and has a structure that parallels those of the other Churches. While some of these Churches are in Eastern Europe or India, most are based in the Middle East.

Eparchies are concentrated in Asia, as are patriarchates. Outside of Asia, there is one patriarchate in Africa and two in Europe. Growth has occurred almost exclusively through natural increase. Thus, while the number of dioceses of the Western Church has grown rapidly and spans the globe, the number of eparchies of the Eastern Churches has increased relatively more slowly. The greatest number of new eparchies have been established in places that have attracted immigration from lands where the Eastern Churches have historically been centered. Thus, new eparchies have been created in certain cities in the Americas, Oceania (particularly Australia), and Europe to provide more effective pastoral care for these Church communities. Such immigration has continued throughout the twentieth century as a result of political unrest, economic challenges, and religious discrimination.

Mission Status

Throughout the history of the Catholic Church, missionary expansion has taken many institutional forms. It was only in about 1500 that the Church began to grow by planting diocesan structures and through the labor of specifically missionary-oriented religious orders. Before that time, Catholic expansion in Northern Europe had been largely through the foundation of monasteries, which over time came to establish and govern parishes. Many of the leaders of these monasteries functioned as bishops and to this day there are a number of abbot-bishops. Territorial abbacies are a type of ecclesiastical territory still found in Europe and more recently established in a few other places around the world.

Over the last quarter of the twentieth century, the number of territorial abbacies declined, while other missionary-oriented ecclesiatical territories grew only modestly.

Table 2.2 Selected Ecclesiastical Territories: 1975-2000*							
		Africa	Americas	Asia	Europe	Oceania	World
Territorial	1975	1	4	0	13	1	19
Abbacies	2000	0	2	0	11	0	13
		-100%	-50%	0%	-15%	-100%	-32%
Territorial	1975	1	82	12	6	0	101
Prelatures	2000	0	39	6	6	0	51
		-100%	-52%	-50%	0%	0%	-50%
Apostolic	1975	17	12	7	0	0	36
Prefectures	2000	7	2	6	0	1	16
		-59%	-83%	-14%	0%	100%	-56%
Apostolic	1975	15	39	17	3	1	75
Vicariates	2000	15	42	18	1	0	76
		0%	8%	6%	-67%	-100%	1%
Apostolic	1975	2	2	1	7	0	12
Administrations	2000	1	0	5	7	0	13
		-50%	-100%	400%	0%	0%	8%
Independent	1975	0	0	2	0	1	3
Missions	2000	1	2	5	1	2	11
		100%	200%	150%	100%	100%	267%
*The percent change between 1975 and 2000 is given in the shaded areas.							

Parishes and Pastoral Centers

The Catholic Church defines a parish as a "definitive community of the Christian faithful established on a stable basis within a particular Church," in the words of the Code of Canon Law for the Western Church. Parishes cannot be created where priests, financial resources, or other aspects critical for parish life are missing. The term "pastoral center" includes parishes and other pastoral settings not established as parishes, including mission stations and chapels within a parish.

Many parts of the world, especially Africa and Asia, have large numbers of "pastoral centers" not formally established as parishes. Instead, a priest or team of priests visits these centers at regular intervals. In Africa, the number of such mission stations is roughly six times the number of parishes and most do not have resident priests. In Africa, only 218 of the 69,074 mission stations have a resident priest. However, nearly all of the 32 mission stations in Europe have a resident priest.

The table that follows shows that both parishes and missions have grown at approximately the same pace in Africa, but the number of missions is much larger. In the rest of the world, the number of missions has declined and trends regarding other pastoral centers are more varied.

Table 2.3 Pastoral Centers: 1975 and 2000*							
		Africa	**America**	**Asia**	**Europe**	**Oceania**	**World**
Parishes	1975	6,099	44,210	10,866	136,718	2,223	200,116
	2000	11,022	54,682	20,543	129,565	2,384	218,196
		81%	24%	89%	-5%	7%	9%
Missions	1975	38,705	14,167	28,536	426	1,546	83,380
	2000	69,074	5,992	28,427	32	839	104,364
		78%	-58%	0%	-92%	-46%	25%
Other	1975	12,797	13,353	5,702	7,027	512	39,391
	2000	2,572	61,839	3,205	18,031	430	86,077
		-80%	363%	-44%	157%	-16%	119%
Total	1975	57,601	71,730	45,104	144,171	4,281	322,887
	2000	82,668	122,513	52,175	147,628	3,653	408,637
		44%	71%	16%	2%	-15%	27%
*The percent change between 1975 and 2000 is given in the shaded areas.							

Educational Institutions

In 2000, Africa had the largest number of Catholic primary schools and the largest total number of educational institutions, about 30 percent of all Catholic educational institutions worldwide. However, about four in five Catholic schools in Africa are at the elementary level. In the Americas, which has the second highest concentration of Catholic schools worldwide, seven in ten Catholic schools are elementary schools. Europe has the highest proportion of Catholic schools at the secondary level. Nearly 40 percent of its educational institutions are secondary schools.

		Africa	America	Asia	Europe	Oceania	World
Primary	1975	18,649	22,865	11,375	23,915	2,620	79,424
	2000	30,245	23,860	14,625	18,006	2,721	89,457
		62%	4%	29%	-25%	4%	13%
Secondary	1975	2,138	8,565	5,747	10,385	707	27,542
	2000	7,297	9,409	7,976	10,226	651	35,559
		241%	10%	39%	-2%	-8%	29%
Total	1975	20,787	31,430	17,122	34,300	3,327	106,966
	2000	37,542	33,269	22,601	28,232	3,372	125,016
		81%	6%	32%	-18%	1%	17%

Table 2.4 Selected Catholic Educational Institutions: 1975 and 2000*

*The percent change between 1975 and 2000 is given in the shaded areas.

Europe also has 19 universities established officially under the auspices of the Holy See as "pontifical universities" and another 44 advanced theological schools recognized by the Vatican. Worldwide, there are perhaps 30 universities of pontifical rank outside Europe, all of which are in the Americas. In addition, there are approximately 39 advanced Catholic theological schools outside of Europe, seven of which are in the United States and nine in the rest of the Americas. In the United States, there is a particularly large number of general purpose Catholic institutions of higher education, about 221 in all, thanks to the unique freedom the Church has enjoyed in the sphere of higher education, together with the creativity of the religious who founded these institutions. For this reason, the table below

Table 2.5 Catholic Universities: 2000

	Total Universities	Ecclesiastical Universities	University Colleges	Specialized Institutions
Africa	11	0	5	3	3
Asia	369	40	11	282	36
North America	267	50	11	178	28
Latin America	172	79	4	41	48
Europe	221	23	71	20	107
Oceania	6	0	1	5	0
Total	1,046	192	103	529	222

divides the Americas into North America (the United States and Canada) and Latin America (including Mexico and the Caribbean).

Over the centuries, the number of Catholic universities expanded very slowly. It was only in the 1800s that their numbers began to grow, primarily in North America. The high water mark for the creation of Catholic universities in the United States was in the early twentieth century. Elsewhere in the world, particularly in Asia but also in Latin America, the period after World War II saw the greatest growth in numbers of Catholic institutions of higher education.

Charitable Institutions

Charitable institutions conducted under Catholic auspices around the world include a wide variety of hospitals, dispensaries, leprosaria, homes for the elderly, homes for the chronically ill, orphanages, nurseries, and counseling centers, among others. As a result of the range and complexity of these kinds of institutions, comparisons across continents or even between countries must be done with caution. Some charitable institutions may be relatively small and less organized operations while others may be very large, heavily funded enterprises.

In some countries, government funding may be permitted for Church-related charitable institutions and in others the Church may be effectively prevented from providing such services in any form. In still others, economic or other pressures may force a number of previously existing Catholic charitable institutions to merge or close altogether.

Unlike Catholic parishes, which are faith communities designed specifically to serve the religious needs of Catholics, the services provided by Catholic charitable institutions are generally provided to all without distinction as part of the Church's social apostolate. Thus, simply comparing the number of these institutions to the number of Catholics may not be as helpful as considering the distinct human needs and realities particular to each country or region. The number of charitable institutions also often reflect the vitality of religious institutes of sisters, brothers, and religious priests, who often provide staff or sponsor such institutions as part of their particular charism or mission.

About one-third of reported charitable institutions are in the Americas and another one-third are in Europe. Asia has 20 percent of all charitable institutions. Of Catholic charitable institutions in Asia, a remarkable 75 percent, or 15,090 of the 20,525 charitable institutions reported, are in India. This reflects the strong presence of religious within the Catholic community in India, as well as the unique impact of such religious institutes as Mother Theresa's Missionaries of Charity. Finally, while only one in three Catholic charitable institutions is in Europe, more than half of all homes for the sick and elderly are located in that continent. This underlines the demographic reality of an increasingly older European population relative to the rest of the world.

Table 2.6 Selected Catholic Charitable Institutions: 2000*				
	Hospitals	Orphanages	Homes**	Other***	Total
Africa	819	859	890	11,628	14,196
America	1,946	2,516	3,465	28,439	36,366
Asia	1,548	2,851	1,548	14,542	20,525
Europe	1,330	2,411	7,679	19,388	30,808
Oceania	174	58	351	939	1,522
World	5,853	8,695	13,933	74,936	103,417

*No comparable data are available for 1975.
**These are primarily homes for the elderly and handicapped.
*** These include dispensaries, leprosaries, nurseries, and other institutions.

Religious Institutes, Secular Institutes, and Apostolic Movements

As noted above, the key source behind the founding and vitality of many Church structures, particularly its charitable, educational, and missionary enterprises, comes from institutes of consecrated life–distinct organizations within the Church such as the Franciscans, Jesuits, Christian Brothers, or Missionaries of Charity. Members of these groups commit to living a life of unique fidelity to the evangelical counsels of poverty, chastity, and obedience along with a particular commitment to the mission and spirituality of their founder and the tradition of which they are a part.

Unfortunately, data are very incomplete on the number of religious institutes worldwide. In part, this is because some exist only within a single diocese, or are in the process of being recognized on a broader basis. Of those institutes recognized worldwide, some have a limited presence beyond a particular geographic area, while others are very large and have a great number of intermediary levels of governance such as provinces or similar subdivisions.

No reliable numbers are available on the number of distinct organizations of religious institutes in the different countries or regions of the world. Available reports for individual communities are often so incomplete and the number of different communities so vast as to make summations at a global level impossible. This is further complicated by the fact that many religious institutes have the same names even though their governing structures, histories, and countries in which they are based may be completely distinct.

In comparison to religious institutes, which trace their beginnings to the ancient monastic orders, secular institutes are a much more recent phenomenon. These groups, many fewer in number, were first founded in 1946. They emphasize living in the world and pursuing a secular vocation without the ties to community living that are part of traditional religious life.

Another source of Church life that serves to strengthen parish life and other Church enterprises comes from apostolic movements and renewal groups of the laity such as *Cursillos de Cristiandad*, Legion of Mary, and a host of others. Unfortunately, the sheer complexity of these groups means that no summary information is available on an international or global basis for these different kinds of movements or groups. This absence of reliable centralized data is particularly problematic since the second half of the twentieth century saw dramatic growth and changes with respect to such Church groups and lay movements. However, limitations of available data prevent this topic from being suitably explored in this book.

INSTITUTIONAL DISTRIBUTION AND GROWTH

As the proportion of world Catholic population grew in Africa, the Americas, and elsewhere, the presence of dioceses and parishes also increased, but at a level less rapid than the growth of the Catholic population. Schools and charitable institutions grew relatively faster and therefore reflect Catholic population more closely.

Table 2.7 Catholic and Institutional Distribution: 1975 and 2000

		Africa	America	Asia	Europe	Oceania
Catholics	1975	7%	48%	7%	37%	1%
	2000	12%	50%	10%	27%	1%
Dioceses	1975	16%	35%	15%	31%	3%
	2000	18%	36%	17%	26%	3%
Parishes	1975	3%	22%	5%	68%	1%
	2000	5%	25%	9%	59%	1%
Schools	1975	19%	29%	16%	32%	3%
	2000	30%	27%	18%	23%	3%
Charitable*	2000	14%	35%	20%	30%	1%

* Comparable data on charitable institutions for 1975 are unavailable.

Changes in proportion between 1975 and 2000 reflect different rates of growth in different parts of the world. In general, available data show broad increases in most categories for most continents and regions. However, between 1975 and 2000 some declines may be observed, particularly within the data available for Africa, where counts of charitable institutions declined, and Europe, where counts of both educational and charitable institutions declined. In both cases these shifts are largely due to changes that took place in areas subject to Church-state tension or conflict, such as Eastern Europe under communist rule and the immediate post-independence period in Africa.

CONTRASTING RELATIVE "INSTALLED CAPACITY"

"Installed capacity" refers to the existing reach of Church institutions. In the case of parishes, for example, the number of Catholics per parish offers a means to compare the relative reach of parishes in two different places. Contrasting regions in terms of the number of Catholics an average parish or other institution must serve thus offers a way to understand the relative strengths and challenges in which the Church operates worldwide.

Table 2.8 Selected Church Institutions: 2000					
	Average Diocese Size (km²)	Catholics per Diocese	Catholics per Parish	Catholics per School	Charitable Institutions per Parish
Africa	61,226	279,009	11,796	3,463	1.4
America	37,985	550,202	9,498	15,612	0.7
Asia	70,100	245,542	5,223	4,748	1.0
Europe	13,644	414,416	2,162	9,923	0.2
Oceania	109,089	113,919	3,441	2,433	0.6
World	43,265	407,430	4,789	8,359	0.5

The number of Catholics per parish is one such measure. Others might be the number of Catholics per diocese or the number of Catholics per school. And, just as one might contrast the number of parishes to the total number of Catholics, one could also compare the total number of charitable institutions to the total number of parishes in order to contrast the relative presence of these two kinds of institutions. Compared to the presence of parishes, Catholic charitable institutions are relatively more present in Africa and Asia than in Europe.

The number of Catholics per diocese is much larger in Europe and the Americas than elsewhere in the world. On the other hand, the average population size per diocese, including both Catholics and non-Catholics, is much larger outside of the Americas and Europe. There are also many fewer parishes per ecclesiastical territory outside of the Americas and Europe. There are 177 parishes per territory in Europe, 52 in the Americas, and an average of 28 parishes per territory in the rest of the world. Finally, the sheer geographical extent of dioceses outside of Europe is on a very different, much more massive scale. In short, outside of Europe–and to a lesser extent outside of the Americas as well–the Church's diocesan structure is less complex insofar as there are fewer Catholics and parishes but much more challenging given the vastly greater distance and size of the general population within which a diocese is situated.

Table 2.9 Ecclesiastical Territories and Parishes: 1975 and 2000						
	Ecclesiastical Territories			Parishes		
	1975	2000	Change	1975	2000	Change
Africa	368	495	35%	6,099	11,022	81%
America	868	1,050	21%	44,210	54,682	24%
Asia	358	492	37%	10,866	20,543	89%
Europe	685	732	7%	136,718	129,565	-5%
Oceania	63	77	22%	2,223	2,384	7%
World	2,342	2,846	22%	200,116	218,196	9%

The shift in the distribution of Catholics around the world has not been accompanied by a change in the distribution of parishes. In 2000, Europe contained 60 percent of all parishes but only 27 percent of the world's Catholics. The Americas have 25 percent of the world's parishes but 50 percent of all Catholics. Institutional capacity in Africa is weak according to these measures. Its parishes are only 5 percent of all parishes in spite of a number of Catholics that represents 12 percent of the figure worldwide. Over the past fifty years, the creation of new parishes has simply not kept up with population shifts.

By the year 2000, Africa had approximately 3,463 Catholics for every Catholic elementary or secondary school. The rate for the Americas was considerably higher, at one such school for every 15,612 Catholics. The European figure was also high, although not nearly as high as that for the Americas, at 9,923 Catholics per school. Oceania had the most favorable ratio of 2,433 Catholics per school.

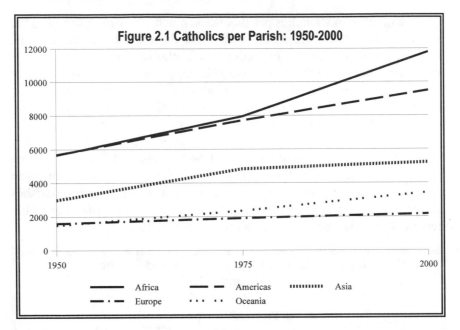

Figure 2.1 Catholics per Parish: 1950-2000

COMPOSITE REGIONAL PORTRAITS

For purposes of this book, the world is divided into 18 different regions. Oceania is treated as a single region and the other four continental areas used in this book have between three and six regions.

These regions are adapted from generally used geographic or cultural divisions that would be most relevant for Church purposes. They are certainly not meant to represent roughly similar shares of the world population or similar shares of the Catholic population. They are simply more or less homogeneous areas drawn together for broad purposes of comparison. As such, they offer an opportunity to understand the wide variations often observable within particular continent-wide areas. Later chapters will explore these nuances in greater detail. At this point some preliminary comparisons may help to underline broader trends.

Africa accounts for 12 percent of the world's Catholic population, 18 percent of ecclesiastical territories, and 5 percent of parishes. Although this would appear to indicate a very underserved population with respect to local pastoral structures, Africa also has a reported total of 69,074 mission stations, two-thirds of all such mission stations worldwide. It also has 30 percent of all educational institutions. Roughly 10 percent of all educational institutions are located in Central Africa, and another 10 percent are concentrated in East Africa. These two regions comprise two-thirds of Africa's educational institutions and 7 percent of global Catholic population. For comparison, North America, home to roughly the same proportion of Catholics, reports only 8 percent of the total number of educational institutions worldwide.

Table 2.10 Distribution of Selected Church Institutions, by Region: 2000						
	Catholics	Dioceses	Parishes	Catholics per Parish	Schools	Charitable Institutions
Africa	12%	18%	5%	11,796	30%	14%
Central	4%	4%	1%	15,899	10%	4%
East	4%	4%	1%	13,566	10%	5%
Indian Ocean	<1%	1%	<1%	11,186	2%	0%
North	<1%	1%	<1%	1,160	0%	0%
Southern	2%	3%	1%	10,609	1%	2%
West	3%	5%	1%	8,530	6%	3%
America	50%	36%	25%	9,498	27%	35%
Caribbean	2%	2%	1%	14,282	2%	3%
Mesoamerica	11%	5%	3%	16,089	5%	5%
North	7%	10%	11%	3,138	8%	7%
South	28%	19%	10%	14,175	12%	20%
Asia	10%	17%	10%	5,223	18%	20%
Northeast	1%	2%	1%	2,304	1%	1%
South	2%	6%	4%	2,195	12%	15%
Southeast	7%	6%	3%	10,468	5%	3%
Western	<1%	3%	1%	2,812	1%	1%
Europe	27%	26%	59%	2,162	23%	30%
Eastern	7%	6%	12%	2,595	1%	5%
Northwestern	10%	8%	23%	2,161	16%	14%
Southwestern	10%	12%	24%	1,942	6%	11%
Oceania	1%	3%	1%	3,441	3%	1%
World	100%	100%	100%	4,789	100%	100%

The Americas have half of all Catholics in the world, 36 percent of all ecclesiastical territories, and a quarter of all parishes and educational institutions. Its various regions offer a number of important contrasts. North America is home to 7 percent of the world Catholic population and as many as 10 percent of the world's dioceses and 11 percent of the world's parishes.

On the other hand, South America has twice as many of the world's dioceses as of its parishes. It also contains a considerable concentration of Catholic educational and charitable institutions relative to other regions, but not in comparison to the large proportion of the world's Catholics who live in South America.

Asia has about one-sixth of the world's ecclesiastical territories despite having one-tenth of the world's Catholic population. Relative to other world regions, South Asia stands out as a particularly exceptional case. It contains 6 percent of all ecclesiastical territories and the number of Catholics per parish is quite low, not far from the traditionally very favorable figures found in Western Europe. Furthermore, 12 percent of Catholic educational institutions and 15 percent of Catholic charitable institutions worldwide are concentrated in South Asia, home to just 2 percent of the world's Catholic population.

Although Europe has a disproportionate number of parishes given their Catholic population, the effects of decades of communist control in Eastern Europe–as well as the historic divide between Catholic and Orthodox Europe–are very apparent. Four-fifths of parishes in Europe are concentrated in Northwestern and Southwestern Europe. Northwestern Europe has the majority of the educational and charitable institutions on the continent. Sixteen percent of schools and 14 percent of charitable institutions can be found here, compared to Eastern Europe, which has 1 percent of all Catholic schools worldwide and 5 percent of Catholic charitable institutions.

Finally, Oceania, with just 1 percent of the world's Catholic population, has 3 percent of all Catholic schools worldwide, a significant concentration of educational institutions relative to its size.

In Catholic institutional life, having more institutions does not always correlate with a vibrant local Church. Indeed, the opposite is also possible. For example, a large concentration of educational or other institutions can overwhelm a local Catholic community with the demands and expectations of institutional life and institutional maintenance issues that may actually hinder its religious mission. As a result, in these numbers and elsewhere in this book, such figures can only be suggestive of broader issues and pastoral realities. Statistics on Church demographics and institutional life reflect a context but they do not predetermine it.

CHAPTER 3

Church Personnel

Changes in the numbers of priests, sisters, and others who serve the Church's workforce show much more nuanced and complex patterns than comparable figures for Catholic population or institutions. This chapter considers the broad trends for each type of Church personnel for whom reliable data exists on a worldwide basis. The chapter also explores likely growth patterns in future years for numbers of priests, particularly as based on numbers of seminarians and ordinations. Finally, the worldwide distribution of Church personnel is presented comparatively, along with the worldwide distribution of Catholic population as a whole.

NEW PATTERNS

After 1950, the number of dioceses grew more dramatically and more globally than ever before, nearly doubling in 50 years. The number of parishes increased more slowly, but still increased by 22 percent during the same period. They accommodated a growing and maturing Catholic community worldwide, one both increasingly denser and more globally dispersed. By the end of the twentieth century, the Catholic population was nearly two and a half times larger than it had been 50 years earlier, and it was much more widely distributed.

In contrast to such dramatic growth in Catholic population and Church structures between 1950 and 2000, Church personnel trends were much more fluid. As a result of the Second Vatican Council, broad cultural and social changes, and a diversity of emerging ministries, the late twentieth century was witness to great changes and new developments within the Church. Many cannot be discussed here in any detail, primarily because the Church has yet to develop effective means of collecting data on the type and presence of these new ministries. In any case, all these changes make for a much more fluid situation in the case of Church personnel.

One of the developments during this time is represented by the Second Vatican Council's restoration of the diaconate as a separate ministry in the Latin Church. While this formal role had never been lost in the Eastern Catholic Churches, the diaconate had become in the West only a transitional step on the way to priestly ordination. Now the diaconate, with its distinctive charism of service, has taken its place again as a key ministry within the Church and the deacon has again become an important part of Church personnel.

Worldwide, vocations to religious orders, including to the priesthood within religious life, had increased more than vocations to diocesan priesthood during the mid-1900s, particularly in Western Europe and North America. However, by the last few decades of the century this trend had disappeared and the number of religious began to decline, particularly in the places where they had grown so notably earlier in the century.

The Second Vatican Council placed great emphasis on the universal call to holiness and called for lay participation in a variety of Church ministries. Many Catholics called neither to priesthood nor to membership in religious institutes have responded to this call to serve. Simultaneously, many religious have worked to share their traditions of education, service, and spirituality with increasing numbers of others who collaborate in their mission.

All of this means that the relatively low increases, or absolute declines, in numbers of priests need to be carefully nuanced to distinguish between diocesan priests who are typically assigned to parish or related forms of ministry, and religious priests, who often minister in the schools or other institutions or serve as missionaries. From a pastoral point of view, a focus on these figures, including the often rapidly increasing numbers of Catholics per priest, do not necessarily present the complete picture. Simple overall figures for total numbers of priests–which are typically all that is available–do not ordinarily discriminate between priests in active ministry and those in retirement, nor between those who serve in direct pastoral ministry and those who serve the Church in other activities, many of which are increasingly performed by qualified lay people.

Unfortunately, figures on lay Catholics who do not belong to religious institutes and who are engaged in Church ministry, while vital to understanding today's personnel reality, are mostly unavailable on a consistent worldwide basis. When available, these figures are often reported in such ways as to make the figures of very limited usefulness. For this reason, little can be said about the numbers of catechists, lay missioners, and others who increasingly form part of the pastoral workforce of the Church.

In part, the lack of consistent reporting is due to the profoundly sacramental and decentralized nature of Catholicism. Priests and deacons have a unique, sacramentally based relationship to the bishop in whose diocese they serve. And, by extension, members of institutes of consecrated life also have a unique relationship with their diocesan bishop as well as with the Church universal through their vows. Those in ministry who have not been ordained or taken vows of consecrated life are linked differently to the local Church. Their tie is primarily to the site or institution in which they minister rather than through an ecclesiastical relationship to the diocesan bishop.

Each diocese, parish, or other ministry site defines the kinds of skills and roles needed for ministry, or for service on a pastoral council or other consultative body that is part of Church structures for shared decision-making. In any case, lay ecclesial ministers, including those entrusted with religious education, youth ministry, and other parish responsibilities, as well as those entrusted with the pastoral care of an entire parish, are relatively new categories. Such roles have emerged in light of the Second Vatican Council (1963-65), the promulgation of the revised Code of Canon Law (1983), and specific local developments. All of this underlines the sheer impossibility of accounting for the dramatically growing presence in the Church ministry of lay people who do not belong to religious communities during the period covered in this book. The situation remains fluid and developing.

BISHOPS

As a result of the increasing density of diocesan structures during the late twentieth century, the number and distribution of bishops has become far more global in nature. In this sense, the Second Vatican Council may be said to be the last in a series of largely European ecumenical councils. In 1963, an ecumenical council of the world's Roman Catholic bishops or Eastern Catholic eparchs meant that all 2,500 persons were called to Rome. If such a council had been called in 2000, 4,541 bishops or eparchs worldwide would have been called to participate.

Future ecumenical councils of the world's bishops are by definition likely to be far more global and far less European than councils of the past millennium, as are the highest levels of Church leadership and decision-making. These trends are likely to accelerate in the future as more dioceses and archdioceses are created in places where the Catholic population continues to expand. Increasing numbers of Catholics per diocese will also lead to the appointment of more auxiliary bishops to assist diocesan bishops. At present, about 57 percent of all bishops or eparchs are diocesan or eparchial bishops, meaning that they are charged with the fullness of leadership of the local Church. Currently about a quarter of all bishops are auxiliaries and a fifth are retired.

As more dioceses and archdioceses become established, more bishops and archbishops will attain 75 years of age, the age when submission of their resignation is mandatory. Due to this, the number of retired bishops and archbishops is likely to continue to increase fairly dramatically, given that so many dioceses–and therefore diocesan bishops–are of relatively recent origin. Statistics show that the number of archbishops has increased significantly over the last few decades of the twentieth century. Typically, cardinals–those who have a unique share in Church governance, particularly with respect to the election of the successor of the Pope–are selected from among archbishops. Although cardinals remain disproportionately European in comparison to the worldwide Catholic population, archbishops and especially bishops are relatively representative of the worldwide distribution of Catholics.

The changes in the last quarter of the twentieth century, a time that almost entirely overlaps with the pontificate of John Paul II, are most revealing of the increasingly global distribution of Church leadership. By the beginning of the twentieth century, there were as many as 306,000 Catholics per bishop in the Americas but only about 67,700 Catholics per bishop in Oceania. The average number of Catholics per bishop was 230,000.

Table 3.1 Bishops, Archbishops, and Cardinals: 2000						
	Bishops		Archbishops		Cardinals	
	Number	*Percent*	*Number*	*Percent*	*Number*	*Percent*
Africa	473	14%	115	13%	16	9%
America	1,391	40%	275	30%	50	27%
Asia	458	13%	150	16%	17	9%
Europe	1,059	30%	350	38%	96	52%
Oceania	94	3%	24	3%	4	2%
World	3,475		914		183	

GROWTH AND DISTRIBUTION OF PRIESTS WORLDWIDE

During the last half of the twentieth century, almost all of the increase in the number of priests occurred between 1950 and 1975, and almost all of that increase is explained by the growth in the number of religious priests that took place before 1975. The relatively rapid 33 percent growth in the number of religious priests between 1950 and 1975 was followed by a slight but absolute decline in numbers of religious priests in the following two and a half decades, making for a total increase of 28 percent during the last half of the century as a whole.

Table 3.2 Catholic Clergy: 1950, 1975, and 2000					
	1950	1975	2000	1950-2000 Change	1975-2000 Change
Diocesan Priests	254,612	259,331	265,781	4%	2%
Religious Priests	109,209	145,452	139,397	28%	-4%
Total Priests	363,821	404,783	405,178	11%	0%
Permanent Deacons	na	2,686	27,824	na	936%

Diocesan priests are responsible for most parish ministry, serve as a representative of the diocesan bishop, and generally minister within their diocese for life, within the diocesan structures of the Church. Religious priests, on the other hand, often belong to transnational communities with generals superior based in other dioceses and often in Rome. They are much more mobile than diocesan priests and much less likely to serve in parish ministry. The missionary religious communities responsible for the dramatic extension of the Church during the later part of the second millennium served mission areas with relatively few native Church personnel. Such mission areas were often dependent on proportionately large numbers of religious priests for extended periods.

From 1950 to 2000, the number of diocesan priests increased steadily but very modestly, and the total number of priests slightly more so, as a result of early increases in religious priests. In worldwide terms, increases of such few percentage points are dwarfed by the huge increases in Catholic population during the same period.

These subtle shifts look very different on a continent by continent basis. The number of priests in Europe declined dramatically over the past 25 years (diocesan priests by 17 percent and religious priests by 10 percent) while the numbers of priests in other continents increased much more than worldwide figures would suggest. This is particularly the case due to considerable shifts in the proportion of diocesan and religious priests. In the Africa of 1950, only 24 percent of all available priests were diocesan. Within a half century, the rapid growth of diocesan clergy on the continent had shifted this proportion to 62 percent, underlining a remarkable proportional increase in diocesan clergy.

Table 3.3 Diocesan and Religious Priests: 1950,1975, and 2000						
		1950	1975	2000	1950-2000 Change	1975-2000 Change
Africa	Diocesan	2,410	5,034	16,962	604%	237%
	Religious	7,581	10,944	10,203	35%	-7%
	Total	9,991	15,978	27,165	172%	70%
America	Diocesan	49,865	65,140	75,121	51%	15%
	Religious	35,525	49,899	45,720	29%	-8%
	Total	85,390	115,039	120,841	42%	5%
Asia	Diocesan	10,550	12,024	25,716	144%	114%
	Religious	8,331	12,068	17,850	114%	48%
	Total	18,881	24,092	43,566	131%	81%
Europe	Diocesan	190,345	174,225	145,268	-24%	-17%
	Religious	58,782	70,046	63,391	8%	-10%
	Total	249,127	244,271	208,659	-16%	-15%
Oceania	Diocesan	2,074	2,908	2,714	31%	-7%
	Religious	1,456	2,495	2,233	53%	-11%
	Total	3,530	5,403	4,947	40%	-8%
World	Diocesan	255,244	259,331	265,781	4%	2%
	Religious	109,675	145,452	139,397	27%	-4%
	Total	364,919	404,783	405,178	11%	<1%

Expressed in terms of the relative changes in the distribution of priests worldwide, one can observe a clear decline in the proportion of priests worldwide who are in Europe, compared to notable increases in other continental areas, with the exception of Oceania where the relative distribution remained unchanged throughout the period.

In short, the number of priests has not kept up with the number of Catholics. The result has been inevitable, dramatic increases in the number of Catholics per priest. While this is only a moderately useful figure since it includes all priests who have not been granted formal laicization, including all diocesan and religious priests, active and retired, it does illustrate general trends. While these comparisons are useful, of course, continents and regions are not exactly comparable. Some tend to have more religious priests who are not directly engaged in pastoral ministry, and others may have higher or lower proportions of older, sick, or retired priests not engaged in pastoral ministry, and of priests on leave or who still belong to the diocese in a particular continent but serve in another part of the world.

	1950	1975	2000	1950-2000 Change	1975-2000 Change
Table 3.4 Catholics per Priest, by Region: 1950, 1975, and 2000					
Africa	1,522	3,037	4,786	214%	58%
Central	1,521	4,030	6,107	302%	52%
East	1,750	2,867	4,955	183%	73%
Indian Ocean	2,230	2,762	3,818	71%	38%
North	1,159	359	524	-55%	46%
Southern	1,079	3,059	6,103	466%	100%
West	1,937	2,657	3,502	81%	32%
America	2,117	2,967	4,298	103%	45%
Caribbean	6,628	6,795	8,347	26%	23%
Mesoamerica	5,407	6,222	6,780	25%	9%
North	619	834	1,321	113%	58%
South	4,726	6,000	7,081	50%	18%
Asia	1,505	2,183	2,463	64%	13%
Northeast	525	515	1,113	112%	116%
South	909	962	923	2%	-4%
Southeast	3,609	5,556	5,322	47%	-4%
Western	427	760	3,862	804%	408%
Europe	859	1,072	1,343	56%	25%
Eastern	1,607	1,815	1,557	-3%	-14%
Northwestern	672	961	1,404	109%	46%
Southwestern	841	963	1,177	40%	22%
Oceania	622	967	1,658	167%	71%
World	1,203	1,753	2,579	114%	47%

The increase in the ratio of Catholics to priests since 1950 is particularly noticeable in Southern Africa (466 percent), Western Asia (804 percent), and Central Africa (302 percent). On the other hand, these increases do not necessarily exceed the average figure of Catholics per priest. In Western Asia, for example, the ratio of 3,862 Catholics per priest is well below that of Southern or Central Africa, even though it increased at a faster rate.

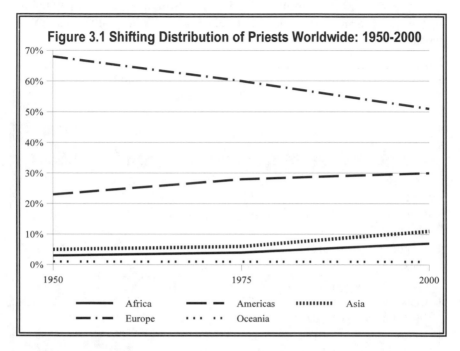

Figure 3.1 Shifting Distribution of Priests Worldwide: 1950-2000

Increases in the numbers of priests have been much more steep in some places than in others. As already noted, these increases have been particularly steep on the continent with the greatest growth in Catholic population. Africa posted a 708 percent Catholic population growth over the past fifty years and a priest population growth rate of 172 percent, moving from 9,991 to 27,165 priests within 50 years. However, this is not the full picture. While the number of seminarians in Africa grew 1,144 percent over that period, well in excess of actual Catholic population growth, Africa had only 3 percent of all Catholic seminarians in 1950 and today still has only 18 percent of all seminarians worldwide. That is, until recently priests in Africa were more likely to arrive through the incardination, or importation, of priests born and ordained outside of Africa rather than through the recruitment of local Africans into the seminary. This pattern has changed dramatically by the end of the twentieth century.

A similar but somewhat more moderate trajectory is observable in Asia. Here, the growth in the number of Catholics per priest is much higher than the worldwide figure. Priests increased by 131 percent–and seminarians by

590 percent–while the total increase for Catholic population was 278 percent. As in the case of Africa, the much greater increase in seminarians relative to the increase in priests suggests an important dynamic in local presbyterates. In 1950, foreign-born priests from missionary orders or established missionary-sending dioceses still provided the bulk of the pastoral workforce. Over the past half century, local dioceses in Africa and Asia have grown in the strength of their internal resources, particularly in terms of vocations to priesthood. At the same time, missionary orders and other sources of foreign-born priests began to have fewer available personnel to replace their members as they died or retired home from the missions.

Again, it was during the last few decades of the twentieth century that the source of the local presbyterate in many younger parts of the Church worldwide shifted from the importation of already ordained clergy from Europe to the successful recruitment of priesthood candidates to fill local seminaries.

SEMINARIANS AND PRIESTLY ORDINATIONS

As noted above, there have been dramatic increases in seminarians in Africa, Asia, and other places where there had been relatively few seminarians in 1950. These increases are particularly impressive precisely because initial figures for local seminarians were so low. As Catholic populations in these parts of the world stabilize and the dramatic increases in new diocesan and parish structures slow, such percentage increases will inevitably slow as well. At the same time, existing trends suggest that the larger numbers of seminarians found in these parts of the world will remain.

Table 3.5 Diocesan and Religious Seminarians: 1950, 1975, and 2000					
	1950	**1975**	**2000**	**1950-2000 Change**	**1975-2000 Change**	**Percent of Total 2000**
Africa	1,638	4,395	20,383	1,144%	364%	18%
America	16,028	20,231	36,392	127%	80%	33%
Asia	3,770	10,322	26,006	590%	152%	24%
Europe	39,212	24,183	26,879	-31%	11%	24%
Oceania	690	1,019	923	34%	-9%	1%
World	61,338	60,150	110,583	80%	84%	100%

The figures underline the fact that the relative distribution of priests has definitely shifted outside of Europe, and continues to do so at an accelerated pace. These dynamics are likely to be long term, given the higher proportion of older priests in Europe, the high proportion of younger priests elsewhere in the world, and the generally lower birth rate in Europe.

It is helpful to focus most on diocesan seminarians and diocesan ordinations for more direct comparisons. In this light, the number of diocesan priests per diocesan seminarian is particularly revealing. Europe, followed by Oceania and the Americas, is in one group, and Africa and Asia are in another. The percentage of seminarians worldwide is also broadly similar to the percentage of priestly ordinations shown in Table 3.7. These comparisons suggest that the percentage of those who abandon seminary studies and are ultimately not ordained is relatively similar worldwide, making the numbers and distribution of diocesan seminarians relatively good predictors for the size of presbyterates worldwide in the early decades of the twenty-first century.

Table 3.6 Diocesan Priests and Diocesan Seminarians: 1975 and 2000					
		Diocesan Seminarians	1975-2000 Change	Diocesan Priests per Seminarian	Diocesan Seminarians Worldwide
Africa	1975	3,883		1.3	10%
	2000	14,675	278%	1.2	20%
America	1975	12,288		5.3	31%
	2000	24,353	98%	3.1	34%
Asia	1975	6,351		1.9	16%
	2000	14,513	129%	1.8	20%
Europe	1975	15,960		10.9	41%
	2000	17,611	10%	8.2	25%
Oceania	1975	573		5.1	1%
	2000	604	5%	4.5	1%
World	1975	39,055		6.6	100%
	2000	71,756	84%	3.7	100%

Another way of looking at likely trends with respect to priests is by focusing on baptism trends together with ordination trends. In 1950, European Catholics represented 48 percent of all Catholics. Priests in Europe comprised 68 percent of all priests, and priestly ordinations in Europe were 66 percent of all such ordinations. At that time, many priests ordained in Europe were destined for permanent or near permanent missionary service. Europe was continuing to export substantial numbers of its recently ordained priests, as they had been for centuries–particularly from certain vocation-rich dioceses and countries.

Table 3.7 Diocesan Priestly Ordinations: 1975 and 2000					
		Diocesan Ordinations	1975-2000 Change	Diocesan Priests per Ordinand	Diocesan Ordinations Worldwide
Africa	1975	284		18	7%
	2000	1,177	314%	14	17%
America	1975	1,371		48	33%
	2000	2,156	57%	35	32%
Asia	1975	448		27	11%
	2000	1,094	144%	24	16%
Europe	1975	1,966		89	47%
	2000	2,321	18%	63	34%
Oceania	1975	71		41	2%
	2000	66	-7%	41	1%
World	1975	4,140		63	100%
	2000	6,814	65%	39	100%

Today, Catholics in Europe are 27 percent of all Catholics, and Catholic baptisms in Europe are 14 percent of all Catholic baptisms worldwide. Although priests in Europe still represent as many as 51 percent of all priests worldwide, priestly ordinations in Europe are only 34 percent of all such ordinations worldwide, and only 25 percent of all seminarians worldwide. Today, many of those studying in European seminaries are from dioceses outside of Europe. The proportion of European seminarians approximates the proportion of Europeans among Catholics worldwide. Ultimately, however, the number of Church personnel, including priests, is likely to reflect the broader and more long-term trends within the Catholic population as represented by the proportion of Catholic baptisms that occur in Europe.

In continents with the most Catholics, namely the Americas and Europe, the Church has had to struggle the most to keep the number of priests and seminarians growing as fast as Catholic population. In the Americas, where Catholic population grew 187 percent since 1950, the number of priests increased by only 42 percent, although the number of seminarians rose by 127 percent. In Europe, the number of both priests and seminarians actually declined by 16 and 31 percent, respectively, by 2000.

Table 3.8 Distribution of Diocesan Priests, Seminarians, and Ordinations: 2000			
	Diocesan Priests	Diocesan Seminarians	Ordinations to Diocesan Priesthood
Africa	6%	20%	17%
America	28%	34%	32%
Asia	10%	20%	16%
Europe	55%	25%	34%
Oceania	1%	1%	1%
World	100%	100%	100%

Though Europe showed the smallest growth in Catholic population of all the continents between 1950 and 2000 (32 percent), the distribution of ordinations to the diocesan priesthood in Europe significantly exceeds the proportion of seminarians reported for Europe. This may be due to differences in how the data are reported or the nature of seminary life in Europe, rather than underlying trends. Nonetheless, such falling numbers in Church personnel represent a challenge for Catholic vitality, and may be in part a reflection of reduced vitality in themselves.

Despite falling numbers, Europe continues to have a large proportion of the world's priests. In 1950, 68 percent of the world's priests lived in Europe, alongside 48 percent of the world's Catholics. In 2000, Europe's share of the Catholic population fell to just 27 percent, but now the difference between the percentage of priests worldwide has become almost twice as high, approximately 51 percent of the Church's total priests.

In the Americas, the growth in the already large Catholic population made it the home to half of the world's Catholics by 2000, as compared to being home for 41 percent of the world's Catholics in 1950. The Americas are served by 30 percent of all priests and contain 33 percent of the world's seminarians.

PERMANENT DEACONS

In 1967, the permanent diaconate, which since the seventh century had become only a transitional step toward priestly ordination in the Latin Rite, was restored as a separate ministry in the Western Church. In the Eastern Catholic Churches, the diaconate had remained as a separate and permanent state. By the mid-1970s, many dioceses that had chosen to develop this ministry had recruited and formed permanent deacons. Married candidates for ordination to the diaconate must be over the age of 35, and are often a good deal older than that, since they are expected to provide for their own livelihood. Nearly all permanent deacons are diocesan, although some men's religious communities have a few members who are ordained as permanent deacons. Growth has been strong since the restoration of the diaconal ministry within the Western Church, particularly within certain world regions. Church figures for the year 2000 show a total of 27,824 permanent deacons.

Table 3.9 Permanent Deacons, by Region: 1975 and 2000				
	1975	2000	1975-2000 Change	Parishes per Deacon
World	2,686	27,824	936%	16
Africa	55	361	556%	31
Central	23	28	22%	97
East	3	12	300%	229
Indian Ocean	0	14		33
North	3	14	367%	22
Southern	26	273	950%	6
West	0	20		160
America	1,807	18,342	915%	3
Caribbean	17	789	4,541%	2
Mesoamerica	25	779	3,016%	10
North	1,344	13,889	933%	2
South	421	2,885	585%	7
Asia	57	128	125%	161
Northeast	0	12		229
South	5	26	420%	339
Southeast	26	45	73%	164
Western	26	45	73%	37
Europe	729	8,813	1,109%	15
Eastern	4	263	6,475%	102
Northwestern	630	5,751	813%	9
Southwestern	95	2,798	2,845%	19
Oceania	38	180	374%	13

As the table above and the figure on the next page suggest, the world distribution of deacons is very uneven. Fifty percent are located in North America, and 31 percent are in Northwestern and Southern Europe. The remaining 19 percent of all permanent deacons are dispersed around the globe. While diaconal ministry has grown dramatically, its growth has largely been restricted to a few parts of the world. Although one of the hopes for the permanent diaconate at the time of its restoration in the Western Church was to address the needs of the church in Africa and other parts of the world in need of ordained ministers, the diaconate is found in much larger numbers within the relatively priest-rich parts of the world.

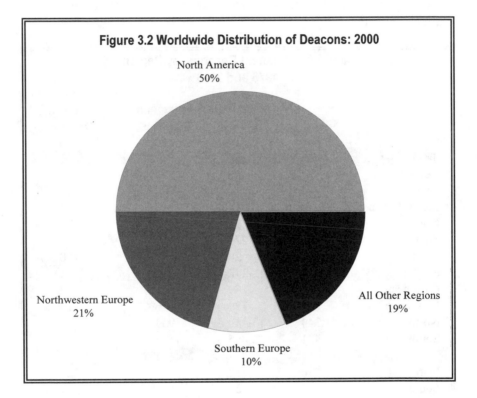

Figure 3.2 Worldwide Distribution of Deacons: 2000

Since the majority of deacons are assigned to parishes, the ratio of parishes to deacons suggests the relative degree to which Catholics are likely to experience deacons in the course of typical parish life. In the Americas, there are three parishes for every deacon, and in Europe there are 15 parishes for every deacon. Elsewhere in the world, the average is much higher, close to 98 parishes per deacon.

Given that North America and Northwestern Europe are the two regions with the strongest presence of deacons, it is not surprising that these are also the ones with the most parishes entrusted entirely to the pastoral care of permanent deacons. In 2000, 136 parishes were entrusted to the pastoral care of deacons in the absence of a priest in North America, and there were 294 such parishes in Northwestern Europe. The total number of parishes entrusted to deacons elsewhere in the world is 146.

MEN RELIGIOUS

Men who are vowed religious include both religious priests–already discussed above–and men religious who remain laity and are not ordained as priests. Historically, European religious institutes of priests and lay brothers with a missionary charism were on the front lines of the Catholic effort to extend the Gospel and develop the Church. To this day, the presence of men religious–particularly religious brothers– among Catholics remains relatively higher in Africa, Asia, and Oceania, reflecting this long history.

Table 3.10 Men Religious: 2000				
	Religious Priests	Religious (Lay) Brothers	Total Men Religious	Lay Brothers as Percent of the Total	Percent of Total Men Religious
Africa	10,203	7,256	17,459	42%	9%
America	45,720	16,615	62,335	27%	32%
Asia	17,850	7,659	25,509	30%	13%
Europe	63,391	21,691	85,082	25%	44%
Oceania	2,233	1,836	4,069	45%	2%
World	139,397	55,057	194,454	28%	100%

At the beginning of the twenty-first century, about one in three (28 percent) of all religious worldwide are lay brothers. However, the proportion varies considerably from continent to continent. The presence of religious brothers among men religious is much higher in Africa and Oceania and less so in Europe, the Americas, and Asia. Lay brothers make up nearly a third of all men religious serving in Asia and more than 40 percent of men religious serving in Africa and in Oceania.

Men religious continue to be concentrated in Europe, however. More than two in five men religious were in Europe in the year 2000, and one in three were in the Americas.

WOMEN RELIGIOUS

There are more women religious than deacons, diocesan priests, and men religious combined. Taken together, women religious represent nearly two-thirds of the total. There are more than three women religious for every diocesan priest and more than four women religious for every male religious.

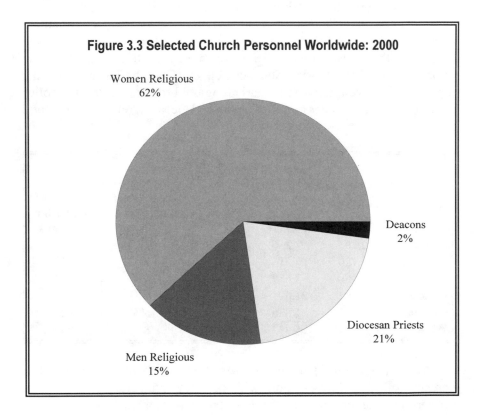

Figure 3.3 Selected Church Personnel Worldwide: 2000

Women Religious 62%

Deacons 2%

Diocesan Priests 21%

Men Religious 15%

Nearly half of all women religious are in Europe. About a third are in the Americas. Asia claims a fifth of women religious, well over half of whom are in India. Given the large numbers of women religious compared to other Church personnel shown in the figure above, the number of Catholics per woman religious is much lower than that for men religious or diocesan priests. On average there are 1,359 Catholics per woman religious, worldwide. In Oceania, there are 739 Catholics per woman religious. There are as many as 2,473 Catholics per woman religious in Africa, a larger number than elsewhere, but still much smaller than the corresponding figure of 7,447 Catholics per men religious. Although the Americas have a large proportion of women religious worldwide, its large Catholic population yields a relatively high proportion of 2,584 Catholics per woman religious.

Table 3.11 Women Religious: 2000		
	Women Religious	**Catholics per Woman Religious**
Africa	52,583	2,473
America	200,943	2,584
Asia	138,195	776
Europe	366,326	765
Oceania	11,095	739
World	769,142	1,359

Between 1950 and 2000, the number of women religious declined from 806,233 to 769,142. However, these numbers mask both steep decreases and increases. Significant declines are found in Europe (from 528,893 in 1950 to 366,326 in 2000), North America (from 183,740 to 90,529) and to some degree in Oceania as well (from12,177 to 11,095). In the rest of the world, the number of women religious increased considerably (from 21,242 to 138,195 in Asia, from 3,280 to 52,583 in Africa, and from 56,901 to 110,414 in Latin America).

A COMPOSITE GLOBAL PORTRAIT

These differences in Church personnel are even more striking in a region by region comparison, such as that offered below. The five chapters that follow will examine the broad themes of these first three chapters in light of the concrete reality of each separate continental area and the regions that comprise it. This review of Catholic population, institutions, and personnel in each distinct continental context will also include a comparison across time, particularly the last quarter of the twentieth century, as well as a comparison across the various regions of each continent. The concluding chapter will present a few broad themes comparable across the continents.

Table 3.12 Distribution of Selected Church Personnel, by Region: 2000

	Catholic Population	Bishops	Diocesan Priests	Religious Priests	Religious Brothers	Religious Women
Africa	12%	13%	6%	7%	13%	7%
Central	4%	3%	2%	2%	4%	1%
East	4%	3%	2%	2%	4%	2%
Indian Ocean	1%	1%	0%	1%	1%	1%
North	<1%	1%	0%	0%	0%	0%
Southern	2%	2%	0%	1%	1%	1%
West	3%	3%	2%	1%	3%	1%
America	50%	37%	28%	33%	30%	29%
Caribbean	2%	2%	1%	1%	1%	1%
Mesoamerica	11%	4%	5%	4%	3%	4%
North	7%	12%	14%	15%	14%	13%
South	28%	19%	9%	13%	12%	11%
Asia	10%	14%	10%	13%	14%	17%
Northeast	1%	2%	1%	2%	2%	2%
South	2%	5%	4%	6%	5%	11%
Southeast	7%	5%	4%	4%	6%	4%
Western	0%	2%	0%	1%	1%	1%
Europe	27%	33%	55%	47%	39%	46%
Eastern	7%	7%	13%	8%	4%	5%
Northwestern	10%	10%	20%	17%	18%	18%
Southwestern	10%	15%	22%	21%	17%	23%
Oceania	1%	3%	1%	2%	3%	1%
Total World	100%	100%	100%	100%	100%	100%

CHAPTER 4

Africa

This chapter presents information on Catholic population, institutions, and personnel in Africa over the twentieth century. Summary information is presented first, followed by a discussion of the six different regions identified within Africa for purposes of this book. These regions are designed to be as consistent as possible with geographical, geopolitical, and cultural divisions used by both Church and secular sources. This presentation of regional data also contains specific information on particular countries within each region to illustrate overall patterns.

OVERVIEW

The growth in Catholic population that took place in Africa over the twentieth century has been remarkable. This is all the more impressive given the geography involved: Africa is larger than South America and Europe combined. At the beginning of the twentieth century, there were 14 dioceses in Africa, almost half of which had been established in the 1500s and were related to the Archdioceses of Seville or Lisbon. A similar number of dioceses had been founded in the second half of the nineteenth century and were related to the French colonial presence. The Catholic presence in Africa extended no further than these limited enclaves.

By 1975, the Catholic population in Africa had risen to about 48 million, a 15-fold increase since 1950. Over the following quarter century the number of Catholics further expanded to 130 million, a growth rate of 168 percent. This rate far outstrips worldwide Church growth (46 percent) and growth within the African population as a whole (97 percent). By the year 2000, Africa's 52 countries together contained 12 percent of the global Catholic population. A half century earlier, Africa had contributed only 4 percent of total worldwide Catholic population.

Of Africa's 789 million inhabitants in the year 2000, 16 percent could be counted as Catholic. These 130 million Catholics, 11,022 parishes, and 495 dioceses or other Church territories were served by 27,165 priests, 7,256 religious brothers, and 52,583 women religious.

POPULATION

Baptismal trends best illustrate the growth dynamics of the Church in Africa. In all, there were 3,574,219 baptisms recorded by the Catholic Church in Africa in 2000, about 1.8 million more than the 1.7 million baptisms recorded in 1975, a 105 percent increase. By the beginning of the twenty-first century, Africa accounted for 20 percent of Catholic baptisms worldwide, second only to South America's 27 percent.

Table 4.1 Selected Church Population Statistics, Africa: 1975 and 2000			
	1975	**2000**	**Change**
Total Population	400,957,000	789,455,000	97%
Catholic Population	48,528,000	130,018,000	168%
Percent Catholic	12%	16%	36%
Percent of Catholics Worldwide	7%	12%	82%
Ecclesiastical Territories	368	495	35%
Parishes	6,099	11,022	81%
Parishes per Territory	17	22	34%
Catholics per Territory	131,870	262,663	99%
All Baptisms	1,742,822	3,574,219	105%
Baptisms under 7 years old (%)	67%	63%	-5%
Confirmations	na	1,503,878	na
Marriages	170,249	368,653	117%

Baptismal trends also show other differences between Africa and elsewhere in the world. Only about 63 percent of all baptisms recorded by the Catholic Church in Africa are of children under age seven. Corresponding figures for other continents are generally well above 90 percent. This may represent a greater proportion of adult conversions–but it could also point to the difficulty of access to the sacraments, including sacraments of initiation, in Africa's many remote areas.

Marriage is often a challenging point of engagement between Catholicism and African cultures. Many African cultures traditionally witness marriages in stages. While the Church has tried to take account of local customs where possible, traditional practices in direct contradiction to the Catholic understanding of marriage, such as conditioning the marital bond upon the fertility of the wife or the taking of more than one wife, have proven challenging. Nonetheless, marriages officially witnessed by the Church rose by 117 percent between 1975 and 2000, from 170,249 to 368,653. Given the large and young Catholic population in Africa, these figures may suggest that many unions are not being celebrated within the Church. In 2000, about 88 percent of all marriages recorded by the Church in Africa took place between two Catholics. The number of such marriages recorded by the Church rose by 106 percent between 1975 and 2000. Those between Catholics and non-Catholics increased at a slower rate, 71 percent.

INSTITUTIONS

By 2000, the number of ecclesiastical territories that were not dioceses–in other words, mission areas not yet established as a diocese–had declined to only 6 percent of all ecclesiastical territories, and new dioceses were emerging more from portions of established dioceses than from apostolic vicariates or other kinds of mission territories. As a result of a growth rate of about 35 percent between 1975 and 2000, the average geographical size of African ecclesiastical territories had steadily declined. Nonetheless, the average geographical size of approximately 61,226 square kilometers was nearly seven times the average size of Asian ecclesiastical territories–and 45 times the size of European ones.

Because Catholic population grew much faster than the number of dioceses, the average number of Catholics per diocese doubled between 1975 and 2000, to about 262,663 Catholics. On average, each of the 495 dioceses or other Church territories in Africa has only 22 parishes, a lower figure than for any other continent. However, the total number of pastoral centers, including parishes and mission stations, is about 6.5 times larger than the number of parishes alone. This results in a particularly high figure. Thus, Africa's proportion of 167 pastoral centers per territory is higher than for any other continental area except Europe.

The parish system looks very different in Africa than elsewhere. African Catholics make up 12 percent of the world Catholic population, but African parishes comprise only about 5 percent of all Catholic parishes in the world. This represents a greater divergence between the distribution of

Catholic population and parishes in Africa than for any other continent. This is explained by the continuing reliance on mission stations and other pastoral centers as a means of meeting the pastoral, sacramental, and community needs of the African Catholic population.

One of the keys to Catholic institutional life in Africa is the strong presence of Catholic educational institutions, particularly primary schools. In contrast to elsewhere in the Catholic world, and as a reflection of the relatively weak presence of formally established parishes, Africa has about three times as many Catholic elementary and secondary schools as parishes. By 2000, elementary and secondary Catholic schools in Africa numbered 37,542–far more than in Europe or Asia and about 4,000 more than in the Americas. The focus on primary schooling is unique to the continent and reflects the great need for basic education. This is especially the case given Africa's literacy rate, which is lower than for any other continent. About 70 percent of men over 15 and 52 percent of women over 15 are literate.

There are approximately 30,000 primary schools in Africa, a figure three times higher than that for Europe and 7,000 more than those in the Americas, which has the next largest number of Catholic primary schools. In 2000, Africa had nearly half of all 63,125 Catholic primary schools worldwide.

Table 4.2 Selected Church Institution Statistics, Africa: 1975 and 2000			
	1975	**2000**	**Change**
Catholic Population	48,528,000	130,018,000	168%
Percent of Catholics Worldwide	7%	12%	82%
Ecclesiastical Territories	368	495	35%
Dioceses or Eparchies	330	466	41%
% of Territories Worldwide	16%	17%	11%
Total Pastoral Centers	57,601	82,668	44%
Parishes	6,099	11,022	81%
Missions	38,705	69,074	78%
Catholics per Parish	7,957	11,796	48%
Primary Schools	18,649	30,245	62%
Secondary Schools	2,138	7,297	241%
Seminaries	63	180	186%

Catholic social service institutions are generally present in proportions consistent with the proportion of Catholics in Africa. In 2000, the Church in Africa reported some 819 hospitals, 859 orphanages, 890 homes for the elderly or handicapped, and 11,628 other charitable institutions. About 12 percent of all Catholics worldwide are in Africa, and orphanages and hospitals are distributed along fairly similar lines. The exceptions are not particularly surprising: Africa has less than its share of Catholic homes for the elderly and handicapped and more than its share of the kinds of less formed and more basic charitable activities. Those include dispensaries, leprosaries, and nurseries. Within Africa, some of these institutions are much more concentrated in particular regions due to historical and political reasons.

PERSONNEL

Dramatically increasing numbers of Catholics in Africa have created an urgent need for priests, religious, and other Church workers. Though their ranks have grown over the past few decades, growth has not been proportional to that of the Catholic population. For example, over the last quarter of the twentieth century, the number of priests grew dramatically, increasing by two-thirds. The Catholic population increased at a rate that was more than twice as fast.

In 1975, there were 3,037 Catholics for every priest in Africa, but by 2000 the ratio had risen to 4,786 Catholics per priest. In spite of these increases, Africa's current proportion of Catholics per priest is by no means the highest in the world. In South America, there are 7,164 Catholics for every priest. In 1929, the first year for which comparable data exist, the ratio of 1,172 Catholics per priest was quite favorable, largely because there were so few Catholics. Relative to later years, there were very few priests at that time, just 4,530. Within two decades, by the year 1950, the number of priests in Africa had more than doubled to 9,942 priests. By the end of the twentieth century, there were 27,165 priests in Africa.

Priests are by no means the only face of ministry in Africa. Women religious are far more numerous. They are also key to maintaining the ministerial life of the Church in Africa's many Catholic educational and charitable institutions. In 2000, there were 52,583 women religious in Africa, about twice as many priests. As a result, there are 2,473 Catholics per women religious, as compared to 4,786 Catholics per priest.

The increases in numbers of priests in Africa mask two key trends. The presence of religious order priests has been holding steady while the numbers of diocesan priests have increased at a very rapid pace. In 1975, priests belonging to religious orders–in most cases non-African missionaries–outnumbered diocesan, typically native-born priests by more than two to one. In 2000, the number of religious priests had remained more or less unchanged from that of 25 years earlier, but the diocesan clergy had expanded more than three-fold.

These changes are reflected in dramatic increases in ordinations and seminarians. Since 1975, the number of priestly ordinations in Africa has increased four-fold. The number of diocesan seminarians has nearly quadrupled. Available statistics also suggest that religious clergy are much more likely to be native-born in the years to come: the number of candidates preparing for the religious clergy locally is now ten times higher than in 1975.

Table 4.3 Selected Church Personnel Statistics, Africa: 1975 and 2000			
	1975	**2000**	**Change**
Catholic Population	48,528,000	130,018,000	168%
Percent of Catholics Worldwide	7%	12%	82%
Bishops	na	601	na
Total Priests	15,978	27,165	70%
Diocesan	5,034	16,962	237%
Religious	10,944	10,203	-7%
Permanent Deacons	55	361	556%
Religious Brothers	4,940	7,256	47%
Religious Women	33,691	52,583	56%
Diocesan Priest Ordinations	284	1,177	314%
Total Seminarians	4,395	20,383	364%
Diocesan	3,883	14,675	278%
Religious	512	5,708	1,015%
Catholics per Priest	3,037	4,786	58%
Catholics per Woman Religious	1,440	2,473	72%

REGIONS OF AFRICA

The regions of Africa vary significantly in the distribution of Catholic population, institutions, and personnel. In order to better analyze and discuss the variation in the Catholic story across the continent, this chapter presents data on six regions that represent the countries or territories within Africa and its surrounding seas. These regions are designed to be relatively consistent with groupings typically used within the Church as well as by geographers and demographers. In general, these divisions also correspond to areas where different non-African languages have dominance, whether as *lingua franca* or as official languages, often through an extended colonial presence or influence. In the list that follows, territories are always followed by the name of the country generally recognized as having sovereign control in parentheses.

- *North Africa:* Algeria, Egypt, Libya, Morocco, Sahara (Morocco), Tunisia.

- *West Africa:* Benin, Burkina Faso, Cape Verde, Cote d'Ivoire, Gambia, Ghana, Guinea, Guinea-Bissau, Liberia, Mali, Mauritania, Niger, Nigeria, São Tomé and Principe, Senegal, Sierra Leone, Togo.

- *Central Africa:* Burundi, Cameroon, Central African Republic, the Democratic Republic of Congo (formerly Zaire), the Republic of Congo, Chad, Equatorial Guinea, Gabon, Rwanda.

- *Southern Africa:* Angola, Botswana, Lesotho, Mozambique, Namibia, St. Helena (United Kingdom), South Africa, Swaziland, Zimbabwe.

- *The Indian Ocean:* Comoros, Madagascar, Mauritius, Mayotte (France), Reunion (France), Seychelles.

- *East Africa:* Djibouti, Eritrea, Ethiopia, Kenya, Malawi, Somalia, Sudan, Tanzania, Uganda, Zambia.

Taken together, Central Africa and East Africa are home to the majority of African Catholics. Central Africa has approximately 43 million Catholics, representing about 45 percent of the region's overall population, a third of all Catholics in Africa. East Africa has about 37 million Catholics, some 29 percent of the continent's Catholic population, but due to different population sizes, only about 17 percent of that region's population.

NORTH AFRICA

By the middle of the first millennium, North Africa was an important center of the Catholic community and had been the site of rich developments in the tradition, from the desert fathers of Egypt to St. Augustine, whose diocese was located in present-day Algeria. However, since the Arab conquests of the seventh and eighth centuries, Islam has dominated the region. In an effort to preserve the memory of long-gone dioceses, to this day the Church maintains the practice of naming auxiliary bishops and others who are not diocesan bishops in their own right to these former dioceses, now called titular sees, or dioceses in name only. The practice has continued with dioceses in other regions that for one reason or another have also become extinct.

Although European colonization re-introduced Catholicism in the nineteenth and twentieth centuries, its presence was never strong and many left North Africa amid political violence in the aftermath of colonialism. In some countries, particularly Algeria, violence against Church leaders and workers continued through the 1990s.

Table 4.4 Selected Church Statistics, North Africa: 1975 and 2000			
	1975	**2000**	**Change**
Catholic Population	315,000	363,200	15%
% Catholic	0.39%	0.26%	-34%
Ecclesiastical Territories	25	26	4%
Parishes per Territory	16	12	-24%
Dioceses	14	19	36%
Parishes	397	313	-21%
Missions	69	176	155%
Catholics per Parish	802	1,160	45%
Total Catholic Schools	525	297	-43%
Priests	878	693	-21%
% Diocesan	38%	41%	8%
Women Religious	3,632	2,101	-42%
Catholics per Priest	363	524	44%

Three hundred sixty-three thousand Catholics live among 138 million North Africans across 6 million square kilometers. North African Catholics worship in 313 parishes throughout 26 ecclesiastical territories. The total number of priests is 693, a much smaller number than for any other African region. Given the relatively small number of Catholics, however, there are fewer Catholics per priest than anywhere else on the continent.

Catholics make up perhaps 1 percent of the population of Libya, due to the presence of foreign workers in the petroleum industry, and less than 1 percent of the population in four of the five North African countries, Algeria, Egypt, Morocco, and Tunisia. Figures are similar for the Moroccan-annexed territory of Sahara, which had been a Spanish-held territory and was the last of the major European-controlled territories in North Africa.

Egypt's approximately 64 million inhabitants are 46 percent of the total population in North Africa and represent the second highest population in all of Africa. Its approximately 237,000 Catholics far outweigh the approximately 126,000 Catholics in the rest of North Africa. With the exception of Lebanon, Egypt has the largest and most important Catholic community in the Arab world. It also has the most diverse Catholic community in the world, with a wider diversity of traditions and liturgies than may be found anywhere else. There are seven different Catholic Churches separately organized in Egypt–Chaldean, Coptic, Melkite, Maronite, Syrian, and Armenian, as well as the Western Church, or Latin Rite. The largest is the Coptic Catholic Church, which is also the only Catholic Church in Egypt growing in number. Their liturgy is similar to that of the Coptic Orthodox Church and predates the Arab conquest of 640. The Coptic Catholic Church was formed when Coptic communities united with Rome in the eighteenth century under the influence of Jesuit and Franciscan missionaries. Most of the other Catholic Churches in Egypt are holding steady in numbers or declining due to immigration or conversion to Islam.

WEST AFRICA

About 12 percent of the population in the 17 countries of West Africa are Catholic. These more than 27 million Catholics are about 21 percent of all African Catholics. Seventy-seven hundred priests, 76 percent of whom are diocesan, minister in 136 dioceses and three other territories across 6.1 million square kilometers.

This part of Africa is particularly notable for its relatively high number of vocations. In part, this is a function of above average growth in the Catholic population even for Africa. The Catholic population increased by 240 percent in the quarter century between 1975 and 2000, the number of women religious rose by 59 percent, and the number of priests increased by 61 percent. The number of priestly ordinations in 2000 represents about 5 percent of all priests, one of the highest such percentages in the world. In addition, three in four of all priests are diocesan, a proportion 34 percent higher than the figure for Africa as a whole. Nonetheless, these overall trends do not necessarily represent all the countries of West Africa. In particular, there are important differences between smaller and sometimes majority Catholic countries, and the larger countries, especially Nigeria.

Table 4.5 Selected Church Statistics, West Africa: 1975 and 2000			
	1975	**2000**	**Change**
Catholic Population	8,012,000	27,253,000	240%
% Catholic	7%	12%	42%
Ecclesiastical Territories	89	139	36%
Parishes per Territory	13	23	45%
Dioceses	85	136	38%
Parishes	1,123	3,195	65%
Missions	12,252	17,408	30%
Catholics per Parish	7,152	8,463	15%
Total Catholic Schools	5,022	7,378	32%
Priests	3,015	7,783	61%
% Diocesan	35%	76%	54%
Women Religious	3,807	9,180	59%
Catholics per Priest	2,664	3,474	23%

The most Catholic country by population is Cape Verde, which has a population reported to be 94 percent Catholic. The Portuguese arrived in this archipelago of 15 islands off the coast of Senegal in the fifteenth century and the islands remained under Portuguese control until 1975. However, in spite of a long historical presence of the Church and a proportionally large Catholic population, the presence of Catholic institutional life and personnel is weak. There are as many as 13,194 Catholics per parish and only 47 priests to serve 409,000 Catholics. Cape Verde's ratio of 8,702 Catholics per priest is more than double the West African average. Although there are more religious women than priests, their presence is also relatively weak compared to elsewhere in Africa.

Although three-fifths of the countries of West Africa were colonized by the French, the largest and most powerful country in the region is a former British colony. Nigeria has 51 percent of the total West African population and its 115 million inhabitants make it the largest country in the continent. Of the five largest countries in Africa, Nigeria is also the most crowded, with a geographic size of 923,768 square kilometers. This means that it is about twice as large as California or two and a half times as large as Germany. As the table below shows, Nigeria has by far the largest population of any country in Africa–but the smallest territory of any of the five most populous countries.

Table 4.6 Five Most Populous Countries in Africa: 2000		
	Population	Area in Km²
Nigeria	115,220,000	923,768
Egypt	63,980,000	1,001,450
Ethiopia	63,490,000	1,127,127
Congo, Democratic Republic	50,950,000	2,345,410
South Africa	43,690,000	1,216,612

The growth of the Church in Nigeria has been particularly rapid between 1975 and 2000. The number of Catholics rose by 295 percent, dioceses by 67 percent, parishes by 423 percent, priests by 292 percent, and seminarians by 142 percent. Nigerian Catholics number over 16 million and constitute about 15 percent of their country's population. They have a large institutional presence, including 2,744 primary schools and 271 secondary schools, 153 Catholic hospitals, and over 1,000 other Catholic charitable institutions.

Nigeria is also a place of tension between an expanding and increasingly assertive Muslim presence in the north and a Catholic and Christian presence to the south. This is particularly challenging because the Muslim community often calls for the imposition of Islamic religious law in place of secular law where Islam is the majority religion.

Throughout the period since independence, the Church's role as a respected minority has often given it a voice within civil society to speak out in favor of human rights, peace, and democratic reforms. Perhaps the greatest challenge the Church faced came during the late 1960s, when Nigeria experienced a traumatic civil war. This had a particularly negative impact on the Church since the populations most affected were disproportionately Catholic.

In spite of these difficulties, the Church in Nigeria is growing and has been particularly successful in promoting vocations to priesthood and religious life. As many as 83 percent of all priests are diocesan priests, underlining the fact that few priests are foreign-born missionaries and that there are high numbers of local priestly vocations. Figures for Church-recorded marriages also suggest that the Church is relatively strong in this country, and, by extension, West Africa as a whole. The Church in Nigeria reports witnessing twice as many marriages as the Church in the Democratic Republic of Congo, in spite of Nigeria's having only two-thirds the number of Catholics reported for the Congo.

CENTRAL AFRICA

Catholics are most concentrated in Central Africa. Five of its nine countries have populations at least 50 percent Catholic. Indeed, Central Africa has six of the fifteen most Catholic African countries or territories in terms of population. This is all the more impressive when one considers the large size of those countries with proportionately large Catholic populations.

Table 4.7 Top Fifteen African Countries, by Percent Catholic: 2000			
	Region	Percent Catholic	Catholic Population
Guinea, Equatorial	Central	95%	370,000
Cape Verde	West	94%	443,000
Reunion	Indian Ocean	92%	590,000
Seychelles	Indian Ocean	85%	69,000
Sao Tome and Principe	West	83%	107,000
Burundi	Central	63%	4,009,000
Angola	Southern	59%	7,354,000
Congo	Central	57%	1,683,000
Gabon	Central	53%	743,000
Congo, Dem. Rep.	Central	53%	26,080,000
Rwanda	Central	48%	3,533,000
Uganda	East	45%	10,226,000
Lesotho	Southern	44%	878,000
Zambia	East	28%	2,973,000
Togo	West	27%	1,218,000

Christianity was first planted in the fifteenth century when the Portuguese started trading with various native kingdoms in the area. The first native African bishop was ordained in the early sixteenth century. However, by the eighteenth and early nineteenth centuries, the fortunes of the Church had waned and its presence had considerably declined. Evangelization was reinvigorated in the late nineteenth and twentieth centuries during French and Belgian colonization. The influence of those imperial powers became widespread across the region during the nineteenth and early twentieth centuries. As a result, French is the official language in eight of the ten nations and France remains a key trading partner.

The political violence and instability associated with independence and its aftermath led to new conflicts that in turn often define the pastoral challenges confronted by the local church. As elsewhere in Africa, much of the conflict revolves around access to valuable minerals and other natural resources and is colored by long-standing ethnic rivalries.

Table 4.8 Selected Church Statistics, Central Africa: 1975 and 2000			
	1975	**2000**	**Change**
Catholic Population	17,919,000	42,976,000	140%
% Catholic	38%	45%	16%
Ecclesiastical Territories	90	116	22%
Parishes per Territory	18	23	24%
Dioceses	88	114	23%
Parishes	1,589	2,703	41%
Missions	13,034	15,382	15%
Catholics per Parish	11,395	15,990	29%
Total Catholic Schools	3,136	12,454	75%
Priests	4,446	7,037	37%
% Diocesan	31%	66%	53%
Women Religious	7,227	11,826	39%
Catholics per Priest	4,072	6,142	34%

The Democratic Republic of the Congo is by far the largest in sheer geographic size, with a territory more than three times the size of Texas and four times that of France. Its 27 million Catholics represent over half the total population and are the largest number of Catholics in any single African country. Even when compared to elsewhere in Africa, a relatively small proportion (about 64 percent) of Catholics join the Church as infants. This may reflect a continuing large proportion of adult Christian converts or suggest that many Catholic families do not have an opportunity to have their children baptized until they have passed the primary years due to limited contact with parish life or Church personnel.

Rich in natural resources, and twice as large geographically as the rest of Central Africa combined, the country's gross domestic product per capita is nonetheless the lowest in Central Africa at just $600. Its infant mortality rate is the third highest in the region: nearly 10 percent of all babies born in the Congo die before their first birthday. As a result of these and other health-related realities, including the increasing incidence of AIDS, life expectancy is 49 years.

The Church plays an important role in education within this huge country, particularly as war and recurring crises led to the marked deterioration of the public educational system. There are few secondary schools and almost no colleges or universities. As a result, the Church's almost 7,000 primary schools and over 2,000 Catholic secondary schools have a particularly important presence in the life of the country. The social services of the Church in the Congo are also fairly extensive. There are 166 Catholic hospitals, some 97 orphanages, over 100 homes for the elderly, and over 2,300 other service institutions.

The Church's institutional presence within an otherwise weak civil society has often meant that the Church has been the only independent voice available to speak out on behalf of the voiceless. As a result of the Church's leadership against dictatorship and corruption, a variety of governments over past decades have repeatedly targeted Church leaders. These actions have led to the deaths of thousands, including hundreds of Church workers.

With only about 4,000 priests and 7,000 women religious to serve a Catholic population of over 26 million, the front lines of the Church in the Congo have long been filled by catechists, who number about six times the figure for priests and sisters combined. These Church workers have suffered the brunt of attacks on the Church.

SOUTHERN AFRICA

Eighteen percent of those who live in southern Africa are Catholic, representing 13 percent of all African Catholics. On a proportional basis, there are fewer diocesan priests in this region relative to religious order priests. Only 38 percent of all priests in Southern Africa are diocesan, compared to 64 percent for Africa as a whole. In addition, there are fewer priests relative to the Catholic population. The average of 6,031 Catholics per priest for this region is about 2.5 times higher than for Africa overall.

On the other hand, the ratio of Catholics to women religious is close to that for the continent as a whole. And, while there are very few permanent deacons in Africa, over three-quarters are found in Southern Africa, especially in the Republic of South Africa. The concentration of deacons in this country, representing some 64 percent of all African deacons, is consistent with general worldwide patterns that show a correlation between large numbers of deacons and relatively wealthy countries with a strong European presence. In Southern Africa, as throughout all of Africa, the Republic of South Africa is the economic giant. Its GDP per capita of $8,000 dwarfs that of the other countries of the continent. Approximately 13.6 percent of its population, about 6 million people, are of European origin, the highest concentration of white settlers from the colonial era in all of Africa. Reflecting its greater relative wealth, health statistics and life expectancy for South Africa are also at a different level than in the rest of Africa. Three million South African Catholics worship in 729 parishes in 25 dioceses. Priests in South Africa numbered 1,077 in 2000 and women religious numbered 2,658. The number of Catholics per priest or women religious was similar as that for Africa as a whole, 2,861 Catholics per priest and 1,159 Catholics per women religious.

Table 4.9 Selected Church Statistics, Southern Africa: 1975 and 2000			
	1975	**2000**	**Change**
Catholic Population	7,596,000	17,059,100	125%
% Catholic	15%	18%	20%
Ecclesiastical Territories	60	74	23%
Parishes per Territory	18	22	23%
Dioceses	52	69	33%
Parishes	1,064	1,608	51%
Missions	2,908	11,130	283%
Catholics per Parish	7,126	10,483	47%
Total Catholic Schools	3,248	1,778	-45%
Priests	2,483	2,795	13%
% Diocesan	22%	38%	73%
Women Religious	7,620	7,451	-2%
Catholics per Priest	3,053	6,031	98%

In Africa, there generally are more non-Catholic Christians than Catholics, something not the case in Europe or in the Americas. This is particularly true in Southern Africa. Although Catholicism arrived with Portuguese explorers at the Cape of Good Hope in 1488, Catholic influence rapidly waned as French, German, and Dutch Calvinists came to South Africa in the seventeenth and eighteenth centuries, followed by the British by the end of the eighteenth century. Catholic European immigrants, as well as a Catholic missionary presence, only began to grow significantly in the twentieth century. Today, 83 percent of the South African population is Christian but only 8 percent of the total population is Catholic.

This pattern is replicated elsewhere in Southern Africa, where non-Catholic Christians tend to constitute a clearly majority within the Christian population. Non-Catholic Christian bodies include the historical Protestant churches such as Anglican and Lutherans, as well as a large number of flourishing but more localized Christian religious bodies.

Angola is an exception to the typical Southern Africa pattern in two ways: it has a majority Catholic population, and it has a particularly weak presence of priests relative to the number of Catholics. With just over 550 priests for more than seven million Catholics, Angola exceeds 14,000 Catholics per priest. In this sense it is more similar to Central Africa than Southern Africa. The same is true with Angola's large number of catechists relative to its number of priests and sisters. Its 27,389 catechists are more than twelve times the number of priests and sisters, reflecting a particularly strong dependence on the efforts of these key lay church workers. Indeed, Angola is just third after the Democratic Republic of Congo and Mozambique in terms of the absolute number of catechists.

Although rich in natural resources, Angola is one of the poorest countries in the world, and cannot feed itself. Farmers are afraid to cultivate the land because literally millions of land mines remain buried in their fields. Over past decades, the Church's ability to minister to Angolans has been limited by the government, and Church workers have been repeatedly attacked.

THE INDIAN OCEAN

Catholicism came relatively late to this region of islands in the Indian Ocean off the east coast of Africa. Nonetheless, today about one in four Indian Ocean islanders is Catholic. The islands have relatively more priests and women religious than Central, East, or Southern Africa. Almost five million Catholics inhabit the more than 100 islands of this region, worshiping in 456 parishes.

Thirteen hundred priests, 42 percent of them diocesan, minister to these islanders. There are 3,752 Catholics per priest, lower than the overall figure for Africa. In general, the presence of women religious (4,400) and religious brothers (525) is also strong. There is one sister for every 1,139 Catholics, about half the ratio for Africa as a whole.

Early evangelization in the islands during the seventeenth century did not take root. However, in the eighteenth century, the increasingly successful efforts of a French religious community, the Vincentians, began on Reunion and throughout the Seychelles island chain. In the nineteenth century, the Jesuits and others evangelized in Madagascar and Reunion. Most evangelization efforts were connected in some way with the Church in France and the reinvigorated missionary efforts it sponsored during the nineteenth century. An exception to the success experienced by these efforts is the Islamic Republic of the Comorros, which converted to Islam through the influence of Arab traders in the 1500s.

Table 4.10 Selected Church Statistics, Indian Ocean: 1975 and 2000			
	1975	**2000**	**Change**
Catholic Population	2,547,000	5,101,000	100%
% Catholic	27%	27%	0%
Ecclesiastical Territories	21	23	14%
Parish per Territory	13	19	49%
Dioceses	20	23	15%
Parishes	267	456	71%
Missions	4,713	7,058	50%
Catholics per Parish	9,442	10,992	16%
Total Catholic Schools	1,889	3,028	60%
Priests	922	1,336	45%
% Diocesan	28%	42%	50%
Women Religious	2,463	4,400	79%
Catholics per Priest	2,734	3,752	37%

The region is dominated by Madagascar, an island the size of France, where 20 of the 23 dioceses in the Indian Ocean region are located, as are 310 of the 456 parishes. The fourth largest island in the world, and largest island nation, Madagascar contains 86 percent of the region's population. Although it is just 500 kilometers off the coast of Mozambique, its population is primarily descended from peoples of Malaysian and Indonesian origin. About 26 percent of its population is Catholic and there are more than 1,000 priests and 3,500 women religious.

EAST AFRICA

East Africa contains 28 percent of all Catholics in Africa, the second largest concentration of any of Africa's six regions. Over 37 million Catholics live in these ten countries, making this region 17 percent Catholic. Although Catholic population is 13 percent less than in Central Africa, there are more priests in this region than any other. There are some 4,921

Catholics per priest, about average for the continent as a whole. Sixty percent of priests are diocesan. In 2000, the 105 dioceses and 11 other ecclesiastical territories of East Africa together report some 4,800 seminarians, who were studying in 37 seminaries within the region. In that year, a total of 234 diocesan priests were ordained.

Table 4.11 Selected Church Statistics, East Africa: 1975 and 2000			
	1975	2000	Change
Catholic Population	12,139,000	37,266,100	207%
% Catholic	12%	17%	42%
Ecclesiastical Territories	83	116	40%
Parish per Territory	20	24	18%
Dioceses	71	105	48%
Parishes	1,659	2,747	66%
Missions	5,729	17,920	213%
Catholics per Parish	7,163	13,473	88%
Total Catholic Schools	7,056	12,607	79%
Priests	4,234	7,521	78%
% Diocesan	35%	60%	71%
Women Religious	8,942	17,625	97%
Catholics per Priest	2,807	4,921	75%

Catholicism came to East Africa through Egyptian missionaries in the fourth century, Portuguese sailors and religious in the sixteenth century, and a variety of European missionary societies and orders in the late nineteenth century.

Christianity was established in Ethiopia in 332 under the Church in Alexandria, and soon became the religion of the state. As a result of the work of Coptic missionaries, much of what was to become Ethiopia, Eritrea, Djibouti, Somalia, and Sudan became and remained Christian for centuries, in spite of the rise of Islam beginning in the seventh century. In few countries has the Christian tradition been as ancient and unbroken as in Ethiopia and Eritrea. About 58 percent of Ethiopians and 51 percent of Eritreans are Christian, primarily members of the Ethiopian Orthodox Church. Only 440,000 Ethiopians are Catholics, less than 1 percent of the country's population. Nonetheless, Ethiopia has 184 Catholic schools and 438 priests, one for every 1,009 Catholics. Its Catholic clergy is larger than in most African countries of its size. There are proportionally more Catholics in Eritrea, a country that was formerly Ethiopia's northern province and became independent in 1993. However, given Eritrea's smaller population, there are many fewer Catholics in that country.

Located just to the south of Egypt, Sudan is divided between an Islamic north and a Christian south. This divide has made Sudan the scene of considerable religious and political violence, struggles that are often tied to efforts to control access to lucrative oil and mineral rights. Twelve percent of Sudanese are Catholic. However, Islamic political elites have considerably restricted non-Islamic religious practice.

By the year 2000, about a quarter to a third of Zambians, Kenyans, Tanzanians, and Malawians were counted as Catholic, a larger proportion than found in the northern, more Islamic-dominated parts of East Africa. Although the Portuguese had brought Christianity to Zambia and Malawi in the late fifteenth and sixteenth centuries, a significant Catholic presence did not really begin until the late nineteenth century.

By 2000, Kenya had the most dense educational network for any African country among those countries with more than 7 million Catholics. The Catholic Church in Kenya operates some 5,303 elementary schools, more than any other African country except the much larger Democratic Republic of the Congo. The Church in Kenya also operates 1,268 secondary schools and 2,541 charitable institutions.

Evangelization in Uganda began in the late nineteenth century. The Church experienced strong persecution during the initial stages of evangelization as well as during more recent times, first under King Mwanga II from 1885 to1887 and then under President Idi Amin from 1971 to 1979. More recently, the Church has worked under the threat of rebel violence in the northern and southwestern regions of the country, making it difficult for Church workers to minister effectively.

By 2000, Catholics made up about half the population (45 percent) and numbered over 10 million. The Church had become well established and Church growth was relatively more dependent on natural increase than elsewhere in the continent. Of the 320,451 baptisms recorded in 2000, 86 percent were of persons under the age of seven, a much higher proportion than for the continent as a whole. Nationwide, there are about 1,600 priests, 2,711 women religious, and over 12,000 catechists. The number of Catholic primary schools, 3,266, is the third largest in Africa and the number of hospitals, 30, is the sixth highest.

As elsewhere in sub-Saharan Africa, Uganda's greatest recent challenge has been in the form of the AIDS virus. In spite of having a per capita income higher than that of many neighboring countries, life expectancy is only about 42 years, in large part due to the high rate of HIV/AIDS infection. Uganda, however, has become distinguished for taking strong and effective action to reduce the incidence of HIV/AIDS infection. The Church has participated in public health efforts to help HIV/AIDS patients and reduce infection. Over the past few years, the rate of infection has decreased from 14 percent to 8 percent, a noteworthy achievement in a continent where the scourge of AIDS has been dramatically increasing. Nonetheless, the huge challenges of a large population with the terminal infectious disease remain. These realities will likely have a decisive impact on the future of the country, and on many of its neighbors in the continent as well.

Table 4.12 The Catholic Church in Africa, by Region: 2000

	Central	East	Indian Ocean	North	Southern	West
Catholic Population	42,976,000	37,266,100	5,101,000	363,200	17,059,100	27,253,000
% Catholic	45%	17%	27%	.26%	18%	12%
Ecclesiastical Territories	116	116	24	26	74	139
Parish per Territory	23	24	19	12	22	23
Dioceses	114	105	23	19	69	136
Parishes	2,703	2,747	456	313	1,608	3,195
Missions	15,382	17,920	7,058	176	11,130	17,408
Catholics per Parish	15,990	13,473	10,992	1,160	10,483	8,463
Total Catholic Schools	12,454	12,607	3,028	297	1,778	7,378
Priests	7,037	7,521	1,336	693	2,795	7,783
% Diocesan	66%	60%	42%	41%	38%	76%
Women Religious	11,826	17,625	4,400	2,101	7,451	9,180
Catholics per Priest	6,142	4,921	3,752	524	6,031	3,474
Charitable Institutions						
Hospitals	215	237	13	16	100	238
Homes for Elderly	216	441	33	25	116	59
Orphanages	176	261	32	18	235	137
Other	3,626	3,794	371	285	1,317	2,235

CHAPTER 5

America

This chapter follows the precedent established by the 1999 Synod for America and treats all the land mass of North America and South America as a single unit. The initial discussion that follows is accompanied by a general presentation of major trends within the Church in America at a demographic, institutional, and personnel-related level. The main body of the chapter is focused on a detailed discussion of specific realities within particular regions of the Americas–North America, Central America and Mexico, the Caribbean, and South America.

OVERVIEW

The Americas are distinctive in the sense that they can be seen as the great meeting ground of the world. Each country has taproots of language and religion flowing to Europe–but also ties to Africa and Asia, whether through the centuries-long nightmare of the transatlantic slave trade, the ancient migration of Asian peoples to pre-Columbian America, or more contemporary streams.

In secular terms, this area is seldom considered as a single entity, perhaps because its various regions developed from historical ties to rival European powers and cultures. Nonetheless, the Church has come to see the Americas as more similar than different, and in need of cultivating increasing solidarity from the tip of Tierra del Fuego to the northernmost reaches of Canada. Increasingly, representatives of the separate Catholic bishops' conferences of Canada, the United States, Latin America, and the Antilles gather for consultation and common planning. This is likely to deepen further over the course of the twenty-first century.

Taken separately, both North America (defined in geographic terms as stretching to the isthmus of Panama) and South America are smaller than

Europe. Taken together, however, America is second in size only to Asia. In terms of population, America is the most Christian area of the world. It is also the most Catholic. Almost two of every five of the world's Christians are found here–as are one in two of the world's Catholics. Well over 85 percent of the total population is Christian. This is higher than anywhere else in the world. The continent with the next highest proportion of Christians is Europe, where an estimated 77 percent of the population is counted as Christian. Indeed, 27 of the 55 sovereign countries with populations 75 percent or more Catholic are in the Americas.

Table 5.1 Countries with Populations over 75 Percent Catholic: 2000		
	Number of Countries with 75% or More Baptized Catholics	**As a Percent of Each Continent's Countries**
Africa	5	9%
America	27	54%
Asia	2	4%
Europe	17	40%
Oceania	3	13%

America occupies about 30 percent of the world's land mass, whereas Africa includes 23 percent of the world's land mass. However, both Africa and America contain a similar proportion of the world's population (about 14 percent). America's lower population density is in part due to the difficult geography of the tundra, mountainous regions, deserts, and other challenging spaces. This relatively low population density also underlines the appeal America has long had for settlers from other continents. No other part of the world has seen such dramatic changes in the composition of its population over the past five centuries. Today, very little of the population is comprised of full descendants of those who inhabited these lands in 1500, many of whom perished in the massive epidemics accompanying the European invasions. In many cases, the original indigenous populations are entirely extinct; in others they were forcibly removed from economically valuable areas or live only within mixed populations that also contain European and African elements. For the most part, these mixed populations are more characteristic of Latin America than elsewhere in the Americas.

Historically, these countries have had a rich cultural and religious heritage focused on the Catholic Church. As a result, the percentages of the population reported to be baptized Catholics have always been high. However, throughout the second half of the twentieth century, Latin

America has been the site of a noteworthy expansion of Protestant evangelical Christianity. As a result, it is likely that the figures reporting the percentage of the population that is baptized Catholic may not represent those who would currently consider themselves Catholic, or be in the process of raising their children Catholic.

However, precisely because these changes are so recent, their magnitude is difficult to estimate with precision. One set of estimates, calculated by David Barrett and his collaborators, utilizes the Church's numbers of baptized Catholics and compares those figures to membership figures reported by evangelical and other religious bodies together with figures accounting for the religious practices or preferences of the population as a whole. The net result are figures of those termed "doubly affiliated" Christians–persons apparently baptized Catholic but now counted as a member by an evangelical or other religious body that is not Catholic. Of course, such estimates cannot be precise and calculations like these allow for multiple sources of bias. However, compared with other estimates they may be useful to understand broader dynamics within Catholic religious affiliation.

Another tool for estimating the proportion of the population that is likely to currently consider itself Catholic, or likely to be baptized Catholic in the future, is based on the baptism figures for the most recent available year. This approach takes the number of known births in a population and divides it by the number of infant baptisms reported by the Church. Both baptism and birth statistics, of course, may be subject to error and considerable under- or over-reporting. However, it is interesting to note the frequency of cases where the percent of Catholic baptisms to all births is close to the percent of baptized Catholics less the percent estimated to now identify as evangelical Protestants. In any case, the figures reported below raise questions about the high proportion of Catholics often reported for Latin America.

As the figures suggest, there has been dramatic change in some countries, particularly Brazil, which is now not only the world's largest Catholic country, but possibly also the world's second largest Protestant country after the United States. Of course, these figures may be explained by a variety of factors–including poorly reported statistics. For this reason, the three different sources are particularly useful to compare. In order to provide consistency and follow standard Catholic definitions of membership in the Church, however, this book will focus only on the figures representing all baptized Catholics, both adults and children, regardless of their level of practice or involvement with other religious bodies. As the table implies, however, these numbers might not be as useful to predict long-term membership patterns.

	Births Baptized Catholic (est.)*	Catholic Baptisms of Total Population	Percent Evangelicals Baptized Catholic	Evangelicals Baptized Catholic (est.)
Argentina	74%	91%	13%	4,786,128
Bolivia	64%	88%	5%	377,968
Brazil	55%	90%	32%	55,239,391
Chile	63%	78%	20%	3,099,410
Colombia	75%	96%	3%	1,174,912
Costa Rica	98%	96%	8%	304,439
Cuba	52%	43%	0%	na
Dominican Republic	35%	89%	0%	na
Ecuador	72%	97%	2%	245,613
El Salvador	62%	97%	16%	975,378
French Guiana	37%	80%	4%	6,554
Guatemala	91%	94%	11%	1,263,638
Haiti	53%	93%	11%	905,576
Honduras	34%	86%	3%	220,600
Mexico	78%	94%	7%	7,380,873
Nicaragua	40%	85%	5%	266,868
Panama	43%	86%	8%	232,836
Paraguay	61%	90%	1%	37,798
Peru	38%	96%	6%	1,581,451
Puerto Rico	54%	75%	1%	40,409
Uruguay	57%	78%	4%	131,471
Venezuela	66%	94%	5%	1,257,766

Table 5.2 The Changing Face of Christianity in Latin America: 2000

* Catholic baptisms of those under age seven compared to the total number of births over 12 months.

One reason why evangelical Protestant faiths have spread so rapidly in Latin America is due to the cultural and social homogeneity of the region. Common or similar languages and cultures have made communication and cultural and religious change much easier. This common culture offers a great contrast to the enormous cultural diversity of Africa, a continent also heavily affected by European colonialism. In this sense, the two continents could not be any more different. In 1900, Africa entered the twentieth century largely as a set of isolated horticultural societies. Latin America, on the other hand, was and had been long composed primarily of agricultural societies with organized states and recognized national identities.

At the beginning of the nineteenth century, the entire population of the Americas was about 30,400,000 or perhaps 3 percent of the world's population. A sizeable share of the newly arrived populations consisted of those brought from Africa as slaves. Within a hundred years, the population had grown six times larger to over 180 million, largely as the result of European immigration to North America. After 1950, natural population increases began to produce particularly significant gains in Latin America. Thus, while the population of the United States in 1900 represented 41 percent of the population of the Americas, by 2000 the U.S. population was only 34 percent of the total population of the Americas.

POPULATION

Over the 25-year period from 1975 to 2000, Catholic population in the Americas grew somewhat faster than overall population growth. However, in spite of this rapid growth, the numbers of marriages annually recorded by the Catholic Church in the Americas have actually declined by 10 percent. And the number of baptisms performed in 2000 is higher, but only 6 percent higher, than the comparable figure for 1975.

Table 5.3 Selected Church Population Statistics, America: 1975 and 2000			
	1975	**2000**	**Change**
Total Population	555,846,000	826,554,000	49%
Catholic Population	341,290,000	519,391,000	52%
Percent Catholic	61%	63%	2%
Percent of Catholics Worldwide	48%	50%	3%
Ecclesiastical Territories	868	1,050	21%
Parishes	44,210	54,682	24%
Parishes per Territory	51	52	2%
Catholics per Territory	393,191	494,658	26%
All Baptisms	8,929,022	9,433,170	6%
Baptisms under 7 years old (%)	98%	91%	-7%
Confirmations	na	4,401,416	na
Marriages	1,790,791	1,604,687	-10%

However, the proportion of baptisms that were of persons seven years of age or older increased significantly during this time, from about 2 to 9 percent of all baptisms.

INSTITUTIONS

Growth in the number of parishes rivaled population growth during the third quarter of the twentieth century. However, parish growth was far lower than population growth during the final quarter of the century. In fact, from 1950 to 1975, the 121 percent growth in parishes outpaced the 88 percent growth in Catholic population. Between 1975 and 2000, Catholic population grew by 52 percent, but parishes grew by only 24 percent. There was also a slowdown in the creation of new dioceses over these two periods, from 63 percent to 30 percent growth rates.

Table 5.4 Selected Church Institution Statistics, America: 1975 and 2000			
	1975	**2000**	**Change**
Catholic Population	341,290,000	519,391,000	52%
Percent of Catholics Worldwide	48%	50%	3%
Ecclesiastical Territories	868	1,050	21%
Dioceses or Eparchies	725	944	30%
% of Territories Worldwide	37%	37%	0%
Total Pastoral Centers	71,730	122,513	71%
Parishes	44,210	54,682	24%
Missions	14,167	5,992	-58%
Catholics per Parish	7,720	9,498	23%
Primary Schools	22,865	23,860	4%
Secondary Schools	8,565	9,409	10%
Seminaries	470	760	62%

Like parishes, educational institutions grew more quickly when Catholic population was much smaller. There are currently many more Catholics per school, as well as many more Catholics per parish, than had been the case for most of the twentieth century. As a result, there are natural limits on the number of Catholics that may be effectively served in parish life. Churches can be only so big, and only so many Masses or other sacraments may be celebrated at any one time. This is not the case for educational or charitable institutions, which are less hampered by natural size limitations. A Catholic university can have students in the hundreds or tens of thousands; health care institutions or other social services can reach a handful or exponentially larger numbers of people based on how they are organized.

Consequently, the fact that recent decades have been a time of comparatively slower growth in the founding of Catholic institutions may mean that the existing institutions have simply expanded in size and can still serve similar or greater proportions of the population. On the other hand, after a certain point, a slower growth rate of parishes relative to fast-growing populations may mean that it is much more likely that fewer Catholics can actively participate in parish community life.

PERSONNEL

Increases in Church personnel over the past half-century have been significant in their own right but relatively insignificant in comparison to the increase in total Catholic population. Thus, the number of priests increased by 42 percent while the number of Catholics rose by 187 percent. As a result, the average number of Catholics per priest throughout the Americas grew by 103 percent between 1950 and 2000. In 1950, there were 2,117 Catholics per priest; by 1975, there were 2,967 Catholics per priest, and by 2000 that figure had increased to 4,298 Catholics per priest. Taking the Americas as a whole, ordinations have increased between 1975 and 2000, and the proportion of priests per ordinand declined by as much as 25 percent, suggesting continued increases in the number of priests for the years ahead. Nonetheless, Catholic population is also likely to continue to outstrip growth in the number of priests and some regions are likely to have very different growth trajectories.

Overall, the number of seminarians between 1975 and 2000 increased by 80 percent. Seminarians for the religious clergy increased 52 percent and seminarians for diocesan clergy rose 98 percent. In other words, proportionally more men are entering the seminary in order to become diocesan priests. In 1975, these candidates for diocesan priesthood constituted 61 percent of all those preparing for priesthood. By 2000, diocesan priesthood candidates made up 67 percent of all seminarians.

Shifts within the numbers of women religious parallel the relative declines among religious priests over the last half of the twentieth century. In 1950 there were four women religious per priest; by 2000 there were two women religious per priest, representing a significant proportional and absolute decrease.

Table 5.5 Selected Church Personnel Statistics, America: 1975 and 2000

	1975	2000	Change
Catholic Population	341,290,000	519,391,000	52%
Percent of Catholics Worldwide	48%	50%	3%
Bishops	na	1,695	na
Total Priests	115,039	120,841	5%
Diocesan	65,140	75,121	15%
Religious	49,899	45,720	-8%
Permanent Deacons	1,807	18,342	915%
Religious Brothers	21,707	16,615	-23%
Religious Women	296,001	232,986	-21%
Diocesan Priest Ordinations	1,371	2,156	57%
Total Seminarians	20,231	36,392	80%
Diocesan	12,288	24,353	98%
Religious	7,943	12,039	52%
Catholics per Priest	2,967	4,298	45%
Catholics per Woman Religious	1,153	2,229	93%

REGIONS

The definition of Latin America given above is both so vast, and more cultural than geographical, as to not be workable for a nuanced discussion of the continent except for certain broad trends. The regions used in the discussion that follows are designed to provide more detailed analysis.

These groupings also include a number of territories that belong to sovereign states listed elsewhere, typically European countries that continue to have dependencies in the Americas. Often self-governing at a local level, these territories are listed with the country to which they correspond named in parentheses. For the sake of consistency, statistics that pertain to these territories are treated as part of the region in which they are located rather than the country to which they belong. The exception is Greenland, which has a single Catholic parish and is part of the Diocese of Copenhagen. Because it is at once so vast and uninhabited, Greenland's land mass is also excluded from any discussion of the geographic expanse of the Americas, and, along with Antarctica, from any of the land mass calculations given in this book.

The regions within America are defined as follows:

- *North America:* Bermuda (United Kingdom), Canada, Greenland (Denmark), St. Pierre et Miquelon (France), United States

- *Caribbean:* Anguilla (United Kingdom), Antigua and Barbuda, Aruba (Netherlands), Bahamas, Barbados, Cayman Islands (United Kingdom), Cuba, Dominica, Dominican Republic, Grenada, Guadeloupe (France), Haiti, Jamaica, Martinique (France), Montserrat (United Kingdom), Netherlands Antilles (Netherlands), Puerto Rico (United States), St. Kitts and Nevis, Santa Lucia, St. Vincent and the Grenadines, Trinidad and Tobago, Turks and Caicos Islands (United Kingdom), Virgin Islands (United Kingdom), Virgin Islands (United States)

- *Mesoamerica:* Belize, Costa Rica, El Salvador, Guatemala, Honduras, Mexico, Nicaragua, Panama

- *South America:* Argentina, Bolivia, Brazil, Chile, Colombia, Ecuador, French Guiana (France), Falkland Islands (United Kingdom), Guyana, Paraguay, Peru, Suriname, Uruguay, Venezuela

NORTH AMERICA

This northernmost region includes Canada, the United States, an island colony of Britain, Bermuda, located off the coast of the southeastern United States, together with an island dependency of France, St. Pierre et Miquelon, near the eastern coast of Canada. As noted earlier, Greenland also falls within this region.

Twenty-five percent of North Americans are Catholic, representing 15 percent of all Catholics in the Western Hemisphere. More than 76 million Catholics live across a total area of almost 20 million square kilometers. More than 58,000 priests are found in this region, 64 percent of whom are diocesan priests. Nearly 50 percent of all priests in the Americas are in this region.

As measured on a per Catholic basis, Church institutions in this region are in comparative abundance—and thus offer a greater opportunity than elsewhere in the Americas for Catholics to participate in the sacramental and institutional life of the Church. Figures for the number of Catholics per parish, per school, and per charitable institution tend to be between 2 to 4.5 times higher than in the Caribbean, Mesoamerica, or South America.

Table 5.6 Selected Church Statistics, North America: 1975 and 2000			
	1975	**2000**	**Change**
Catholic Population	57,050,000	76,815,100	35%
% Catholic	24%	25%	1%
Ecclesiastical Territories	238	191	-18%
Parishes per Territory	99	92	-7%
Dioceses	234	263	12%
Parishes	23,678	24,480	3%
Catholics per Parish	2,398	3,189	33%
Catholic Schools	11,666	9,709	-17%
Priests	68,420	58,129	-15%
% Diocesan	62%	64%	2%
Women Religious	174,619	103,560	-41%
Catholics per Priest	830	1,343	61%

The relatively low numbers of Catholics per priest in North America that had been a feature of the twentieth-century Church in this region began to change rapidly by the last decades of the century. While the Catholic population in North America grew 35 percent between 1975 and 2000, slightly more than the rate of growth for the total population, the number of priests declined by 15 percent, increasing the ratio of Catholics per priest by over 61 percent. During the same period, the number of religious, especially women religious, declined as well, dropping by 41 percent.

Although Canada occupies a larger share of the land mass of North America than the United States, its total population of almost 31 million represents only about 10 percent of the population of the United States. The presence of francophone Quebec has a particularly striking effect on the Church in Canada, which is organized in two parallel and very different language and cultural groupings. Although English-speaking Catholics have long made up the largest share of Catholics in North America due to the large size of the Church in the United States, French-speaking dioceses far predate English-speaking ones. The first Mass was celebrated in Canada in 1534, and Catholicism took root there when Samuel de Champlain founded Quebec in 1608. Similarly, the first religious community and Catholic hospital founded in the present-day United States was in predominantly French New Orleans.

Jesuit, Franciscan, and other Catholic missionaries began their work among the native peoples from the very beginning. As a result of their work and those of the missionary orders who followed them throughout the region, there is a strong Catholic presence among the native peoples of North America. To this day, native peoples in North America are often more likely to be Catholic than their non-native neighbors.

A period of tension between the government and the Catholic Church in Quebec ensued after England acquired Canada in 1763. However, these issues were largely resolved and Catholicism spread through western Canada after the 1840 Act of Union that brought Upper and Lower Canada together into one country. Forty-four percent of Canadians are Catholic, a total of over 13 million people, making Catholicism the most common religious body in the country. These figures are somewhat misleading given the disproportional French Canadian presence within the Church. Although only about 30 percent of the non-French-speaking population identifies as Catholic, 86 percent of French-speaking Canadians do so. Patterns regarding religious practice also vary by language group. Mass attendance has declined throughout Canada since the 1960s, but nowhere faster than within Quebec. In the mid-1960s, about 75 percent of Catholics attended on a weekly or near-weekly basis. By the mid-1990s, however, about 25 percent of Catholics in Quebec reported weekly attendance and the percentage showed signs of continuing decline. In the rest of Canada, 40 percent of Catholics reported weekly attendance, and the figure has held steady since the mid-1970s, although the proportions generally mirror those within the culture as a whole. Canada's Atlantic provinces thus have some of the highest rates of attendance and the Pacific Coast province of British Columbia some of the lowest. Unlike the situation in the United States, most provincial governments fund the 1,229 primary and 253 secondary schools conducted under Catholic auspices.

The English-speaking Catholic presence in North America began with a small number of wealthy and well-educated English Catholic refugees who created vast estates on land not far from the present-day capital of the United States. In 1789, the same year as the ratification of the U.S. Constitution and inauguration of the first U.S. president, John Carroll became the country's first Catholic bishop. However, outside of a small concentration of Catholic families near Carroll's see city of Baltimore, the Spanish- and French-descended people of southern Louisiana who became incorporated into the United States in 1803, and Mexicans who inhabited the vast expanse from Texas to California that was seized in the 1830s and 1840s, there were few Catholics in the United States until the waves of European immigration during the mid-nineteenth century.

As a result of these immigrants, Catholics in North America have a more diverse set of cultural origins than anywhere else in the world. This includes more than 20 eparchies of the Eastern Catholic Churches, nearly all of which are in the United States. North America is the only place where such eparchies are established in any significant number outside their original homelands. These range from the Syro-Malabar Catholic Church, comprised of Catholics from India, to the Byzantine Catholic Churches of Eastern Europe and the Maronite Church based in Lebanon.

The Catholic Church in the United States also includes millions of African Americans and Asians, as well as a dramatically growing population of Catholics of Latin American origin or heritage. Growth in these latter groups is a major point of departure from the middle of the twentieth century, when over 90 percent of the Church in the United States was of European immigrant origin. Catholic population trends reflect recent U.S. population trends. By the end of the twentieth century, the United States was the fifth largest Spanish-speaking country as measured by native speakers.

Levels of participation, formation, and practice of the faith vary considerably for Catholics of different nationalities, racial or ethnic groups, educational background, and regions of the country. However, overall, surveys suggest that weekly Mass attendance ranges from about 60 percent of Catholics over age 60 to about a little over 20 percent for Catholics under 40.

CARIBBEAN

In comparison to North America's almost 20 million square kilometers, the 24 countries or territories of the Caribbean cover only a little more than 200,000 square kilometers. Population density is much higher, with nearly 161 people per square kilometer in the Caribbean, compared to 16 in North America. Countries or territories in this region include those on the islands of the West Indies, which include the Greater and Lesser Antilles, as well as island chains such as the Bahamas, just outside the Caribbean Sea.

The Caribbean stretches 4,000 kilometers from the southern tip of the United States to Venezuela, dividing the Atlantic Ocean from the Gulf of Mexico and the Caribbean Sea. The historical importance of these diverse islands as trading and military outposts has resulted in a great diversity of separately governed microstates and a variety of official languages. The islands of the northern part are larger and comprise the Greater Antilles. They include Cuba, Jamaica, Haiti, and the Dominican Republic, the Cayman Islands (a British territory), and Puerto Rico (a territory of the

United States). These were the territories first encountered by Christopher Columbus and the first Spanish missionaries in 1492-3.

Table 5.7 Selected Church Statistics, Caribbean Basin: 1975 and 2000			
	1975	**2000**	**Change**
Catholic Population	16,642,100	25,207,200	51%
% Catholic	62%	67%	8%
Ecclesiastical Territories	35	54	54%
Parishes per Territory	34	33	-5%
Dioceses	35	51	46%
Parishes	1,207	1,765	46%
Catholics per Parish	13,716	14,345	5%
Catholic Schools	1,706	2,667	56%
Priests	2,449	3,020	23%
% Diocesan	33%	50%	52%
Women Religious	5,274	5,331	1%
Catholics per Priest	6,760	8,384	24%

Of the 24 nations and territories in the Caribbean, the Dominican Republic has the greatest Catholic population of any of the islands. The Church counts 88 percent of the 8.5 million inhabitants as Catholic. This results in an average of 9,277 Catholics for each of the 804 priests. Forty-seven percent of its priests are diocesan. More than 27,000 catechists and over 1,600 women religious minister to Catholics in 485 parishes in 12 dioceses.

The Lesser Antilles arc southeast from Puerto Rico to Venezuela, and include territories of the Netherlands, Britain, France, Venezuela, and the United States. They include Barbados, Trinidad and Tobago, the Turks and Caicos Islands, Aruba, Curacao, and Bonaire, together with the Leeward and Windward Islands. The Leeward Islands include the British and U.S. Virgin Islands, Guadeloupe, St. Eustatius and Saba, St. Martin, St. Kitts and Nevis, Antigua and Barbuda, Anguilla, and Montserrat. The Windward Islands include Martinique, Dominica, Grenada, St. Lucia, and St. Vincent and the Grenadines.

Catholics comprise about 80 percent of the population of Aruba, Dominica, Guadeloupe, Saint Lucia, Martinique, and the Netherlands Antilles (which include the islands of Curacao, Bonaire, Saint Eustatius and Saba, as well as part of Saint Martin). For the most part the populations of these island territories and microstates are quite small. The largest by far is that of Trinidad and Tobago. As a result, despite the fact that only about one in three persons in Trinidad and Tobago is Catholic, its nearly 400,000 Catholics give it the greatest number of Catholics anywhere in the Lesser Antilles. Within the islands and microstates of the Lesser Antilles, the number of parishes ranges from 61 in Trinidad and Tobago to one in Anguilla, where 3 percent of the population of 7,000 is Catholic.

MESOAMERICA

Given its common colonial origins, the Catholic Church in Mexico has more in common with the nations of Central America than with Canada and the United States. For purposes of this book, therefore, Mexico is treated as part of "Mesoamerica," a region that encompasses all the countries of Central America, including Panama.

In spite of shared cultural roots, the diversity between the countries of this region is great. A wide variety of pre-Columbian languages and cultural phenomena survive in Guatemala. English is the official language of Belize, and Belize shares much in common with the islands of the Caribbean basin. Panama was historically tied to South America as part of Colombia, and only came to be seen as part of Central America in the twentieth century. Finally, Mexico is a separate case in its own right, and its sheer size dwarfs the rest of the region in geographic, demographic, and economic terms.

The Church in Mexico dates to 1519, when Hernando Cortes and his men, together with their native allies, conquered the Aztec Empire. In the aftermath of the colonial period, the history of the Church in Mexico has been punctuated by times of sharp hostility by the state towards the Church. The situation was particularly tense between 1923 and 1940. By 1958, relations between the Church and the Mexican government began to improve. In 1992, Mexico established full diplomatic ties with the Vatican and has since moved to a situation of greater openness and freedom for the Church.

In spite of Church-State tension across previous centuries and the current rapid growth of evangelical Christians, especially among the more indigenous populations in the south of Mexico, approximately nine in ten Mexicans are baptized Catholic. A little over 14,000 priests, 74 percent of whom are diocesan, are present to a Catholic population of nearly 90 million. The distribution of Catholics per parish and per priest is very different in Mexico and its neighbor to the north. Mexico has 15,502 Catholics per parish, and the United States has 3,273. Likewise, Mexico has 6,382 Catholics per priest, and the United States has 1,311. Catholic population in Mexico is 29 percent higher but the number of parishes (5,784) is 70 percent fewer. Mexico, however, has 171,719 catechists, for an average of 30 per parish, far higher than for any other country in the Americas.

	1975	2000	Change
Table 5.8 Selected Church Statistics, Mesoamerica: 1975 and 2000			
Catholic Population	72,425,000	119,914,000	66%
% Catholic	93%	90%	-3%
Ecclesiastical Territories	112	140	25%
Parishes per Territory	41	53	29%
Dioceses	93	128	-27%
Parishes	4,633	7,453	61%
Catholics per Parish	15,621	16,074	3%
Catholic Schools	3,338	5,926	78%
Priests	11,640	17,687	52%
% Diocesan	66%	70%	6%
Women Religious	27,799	35,720	28%
Catholics per Priest	6,217	6,773	9%

Guatemala, Mexico's neighbor to the southeast, has some 9,764 baptized Catholics per priest, a particularly elevated figure. Another reflection of the Church's relative weakness here is that only 37 percent of its 970 priests are diocesan priests, suggesting a continued dependence on international religious orders to supply priests. This compares to the 74 percent of priests in Mexico who are diocesan priests. The challenges the Church faces in Guatemala largely spring from the country's many decades of civil war and endemic violence. Average income is less than half that of Mexico, and the literacy rate is one of the lowest in the Americas. Guatemala's infant mortality rate of 46 per thousand live births is the third highest, after Bolivia and Haiti.

SOUTH AMERICA

Both South America and Europe have similar numbers of Catholics (280,144,000 in Europe compared to 297,455,000 in South America) and a similarly sized land mass (about 20 million square kilometers). However, this is where other comparisons from the perspective of Church statistics demonstrate sharp differences.

Europe has over six times as many Catholic parishes as South America and 20 percent more dioceses and other ecclesiastical territories. South America's dioceses and ecclesiastical territories average about 36 parishes each while Europe's average 202. Europe has about five times as many priests as South America and about six times as many women religious. South America has 7,112 Catholics per priest while Europe has 1,342 Catholics per priest. In terms of parishes, the difference is even larger: South America has 20,984 Catholics per parish and Europe has 2,162 Catholics per parish.

Trends in the numbers of priests and women religious highlight another facet of South America's long relationship with Europe. Historically, large numbers of priests, particularly religious priests, and women religious, came to South America from Europe. When the number of religious in Europe began to decline in the late 1960s, fewer were sent and others returned to Europe. As a result, the proportion of native-born diocesan clergy has been increasing and the overall rate of growth within numbers of priests and women religious has been slow, due to the loss of Europe as a major source for Church personnel.

Table 5.9 Selected Church Statistics, South America: 1975 and 2000

	1975	2000	Change
Catholic Population	195,173,200	297,455,000	52%
% Catholic	81%	87%	6%
Ecclesiastical Territories	483	589	22%
Parishes per Territory	30	36	20%
Dioceses	364	502	38%
Parishes	14,692	20,984	43%
Catholics per Parish	11,840	14,236	20%
Catholic Schools	14,720	14,967	2%
Priests	32,530	42,005	29%
% Diocesan	43%	56%	13%
Women Religious	88,309	88,375	0%
Catholics per Priest	5,347	7,112	33%

Diversity in this large region is defined largely by geography. The Andes mountain chain stretches from Eastern Venezuela to Bolivia and the Southern Cone includes Chile, Argentina, and Uruguay. The largest country, Brazil, occupies about half the land mass along with the vast Amazon River basin and is usually considered separately, as is the relatively small area to the east of Venezuela colonized by the English, Dutch, and French.

The Andean countries historically had the strongest Church presence in this land of mountains and plateaus, where the Church had a well-established place in the life of the large estates and towns. The sparsely settled jungles leading to the Amazon basin, as well as the traditionally less settled coastal regions, tended to have a weaker Catholic presence and practice.

Table 5.10 The Catholic Church in the Americas, by Region: 2000				
	Caribbean	Meso-america	North America	South America
Catholic Population	25,207,200	119,914,000	76,815,100	297,455,000
% Catholic	67%	90%	25%	87%
Ecclesiastical Territories	54	140	267	589
Parishes per Territory	33	53	92	36
Dioceses	51	128	191	502
Parishes	1,765	7,453	24,480	20,984
Missions	238	1,546	50	4,158
Catholics per Parish	14,345	16,074	3,189	14,236
Catholic Schools	2,667	5,926	9,709	14,967
Priests	3,020	17,687	58,129	42,005
% Diocesan	50%	70%	64%	56%
Women Religious	5,331	35,720	103,560	88,375
Catholics per Priest	8,384	6,773	1,343	7,112
Charitable Institutions				
Hospitals	56	341	652	897
Homes	130	349	1,251	1,735
Orphanages	99	357	685	1,375
Other	2,360	4,627	4,486	16,966

The Southern Cone of Chile, Argentina, and Uruguay has a temperate climate and grew rapidly through immigration from Spain and Italy during the nineteenth and early twentieth centuries. As a result, the Church in the

Southern Cone has tended to have the most in common with the Church in Europe. Uruguay, the smallest of these countries, is also the one where Catholicism– and organized religion in general– is most weakly established. The first diocese was created in Montevideo in 1878 and the political climate reflected the relatively strong anticlerical orientation of nineteenth-century immigrants. Between a quarter and a third of the population has counted itself as agnostic and been unaffiliated with Catholicism since the turn of the twentieth century.

The Church in Brazil includes 143 million baptized Catholics. Brazil's 8.5 million square kilometers are divided into some 267 ecclesiastical territories which in turn contain over 8,700 parishes. Although the United States has many more parishes than Brazil, no other country in the world has more dioceses. The average diocese or ecclesiastical territory has 33 parishes. This ratio is about a third of the average for North America and a fifth of the average for Europe.

In comparison to Mexico's average of 1,120,800 Catholics per diocese, there are 577,921 Catholics per diocese in Brazil. The average number of baptisms per diocese, as reported by the Church in Brazil (8,687), is about three times lower than the similar figure for Mexico (25,031). This may suggest that Brazil has a greater proportion of baptized Catholics who do not baptize their children as Catholics.

Catholic history in Brazil has been punctuated with difficulties. After independence from Portugal in 1822, the government took a heavy hand to regulating Church actions and growth. During the dictatorships of the 1960s and 1970s, the Church in Brazil was at the forefront of leadership for change. Many bishops advocating land reform and defending democracy were threatened with violence, echoing the call of missionaries in the seventeenth and eighteenth centuries to stop the exploitation and enslavement of indigenous peoples.

CHAPTER 6

Asia

If there are good reasons to treat North and South America as a single continental unit, there are perhaps just as many reasons to treat Asia as if it were a collection of several entirely separate continents. The distinctions between the several regions identified in this chapter–Western Asia, South Asia, Southeastern Asia, and Northeast Asia–present dramatically contrasting cultural and social contexts.

Nonetheless, there are certain features that the Church in Asia tends to share. These aspects and related trends are discussed in the initial sections of this chapter, followed by a more detailed examination of each of the regions identified for purposes of this book.

OVERVIEW

Asia is the largest and most populous continent, and, although it is the birthplace of the Church, it is also the least Catholic continent. Asia stretches across eight time zones, includes a broad diversity of cultures, and is birthplace of the world's great religions. It is home to the world's only countries with over a billion inhabitants. Yet while it contains one-third of the global population, it is has just one in ten of all Catholics worldwide. In addition, within its Christian population, there are decidedly more non-Catholics than Catholics. Only three countries have majority Catholic populations, and in most countries Catholics make up less than 4 percent of the population. The religions with the greatest number of adherents in Asia are Islam, Hinduism, and Buddhism.

Although the Catholic population, and the Christian population in general, is small compared to other religions in Asia, Catholic population has grown significantly in recent years. In addition, while the proportion of Catholics within the overall population is relatively small, these figures represent larger numbers of people than they would in other continents due to the scale of Asia's population.

POPULATION

During the last quarter of the twentieth century, Asian population increased by 61 percent and Catholic population more than doubled, growing at a rate of 104 percent. While Catholics number only about 3 percent of the total Asian population, the approximately 107 million Catholics in Asia are just slightly fewer than the number of Catholics in Africa. However, Catholics remain concentrated in a relatively few regions of Asia, and then in only a few countries within those regions.

Table 6.1 Selected Church Population Statistics, Asia: 1975 and 2000			
	1975	**2000**	**Change**
Total Population	2,301,291,000	3,698,043,000	61%
Catholic Population	52,589,000	107,301,000	104%
Percent Catholic	2%	3%	27%
Percent of Catholics Worldwide	7%	10%	39%
Ecclesiastical Territories	358	638	78%
Parishes	10,866	20,543	89%
Parishes per Territory	30	32	6%
Catholics per Territory	146,897	168,183	14%
All Baptisms	1,823,274	2,701,555	48%
Baptisms under 7 years old (%)	89%	84%	-7%
Confirmations	na	1,248,515	
Marriages	320,414	696,840	117%

Catholic population growth in the last quarter of the twentieth century outstripped overall population growth. However, the number of Catholic baptisms has not been increasing as quickly as the number of births in Asia. Between 1975 and 2000, the total number of baptisms increased by 48 percent while the total number of all births increased by 240 percent. These figures may suggest that the overall presence of Catholics within the population is not likely to change significantly and may decline as a proportion of the population in the years ahead.

These population trends are within a wider demographic context that includes massive efforts by China to slow population growth through its one-child policy. It also includes the rapidly rising population and soaring growth rates characteristic of many Islamic countries, and the continuing net out-migration patterns of Christians in the Holy Land and other ancient Christian lands due to the twin forces of economic instability and a rising sense of religious discrimination from their Muslim neighbors.

As elsewhere, the proportion of baptisms of persons over the age of seven is increasing and now represents about one in seven of all baptisms performed annually. Finally, the increase in the number of marriages is higher than the overall increase in the Catholic population. This may suggest that overall levels of participation in Catholic life are increasing somewhat faster than the rate of Catholic population growth. However, marriage statistics are subject to many variables and should only be seen as suggestive of longer-term trends.

A special feature of Catholicism in Asia, particularly the Middle East and South Asia, is the presence of a variety of ecclesiastical traditions within the Catholic community. A fifth of all ecclesiastical territories in Asia are of the Eastern Catholic Churches. These include the Maronite Church centered around Lebanon and Syria and the Syro-Malabar Church centered in southern India, as well as many other Churches with similarly ancient liturgies and distinct hierarchies, each headed by its own patriarch.

INSTITUTIONS

By the end of the twentieth century, the approximately 50 countries or other separately reported Asian lands had 638 dioceses or other ecclesiastical territories, and approximately 20,543 parishes. On average, there are 32 parishes per diocese or other ecclesiastical territory, which in turn average 70,100 square kilometers in size.

The effect of a large land mass and a relatively small Catholic population is clear when one compares average figures for Asia and Europe. The average Asian diocese or ecclesiastical territory is about five times larger than the average European diocese or territory–but the number of Catholics per diocese is one-third smaller and the number of parishes more than six times fewer.

A large number of dioceses and parishes were created over the past 25 years as a result of rapid population growth and significant political changes. The total number of parishes nearly doubled, a more rapid rate of growth than for any other continent except Africa. The number of dioceses grew by 45 percent, from 302 to 437, again more rapidly than any continent except Africa.

Table 6.2 Selected Church Institution Statistics, Asia: 1975 and 2000			
	1975	2000	Change
Catholic Population	52,589,000	107,301,000	104%
Percent of Catholics Worldwide	7%	10%	39%
Ecclesiastical Territories	358	638	78%
Dioceses or Eparchies	302	437	45%
% of Territories Worldwide	15%	22%	47%
Total Pastoral Centers	45,104	52,175	16%
Parishes	10,866	20,543	89%
Missions	28,536	28,427	0%
Catholics per Parish	4,840	5,223	8%
Primary Schools	11,375	14,625	29%
Secondary Schools	5,747	7,976	39%
Seminaries	126	352	179%

PERSONNEL

The Church's pastoral workforce increased dramatically in Asia during the last quarter of the twentieth century. In particular, women religious increased from 75,327 to 138,195, an 83 percent increase. This is especially noteworthy since the numbers of religious women declined during the same period in Europe, Oceania, and North America, where the combined total for those three continental areas or regions dropped from 738,126 women religious in 1975 to 480,981 by 2000. This decline of 35 percent is even more steep when calculated from its high water mark of about 1965. In the United States, women religious numbered 179,954 in 1965, but only 79,814 in 2000, a decline of 55 percent. By 2000, there were 776 Catholics per women religious in Asia, indicating that woman religious are generally more common within the Catholic Church in Asia than any continent other than Europe and Oceania, both of which are experiencing continuing declines. The world average is 1,304 Catholics per woman religious.

Increase in the number of priests in Asia is at a similar level, and even higher for diocesan priests alone. Seminarians and ordinations have increased much faster than the number of priests, suggesting an increasing presence of local clergy. Total seminarians increased from 10,322 to 26,006, a 152 percent increase that implies continuing strong gains in total numbers of priests. Diocesan ordinations increased 144 percent, from 448 in 1975 to 1,094 in 2000. Finally, while permanent deacons represent the fastest growing category of clergy in percentage terms, absolute numbers remain negligible, at only 128 deacons for all of Asia.

Table 6.3 Selected Church Personnel Statistics, Asia: 1975 and 2000			
	1975	**2000**	**Change**
Catholic Population	52,589,000	107,301,000	104%
Percent of Catholics Worldwide	7%	10%	39%
Bishops	na	627	na
Total Priests	24,092	43,566	81%
Diocesan	12,024	25,716	114%
Religious	12,068	17,850	48%
Permanent Deacons	57	128	125%
Religious Brothers	5,709	7,659	34%
Religious Women	75,327	138,195	83%
Diocesan Ordinations	448	1,094	144%
Total Seminarians	10,322	26,006	152%
Diocesan	6,351	14,513	129%
Religious	3,971	11,493	189%
Catholics per Priest	2,183	2,463	13%
Catholics per Woman Religious	698	776	11%

While significant increases in clergy are likely to continue, they will produce little increase in the average number of Catholics per priest due to continued growth in the Catholic population. Some dioceses, particularly where up to now there have been relatively few priests, are likely to have increasingly higher numbers of Catholics per priest. Nonetheless, in spite of strong increases in the number of priests, the number of Catholics per priest in Asia actually grew by some 13 percent between 1975 and 2000, from 2,183 to 2,463. However, this is one of the lowest rates of growth for any continent. In Africa, this same figure grew by 58 percent, in America by 45 percent, and in Europe by 25 percent.

REGIONS

The four regions of Asia used in this book are given below. As elsewhere, the names of the countries or territories included in each region are given in alphabetical order, qualified by additional information as necessary.

- *Western Asia:* Afghanistan, Armenia, Azerbaijan, Bahrain, Cyprus, Georgia, Iran, Iraq, Israel, Jordan, Kazakhstan, Kuwait, Kyrgyzstan, Lebanon, Oman, Palestinian territories (West Bank and Gaza Strip), Qatar, Saudi Arabia, Syria, Tajikistan, Turkey, Turkmenistan, the United Arab Emirates, Uzbekistan, Yemen

- *South Asia:* Bangladesh, Bhutan, India, Maldives, Nepal, Pakistan, Sri Lanka

- *Southeast Asia*: Brunei Darussalam, Cambodia, East Timor, Indonesia, Laos, Malaysia, Myanmar, Philippines, Singapore, Thailand, Vietnam

- *Northeast Asia:* China, Japan, Mongolia, North Korea, Russia (Asian territory only), South Korea, Taiwan

The balance of this chapter will compare the various countries within each region to one another, comparing the size of the Catholic population to the total population, the numerical strength of the Church's personnel and institutions, and the special challenges that confront the Catholic Church in that particular region as revealed through a consideration of particular representative countries and trends.

WESTERN ASIA

This region that includes the Holy Land is one of the most challenging to define. This is because these lands are so meaningful from a religious and geopolitical point of view, as well as a great world crossroads. Sometimes the bulk of these lands are termed the "Middle East," referring to the Arab and Islamic countries at the east of the Mediterranean basin. In this sense, North African countries such as Egypt are often included. Other definitions include countries that do not necessarily share Arab culture but are instead connected to on-going political and strategic tensions and stress points, such as Turkey or Iran. These countries in turn have other neighbors in Central Asia and the trans-Caucasus that were formerly part of the Soviet Union. To avoid confusion, and to include the countries of Central Asia, this book avoids the term "Middle East." Western Asia therefore includes the Asian countries typically described as part of the Middle East together with those often classified in Central Asia. The resulting group includes all of Asia to the west of China, the south of Russia, and to the north or east of Nepal, India, and Pakistan. From the perspective of the challenges faced by the Church in these countries, the similarities generally outweigh the dissimilarities, particularly when compared to other regions in Asia.

Table 6.4 Selected Church Statistics, Western Asia: 1975 and 2000			
	1975	**2000**	**Change**
Catholic Population	1,736,000	4,688,500	170%
% Catholic	1%	1%	0%
Ecclesiastical Territories	83	98	18%
Parishes per Territory	19	17	-11%
Dioceses	63	70	11%
Parishes	1,591	1,667	5%
Missions	128	62	-52%
Catholics per Parish	866	1,970	127%
Total Catholic Schools	837	749	-11%
Priests	2,284	2,461	8%
% Diocesan	1	1	1%
Women Religious	5,416	4,975	-8%
Catholics per Priest	603	1,334	121%

Despite Western Asia's location as the cradle of Christianity, only 1 percent of the 328 million inhabitants of these 16 nations are Catholic, approximately 4.7 million people. Further, these numbers are unlikely to grow over the next century. They may even decline as Catholics continue to migrate out of these lands and birth rates of other religious groups continue to far exceed those of Catholics.

The Palestinian Territory (Gaza and the West Bank) and Israel had a low proportion of Catholics at the beginning of the twentieth century (about 2.3 percent in the Palestinian Territory and 2.4 percent in the lands that comprise Israel's recognized boundaries) and a lower proportion at the end of the century (about 1.3 percent in Gaza and the West Bank and 2.7 percent of the population in Israel). Numbering less than 150,000, Catholics include those of a variety of Churches and liturgical traditions. Established in the Holy Land are the hierarchies of Armenian, Chaldean, Maronite, Melkite, and Syrian as well as Latin Catholics. Almost all are resident in Jerusalem.

The only country in this region where Catholics are at or near a majority is Lebanon. Perhaps as many as 52 percent of the 3.5 million Lebanese are Catholic, almost all Maronite Catholics. Unlike other Eastern Catholic Churches, which often share a common history or liturgy with a Church of the Eastern Orthodox tradition, there is no equivalent of the Maronite Catholic Church within the Orthodox tradition.

In some places, particularly the oil-producing Gulf states, the Catholic presence is a recent and probably temporary phenomenon resulting from the presence of non-citizens employed in the petroleum or other industries. Between 12 and 14 percent of those who reside in Qatar and the United Arab Emirates (U.A.E.) are Catholic, primarily Filipino. These countries have the third and fourth highest per capita GDP and are among the richest in the world. However, in spite of the presence of guest workers, the Catholic pastoral presence is very weak and one should not assume that the guest workers share in the affluence of the citizens of these countries. The Kingdom of Qatar has only one priest, while the U.A.E., a federation of sheikdoms, has 17 priests, compared to Lebanon's 1,370.

Three other nations on the Arabian peninsula, Kuwait, Bahrain, and Saudi Arabia, have Catholic populations of between 4 and 7 percent, and again almost all are guest workers. The other nations of the Middle East have Catholic populations that rarely exceed 1 percent.

West of the Caspian Sea and south of European Russia and Georgia is a country sometimes described as the most ancient Christian country in the world. In the year 301, Armenia became the first nation to establish Christianity as its official religion. Today, Armenia is about 78 percent Armenian Orthodox and 4 percent Catholic. Neighboring Azerbaijan, on the other hand, is predominantly Muslim. To the north of Armenia on the other side of the Caucasus Mountains is Georgia, which is classified as part of Europe but shares many similarities both with its neighbors in Western Asia and nearby European Russia.

With the exception of Afghanistan, almost all of the landlocked, often extremely mountainous countries of Central Asia had been part of the Soviet Union. Almost all have a negligible number of Christians. The exception is Kazakhstan, where a little over 16 percent of the population is Christian, and perhaps 1 percent of the population is Catholic. Islam predominates in these countries, as it does throughout the region. Less than 1 percent of the population of these countries is Catholic. In all of Central Asia, there is only one Catholic hospital, compared to 70 Catholic hospitals elsewhere in Western Asia–and more than 1,300 Catholic hospitals in South Asia, where Catholics also comprise about 1 percent of the total population.

SOUTH ASIA

Although South Asia is only 1 percent Catholic, this densely populated area is home to 18 percent of all Catholics in Asia. In Western Asia, 1 percent of the population represents about 4.7 million people and in South Asia it represents 19.3 million. Catholicism in South Asia is unusual among most regions in that the growth of parishes, priests, and women religious has been about equal to the growth of the Catholic population as a whole. In most other regions in Asia, the Catholic population growth far exceeded growth in pastoral institutions and personnel. The only other world region that has similar figures is South Asia's neighbor, Southeast Asia.

Sri Lanka has the densest Catholic presence among the six countries of South Asia. Although the great majority are Buddhist, perhaps as many as 7 percent of the population are Catholic, approximately 1.3 million people in 2000. Sixty-four percent of the 941 priests are diocesan, and there are more than 9,000 catechists.

Table 6.5 Selected Church Statistics, South Asia: 1975 and 2000			
	1975	**2000**	**Change**
Catholic Population	10,682,500	19,323,400	81%
% Catholic	1%	1%	0%
Ecclesiastical Territories	112	170	52%
Parishes per Territory	42	52	25%
Dioceses	103	168	63%
Parishes	4,650	8,802	89%
Missions	19,172	16,043	-16%
Catholics per Parish	1,663	1,502	-10%
Total Catholic Schools	9,350	14,699	57%
Priests	11,104	20,938	89%
% Diocesan	59%	57%	-3%
Women Religious	45,156	85,575	90%
Catholics per Priest	696	631	-9%

India is three times larger in geography and population than the other six South Asian nations combined and contains 85 percent of all Catholics in South Asia. Tradition holds that the Apostle Thomas introduced Christianity in southern India. The oldest Catholic diocese in India, Goa, was founded in 1533. Through the work of Jesuit missionaries, many of those who had worshiped according to the ancient Syro-Malabar and Syro-

Malankara liturgies came into communion with the Catholic Church. Over 16 million Catholics live in this primarily Hindu country, and most of these continue to be concentrated toward the southern tip of the subcontinent. In some areas, Catholics make up a sizeable minority. However, taken together, the world's second most populous country–and South Asia as a whole–is only 1 percent Catholic.

Catholic religious life thrives in India. With over 81,000 women religious, there are only 204 Catholics per woman religious. While there are many thriving religious communities in India, perhaps the best known is the Missionaries of Charity, established in 1950 by Mother Teresa. Originally born in Macedonia, she began her ministry to the poor, sick, and dying in the slums of Calcutta in 1948. By the time she died in 1997, 4,000 sisters, novices, brothers, and priests of the Missionaries of Charity were serving in 450 sites around the world.

Men's religious communities are also experiencing remarkable growth. There are 8,400 religious priests and 2,471 religious brothers in India. India has the sixth largest number of men religious for any country in the world. This is particularly striking given that India's Catholic population is only the sixteenth largest in the world. In addition, unlike the situation in many other regions, religious in India tend to be local vocations.

SOUTHEAST ASIA

Seven in ten Asian Catholics live in Southeast Asia, and most of them are in the Philippines or East Timor. Available figures suggest that as many as eight in ten Filipinos are Catholic and perhaps as many as 94 percent of the population of the newly independent East Timor are Catholic. As a result of the Catholic presence in these countries and the Catholic presence in Vietnam, about 15 percent of all Southeast Asians are Catholic, more than 77 million people.

The 11 nations of Southeast Asia are usually divided into two general categories based on whether they are part of the continental land mass or located on one of the many islands of Southeast Asia. The first group includes Myanmar (formerly Burma), Thailand, Laos, Cambodia, and Vietnam. The island nations are Brunei, East Timor, Indonesia, Malaysia, and Singapore. Buddhism tends to be more present on the continent and Islam in the islands. Sharp economic differences separate the regional economic powers of Singapore, Malaysia, and Brunei from the eight other poorer and generally much larger countries.

Table 6.6 Selected Church Statistics, Southeast Asia: 1975 and 2000			
	1975	**2000**	**Change**
Catholic Population	38,198,000	77,220,000	102%
% Catholic	12%	15%	25%
Ecclesiastical Territories	122	181	48%
Parishes per Territory	24	41	72%
Dioceses	96	158	65%
Parishes	2,887	7,377	156%
Missions	6,547	11,803	80%
Catholics per Parish	13,275	10,601	-20%
Total Catholic Schools	6,188	6,503	5%
Priests	6,875	14,510	111%
% Diocesan	43%	64%	49%
Women Religious	13,035	31,369	141%
Catholics per Priest	5,574	5,390	-3%

Two-thirds of the priests in Southeast Asia are diocesan priests, the highest proportion of diocesan priests for any region of Asia. Another distinction is that Southeast Asia has by far the greatest number of Catholics per priest in Asia, twice the average for the continent as a whole.

Magellan's voyage brought the first Christians to the Philippines in 1521, but evangelization did not start until the 1560s. Spanish rule of the Philippines lasted from the sixteenth century to 1898. In that year, the United States seized the Philippines from Spain, expelled 500 missionary priests, and facilitated the arrival of Protestant missionaries from the United States. This nation of more than 7,000 islands was of great strategic importance during World War II, when it was occupied by the Japanese. The United States granted independence in 1946.

The Philippines' population of 76.3 million is about average for the continent, but its large Catholic population makes it atypical in religious terms. Indeed, certain parallels may be drawn between Latin America and the Philippines since both had a long-term Spanish colonial presence, are predominantly Catholic, and share certain socio-religious cultural characteristics. In this sense, India, where Catholics comprise only 2 percent of the population, is more representative of the Church in Asia. In the Philippines, unlike the situation in most of the rest of Asia, dioceses tend to be geographically smaller but contain many more Catholics.

Unlike almost anywhere else except Latin America, the Philippines has a large proportion of persons who were likely baptized Catholic but who now appear on the membership totals of evangelical and other Christian religious bodies. In 2000, it was estimated that perhaps as many as 14.8 million Filipinos, or almost 20 percent of the population, were baptized Catholic but also participate in the membership of another religious body.

East Timor has the second smallest population of any country in Southeast Asia but the largest percentage of Catholics within its population. Catholicism came to East Timor and Indonesia with the Portuguese in the fifteenth century. By the seventeenth century, Islam began to dominate the islands, particularly the area then controlled by the Dutch East India Company and which later became Indonesia. East Timor was forcibly taken from Portuguese control by Indonesia in 1975, and Catholics experienced considerable repression under Indonesian rule, which claimed the lives of perhaps as many as one-third of the population. By 1999, the territory was turned over to United Nations administration, and it became an independent country in 2002. A little over one hundred priests serve 750,000 Catholics, representing a relatively high ratio of some 7,425 Catholics per priest.

NORTHEAST ASIA

More than eight million Catholics in Northeast Asia are spread across nearly 25 million square kilometers, a land mass defined here as including Siberia and all of Asian Russia, together with China, Mongolia, Korea, and Japan. In all, Northeast Asia includes about 55 percent of the land mass of Asia, although much of the land is only sparsely inhabited. Catholics are most concentrated in South Korea. This part of the Korean peninsula is home to 64 percent of all Catholics in Northeast Asia but only 0.2 percent of the population of the region taken as a whole. In part, this is because reliable figures do not exist for North Korea and China, where the Church was persecuted and severely restricted during the latter half of the twentieth century.

Nine percent of South Korea's total population is Catholic. Christianity is the largest religion in South Korea. Taken together, Christians make up about 40 percent of the population. The next largest religion in South Korea is Buddhism, which claims about 15 percent of the population.

South Korea has the greatest number of priests (2,731) in Northeast Asia. It also has the greatest number of women religious (7,938) and the greatest number of brothers (616). Perhaps most distinctively, South Korea has more than six times the number of catechists (12,067) as any other country in the region. In fact, the number of catechists reported by South Korean dioceses is more than the number reported by all the dioceses in

Canada, a country with 3.3 times the Catholic population. Such statistics suggest that the Church in South Korea is particularly vibrant.

About 3 percent of the overall population of Asian Russia is Catholic, well over a million people. However, it has one of the lowest numbers of priests for any country in Northeast Asia. Unlike South Korea, Russia has a high infant mortality rate and low life expectancy. One hundred twenty infants per 1,000 live births die before their first birthday, and Russians' life expectancy is 39 years, half that of the Japanese. Within Asia, Russian per capita income is $4,200. Only the People's Republic of China ($3,800) and Mongolia ($2,320) have lower per capita incomes. As is the case in Japan, and historically in Korea, Mongolia has had an important Buddhist presence. It was ruled by Communists between 1924 and 1990. According to available statistics, it has seven priests, one brother, 14 women religious, and a total of approximately 100 Catholics.

Table 6.7 Selected Church Statistics, Northeast Asia: 1975 and 2000			
	1975	**2000**	**Change**
Catholic Population	1,973,000	6,320,100	220%
% Catholic	0.18%	0.40%	122%
Ecclesiastical Territories	41	46	12%
Parishes per Territory	42	60	41%
Dioceses	40	41	3%
Parishes	1,738	2,743	58%
Missions	2,689	519	-81%
Catholics per Parish	1,109	2,251	103%
Total Catholic Schools	742	650	-12%
Priests	3,829	5,679	48%
% Diocesan	34%	57%	68%
Women Religious	11,720	16,319	39%
Catholics per Priest	503	1,087	116%

Japan has 513,000 Catholics, placing it third among Northeast Asian nations in terms of total Catholic population. Given Japan's population of 126.9 million, Catholics are considerably less than 1 percent of the population. Nonetheless, Japan has the second greatest number of priests (1,749), women religious (6,488), catechists (1,294), and brothers (253) in the region. Proportional to the number of Catholics, there are more women religious in the Church in Japan than any other country in the world. While the very favorable proportion of 79 Catholics per woman religious may be due to the overall low numbers of Catholics, it also suggests that religious life, particularly for women, is a strong feature of Catholicism in Japan.

In the sixteenth century, Jesuit missionaries converted thousands of Japanese. The number of Catholics grew rapidly, but then virtually disappeared after three major persecutions in the sixteenth and seventeenth centuries. Throughout the twentieth century, growth has been slow.

Christianity came to China as early as the seventh century and there was an important Catholic missionary presence throughout the sixteenth and seventeenth centuries. Missionary activity heightened again in the mid-nineteenth century. However, these activities helped bring about the Boxer Rebellion in 1900, which was put down by an international force. This identified Christianity as a foreign religion in the minds of many Chinese.

After significant growth in the early twentieth century, the Church's position in China became very difficult after Mao Zedong and the Communist Party came to power in 1949. At that time, there were 2,542 Chinese priests and 3,046 foreign priests serving a population of 3.2 million Catholics. By the end of 1951, all foreign priests had been expelled or arrested. The last seminary was closed in 1955. The government attempted to create a schism in the Catholic Church by establishing the Chinese Catholic Patriotic Association in 1957. By 1975, estimates suggested that only about 500 Chinese priests remained alive in China. While it is known that some bishops in the breakaway association have reconciled with the Vatican, no public data exist on how many bishops have done so, since that would open them to reprisals from the government. In any case, very difficult conditions persist.

Only limited information is therefore available and it only covers about half of the 144 Catholic dioceses or other ecclesiastical territories in China. Based only on those figures, .02 percent of Chinese are Catholic. An estimated 2.4 million baptized Catholics are served by 3,179 priests, 1,173 brothers, and 3,782 women religious. There are 755 Chinese Catholics per priest, and 635 Catholics per women religious. Some estimates put the total number of Chinese Catholics at more than four million. However, because these figures are estimates and are not supplied officially and openly by the dioceses and other territories of the country, they are not used in the summaries and comparisons given in this book. The same is true for statistics on North Korea, where organized Catholic life was entirely extinguished, although a number of Catholics likely remain.

The situation of the Church is much more normal in Macau and Hong Kong. These two cities, recently relinquished colonial outposts of Portugal and the United Kingdom, are designated Special Administrative Regions (SARs) by the People's Republic of China, and the Church enjoys a greater measure of freedom in these territories than in the rest of China. Macau has about 30,000 Catholics, 7 percent of the population, and the distinction of being the oldest diocese in China (1576). Hong Kong is 5 percent Catholic and has an estimated 371,000 Catholics.

Table 6.8 The Catholic Church in Asia, by Region: 2000				
	Northeast	**South**	**Southeast**	**Western**
Catholic Population	6,320,100	19,323,400	77,220,000	4,688,500
% Catholic	0.40%	1%	15%	1%
Ecclesiastical Territories	46	170	181	98
Parishes per Territory	60	52	41	17
Dioceses	41	168	158	70
Parishes	2,743	8,802	7,377	1,667
Missions	519	16,043	11,803	62
Catholics per Parish	2,251	1,502	10,601	1,970
Total Catholic Schools	650	14,699	6,503	749
Priests	5,679	20,938	14,510	2,461
% Diocesan	1	1	1	1
Women Religious	16,319	85,575	31,369	4,975
Catholics per Priest	1,087	631	5,390	1,334
Charitable Institutions				
Hospitals	75	1,248	175	86
Homes	392	890	172	94
Orphanages	190	2,098	475	88
Other	594	11,653	1,779	516

CHAPTER 7

Europe

This chapter describes a continent in transition. The monetary union became an everyday reality in early 2002; continent-wide organizations and expectations are still expanding. At the beginning of the twenty-first century, the continent continues to adjust to a new normalcy after the breakup of formerly Soviet-controlled Eastern Europe. All of these changes have greatly affected the context in which the Church ministers and evangelizes. After a brief consideration of Catholic trends related to population, institutions, and personnel, this chapter contrasts the position of the Church in three key regions: Northwestern Europe, Southwestern Europe, and Eastern Europe.

OVERVIEW

Today, Europe confronts profound changes. The fall of communism in Europe, the increase in immigration from African, Asian, and former communist countries to Western Europe, and the European Union's move to a single currency have contributed to a period of political, economic, social, and cultural transition. For some, this has been a time of disappointment, division, and dashed hopes. For others, this is a time of new opportunity. This includes new opportunity for the Church in Europe, thanks to the decline of age-old Church-State relationships and the disappearance of communism in Europe.

Another reality in Europe by the end of the twentieth century is the demographic transition that occurred as death rates began to exceed birth rates and overall fertility rates went below replacement levels of 2.08 children, on average, per woman. With a fertility rate of 1.8, German population would decline from about 82 million in 2000 to 66 million by 2050, and Italian population would drop from 56 million to 45 million. Both countries currently have fertility rates of 1.3. Naturally, these declines will have a proportional impact on Church membership. Overall in Western Europe alone, population may drop by as much as 20 million from 2000 to 2025.

Over the last quarter of the twentieth century, there was a slight increase in European population, about 6 percent. Likewise, the total number of Catholics increased, by about 7 percent. By the beginning of the twenty-first century, about two in five Europeans are Catholic, a figure lower than in the Americas but higher than in Africa. About one in four of the world's Catholics live in Europe. This later figure can be expected to drop as European population declines while upward trajectories continue elsewhere in the world.

The number of Catholics per parish is much lower in Europe than elsewhere in the world. On average there are 2,162 Catholics for every parish in Europe, a figure that will decline further as population declines unless a considerable number of parishes are closed.

The 1990s marked the definitive end of Soviet communism and the resulting conclusion of the post-World War II period. It saw the beginnings of a discussion around the re-emergence of "Central Europe" as a continental reality apart from the Cold War divisions of "Eastern" and "Western" Europe. The bitter religious wars in the former Yugoslavia also helped define the decade and gave new salience to the ancient religious divisions of Europe. However, the divisions used in this book are based largely on the Cold War divisions that defined Europe throughout the last half of the twentieth century and roughly parallel membership in the European Union in the year 2000.

POPULATION

In Europe, slow population growth, combined with reduced commitment to the practice of the faith, has resulted in declines in the number of baptisms and marriages celebrated within the Church each year. Over the past quarter century the number of infant and adult baptisms, as well as Church-witnessed marriages, have declined by as much as one-third.

Table 7.1 Selected Church Population Statistics, Europe: 1975 and 2000			
	1975	**2000**	**Change**
Total Population	663,128,000	702,661,000	6%
Catholic Population	261,924,000	280,144,000	7%
Percent Catholic	39%	40%	1%
Percent World Catholics	37%	27%	-10%
Ecclesiastical Territories	685	732	7%
Parishes	136,718	129,565	-5%
Parishes per Territory	200	177	-11%
Catholics per Territory	382,371	382,710	<1%
All Baptisms	3,912,637	2,571,180	-34%
Baptisms under 7 years old (%)	100%	96%	-4%
Confirmations	na	2,013,061	na
Marriages	1,757,902	1,033,709	-41%

INSTITUTIONS

Catholic institutional life in Europe continues to have a more developed infrastructure than anywhere else in the world, particularly in those countries where Catholicism has historically had an important presence. For example, Italy, which represents a fifth of European Catholics, has a third of all European dioceses and more than any other country in the world except Brazil. Overall, Europe represents 27 percent of the Catholic world, but has 59 percent of all Catholic parishes worldwide.

Primary and secondary educational institutions in Europe number 28,232–more than anywhere else in the world. Europe's more than 10,000 secondary schools represent 36 percent of all the Church's educational institutions in Europe and considerably exceed the number of such institutions found in the Americas, which has nearly twice as many Catholics.

As with educational institutions, Catholic charitable institutions have a relatively strong presence in Europe. In 2000, there were a total of 1,330 hospitals, 2,411 orphanages, 7,679 homes for the elderly or handicapped, and 19,388 other charitable agencies. These forms of Catholic institutional life vary with the history and political arrangements, especially Church-State relations, of individual countries. In some places, the Church has a long established presence in the social service infrastructure of a country, whereas in other countries, particularly countries where the Church is not as present or where its relationship with the state has been particularly troubled, the Church's presence in social service efforts ranges from weak to non-existent.

Table 7.2 Selected Church Institution Statistics, Europe: 1975 and 2000			
	1975	**2000**	**Change**
Catholic Population	261,924,000	280,144,000	7%
Percent of Catholics Worldwide	37%	27%	-27%
Ecclesiastical Territories	685	732	7%
Dioceses or Eparchies	647	676	4%
% of Territories Worldwide	29%	26%	-12%
Total Pastoral Centers	144,171	147,628	2%
Parishes	136,718	129,565	-5%
Missions	426	32	-92%
Catholics per Parish	1,916	2,162	13%
Primary Schools	23,915	18,006	-25%
Secondary Schools	10,385	10,226	-2%
Seminaries	674	665	-1%

PERSONNEL

The legacy of a time when the population was younger and there were many vocations to priesthood and religious life continues to mark the life of the Church in Europe. The proportion of priests and religious is much higher in Europe than its proportion of Catholics would suggest. Half of the world's priests (208,659), 46 percent of the world's women religious (366,326), and nearly 40 percent of all religious brothers (21,691) live in Europe. However, absolute declines in Church personnel are perhaps more notable than the continuing worldwide preponderance of Europeans among clergy and religious.

Over the past few decades, the number of diocesan priests has contracted by 17 percent and the number of women religious has declined by as much as a third. The number of brothers has declined even further, by almost 40 percent. Given the age distribution of European clergy, the age distribution of the European population, and a declining birth rate, continued contractions in the numbers of priests and religious are likely through the first half of the twentieth century.

Table 7.3 Selected Church Personnel Statistics, Europe: 1975 and 2000

	1975	2000	Change
Catholic Population	261,924,000	280,144,000	7%
Percent of Catholics Worldwide	37%	27%	-27%
Bishops	na	1,497	na
Total Priests	244,271	208,659	-15%
Diocesan	174,225	145,268	-17%
Religious	70,046	63,391	-10%
Permanent Deacons	729	8,813	1,109%
Religious Brothers	34,999	21,691	-38%
Religious Women	546,557	366,326	-33%
Diocesan Priest Ordinations	1,966	2,321	18%
Total Seminarians	24,183	26,879	11%
Diocesan	15,960	17,611	10%
Religious	8,223	9,268	13%
Catholics per Priest	1,072	1,343	25%
Catholics per Woman Religious	479	765	60%

An exception among these expected personnel declines is likely to be seen within the permanent diaconate. Since the restoration of the permanent diaconate in the Western Church after the Second Vatican Council, there has been a significant rise in the number of permanent deacons. Over the last quarter of the twentieth century, the number of deacons grew by more than 10 times. Today, Europe has more than 24 times the number of deacons in Africa, Asia, or Oceania. However, the total figure for all the regions of Europe (8,813) is lower than that for North America (13,889). The United States alone has 12,971 deacons, considerably more than any other country, although even in this case a deacon in every parish is hardly the norm. As a comparison, Europe has 27 percent of all Catholics and about 32 percent of all deacons; the United States has some 6 percent of all Catholics and about 47 percent of all deacons.

REGIONS

This book defines Western Europe in contrast to Eastern Europe largely on the basis of belonging to the European Union. Two regions are then distinguished within Western Europe, the relatively more Mediterranean basin-focused Catholic countries of "Southwestern" Europe and the often more Reformation-influenced and typically Teutonic countries of "Northwestern" Europe. This schema breaks down as follows:

- *Northwestern Europe*: Austria, Belgium, Denmark, Finland, France, Germany, Iceland, Ireland, Liechtenstein, Luxembourg, Monaco, the Netherlands, Norway, Sweden, Switzerland, and the United Kingdom

- *Southwestern Europe*: Andorra, Gibraltar (United Kingdom), Italy, Malta, Portugal, San Marino, and Spain

- *Eastern Europe*: Albania, Belarus, Bosnia, Bulgaria, Czech Republic, Croatia, Estonia, Greece, Hungary, Latvia, Lithuania, Macedonia, Moldova, Poland, Romania, Russia (east of the Urals), Slovakia, Slovenia, Ukraine, and Yugoslavia (Serbia and Montenegro)

The greatest concentration of Catholics is in Southwestern Europe, where approximately 87 percent or more of the population is Catholic. Eastern Europe has the lowest concentration of Catholics and the greatest concentration of Orthodox Christianity within Europe.

Almost half of all European countries are majority Catholic. As the table below shows, the greatest concentration of Catholic-majority countries is in Southwestern Europe, where 100 percent of all countries are majority Catholic. In Northwestern Europe, there are almost as many countries that have no Catholic, Protestant, or Orthodox majority as those with a Protestant majority. In Eastern Europe, there are twice as many Catholic majority countries as Orthodox majority countries. However, half of all countries in Eastern Europe have no single majority Christian tradition.

	Catholic Majority Countries	Protestant Majority Countries	Orthodox Majority Countries	Countries with No Majority
Northwestern	44%	31%	0%	25%
Southwestern	100%	0%	0%	0%
Eastern	32%	0%	16%	52%
Overall, Europe	49%	12%	7%	32%

Table 7.4 European Religious Divisions, by Region: 2000

Over the last decade of the twentieth century, however, the number of these countries with no majority declined. Catholic majority Slovakia split from the Czech Republic, for example, and Catholic majority Croatia and

Slovenia split from then-religiously mixed Yugoslavia, which has since emerged as an Orthodox majority country within smaller boundaries.

NORTHWESTERN EUROPE

Forty percent of the population of Northwestern Europe is Catholic. There are 1,411 Catholics per priest, quite low compared to the average figure of 2,579 worldwide. Over two-thirds of all priests in this region are diocesan priests. Monaco, Luxembourg, Belgium, France, Liechtenstein, Ireland, and Austria are all 75 percent or more Catholic. Switzerland, the Netherlands, and Germany have a significant presence of both Catholics and Protestants. The population of these countries is between 33 percent and 46 percent Catholic.

The United Kingdom is 9 percent Catholic, largely of persons descended from Irish immigrants over the past few centuries. The hierarchy of the Catholic Church in Britain was dissolved after 1536 when King Henry VIII declared himself the head of the Church of England. By 1788, when some of the most discriminatory anti-Catholic laws were repealed, there were only about 60,000 Catholics scattered around the country. The Catholic diocesan system was re-established in Britain in 1850.

Table 7.5 Selected Church Statistics, Northwestern Europe: 1975 and 2000			
	1975	**2000**	**Change**
Catholic Population	107,489,000	107,531,000	<1%
% Catholic	43%	40%	-7%
Ecclesiastical Territories	221	232	5%
Parishes per Territory	299	214	-28%
Dioceses	205	215	5%
Parishes	66,110	49,758	-25%
Catholics per Parish	1,632	2,172	33%
Total Catholic Schools	24,442	19,515	-20%
Priests	111,845	76,596	-32%
% Diocesan	72%	69%	-4%
Catholics per Priest	964	1,411	46%
Women Religious	269,579	144,767	-46%

The Scandinavian countries have 2 percent or fewer Catholics, and a similar history of the extinction of the ancient dioceses and their re-establishment many centuries later. In contrast to the situation in Britain, there has been far less controversy over religion since the Reformation and as a result many of the worship patterns in the dioceses and parish churches taken over during the Reformation changed relatively little. Formal re-establishment of Catholic dioceses in the Netherlands took place beginning in 1853. In the mid-nineteenth century, the Netherlands and its neighbor Belgium were world centers of Catholic revival and missionary-sending countries, second only to France.

The size of the French population and its comparatively large number of Catholics account for the single largest proportion of Catholics for any country within this region (44 percent). Neighboring Belgium and Switzerland, with approximately a third and a fifth, respectively, of their population native French-speakers, contribute to Francophone Catholicism's predominance in this region of Europe. French men and women religious account for one-third of all men and women religious in the region, and France has 56 percent of all of the region's catechists. Seventy-six percent of the 25,353 priests in France are diocesan. Within northwestern Europe, only Germany has such a preponderance of diocesan priests among all priests.

Historically, the Church in France played a very important role in the missionary expansion of the nineteenth century. Its funds and personnel for evangelization efforts in Africa, Asia, and Oceania were probably greater than the sum total of that provided by all other countries during that period. However, France is also the center of Church-State conflicts that intensified during the French Revolution and continued through the nineteenth and twentieth centuries throughout the Catholic world. Anticlericalism, including complete alienation from Christianity and formal religion of any kind, has long been part of the French experience. In the 1881 census, for example, 7,684,000 persons, more than one in four citizens, claimed no religious identity of any kind. Perhaps it is not surprising then, that France has one of the lowest rates of weekly church attendance in Europe and the lowest for any country where Catholics are at least a nominal majority of the population. A 1990 survey, for example, found that no more than 10 percent of those surveyed reported attending church on a weekly basis.

Absolute numbers of priests have been declining in France since 1938, with ordinations dropping from 1,355 at that time to 170 in 2000. Declines in the number of priests have been greater in France than anywhere else in Europe.

The Republic of Ireland, independent since 1922, is 93 percent Catholic. Northern Ireland, part of the United Kingdom, is 47 percent Catholic. Due to a variety of historical factors, this relatively small island (the Republic had a population of 3.6 million people in 2000, and Northern

Ireland a population of about 1.07 million) has had a far greater impact on global Catholicism than its numbers would suggest. Ireland has provided the model, and often the bishops, priests, religious, and Catholics, for many much larger countries of the world over an extended period of time. This includes countries of recent European settlement such as the United States, Canada, Australia, New Zealand, and South Africa. It also includes many other mission territories around the world. Mass attendance remains at among the highest levels in Europe. However, available figures show that the decline in Mass attendance by young adults is perhaps greater than for any other country. This is in part a result of rapid changes in Irish society, issues internal to the Church, and the stratospheric levels of attendance that had been the rule until the late twentieth century. In the 1990s, the International Social Survey found that 92 percent of those over age 60 report attending church at least once a month compared to 46 percent of those age 29 or under.

SOUTHWESTERN EUROPE

While Northwestern Europe is about 40 percent Catholic, Southwestern Europe is nearly 90 percent Catholic. The region is dominated by the Iberian and Italian peninsulas. It includes three relatively large countries (Italy, Spain, and Portugal) and five microstates or territories (Andorra, Gibraltar, Malta, San Marino, and Vatican City). The population of the Italian peninsula (nearly 60 million) is larger than that of the Iberian peninsula, where Spain has a population of about 40 million and Portugal about 10 million. The Catholic presence in these areas was well established during the Roman Empire. In the Iberian peninsula it was re-established during more than seven centuries of fighting after the eighth-century conquests by Islamic forces.

Saints Peter and Paul were martyred in Rome in the 60s. Church-State relationships have been vital to the history of the Church in Italy since the early persecutions, culminating in Constantine's recognition of the Church in 315 and then its establishment as the state religion in 380. For more than a thousand years the Pope enjoyed political power over Rome and a wide portion of central Italy. When this ended by force in 1870, Pope Pius IX declared himself the "prisoner of the Vatican" and the independence of the Holy See was threatened by direct external political control. The problem was resolved when the 1929 Lateran Pacts between the Republic of Italy and the Vatican established the Pope's sovereignty as an elected absolute monarch over the .44 square kilometers comprising Vatican City and extended rights of extraterritoriality to a number of buildings and churches in Rome deemed crucial to the Church's independence. As a result, Vatican City is the world's smallest fully independent sovereign territory.

Table 7.6 Selected Church Statistics, Southwestern Europe: 1975 and 2000			
	1975	**2000**	**Change**
Catholic Population	98,342,000	102,910,000	5%
% Catholic	98%	96%	-2%
Ecclesiastical Territories	370	320	-13%
Parishes per Territory	146	172	18%
Dioceses	356	307	-14%
Parishes	54,029	52,948	-2%
Catholics per Parish	1,820	1,944	7%
Total Catholic Schools	9,801	7,473	-24%
Priests	102,114	87,433	-14%
% Diocesan	68%	67%	-1%
Catholics per Priest	963	1,177	22%
Women Religious	239,619	181,549	-24%

Because Italy has been home to the See of Peter and his successors since the first century, it has collected more than its share of historical accretions and concentrations of Catholic institutions. By 1930, there were at least 296 dioceses in Italy, including 11 abbeys whose abbots governed as a bishop. Many of these dioceses had very low populations and often consisted of just a single small town. Other dioceses could be traced to ancient times when there was a bishop overseer in every parish. After considerable efforts to reduce the number, this figure declined by 1975 to 271 dioceses and 13 other ecclesiastical territories. By 2000, there were 217 dioceses in 2000 and 11 other territories. The country with the largest number of dioceses is now Brazil, with 249 dioceses and 18 other ecclesiastical territories. The United States has the third highest number of dioceses (195 dioceses in 2002, excluding the seven dioceses in Puerto Rico, Guam, and American Samoa that do not belong to the United States Conference of Catholic Bishops).

Although the number of dioceses in Italy has been reduced, the number of Catholics per diocese remains much smaller than in Brazil or the United States. For comparison, there are an average of 538,951 Catholics for each ecclesiastical territory in Brazil and 328,223 for each in the United States. This compares to 245,074 Catholics per diocese or other ecclesiastical territory in Italy.

The Archdiocese of Rome is an ordinary archdiocese as well as the location of the Vatican, which is simply part of archdiocesan territory in an ecclesiastical sense. Rome contains 17 pontifical universities, institutes, and faculties of theology; 89 ecclesiastical institutes for diocesan or religious clergy; and 10 pontifical academies. The total number of clergy represented within the Archdiocese is 5,867. The vast majority, however, does not serve its 335 parishes but rather serve the global Church. Such high numbers of priests make figures for the Church in Italy less comparable. For example, there are 439 Catholics per priest in the Archdiocese of Rome but the figure is 1,079 in the rest of Italy. Similarly, there are 104 Catholics per woman religious in the Archdiocese of Rome; in the rest of Italy, the figure is 590. In the Archdiocese of Rome, 26 percent of all priests are diocesan priests. In the rest of Italy, 70 percent of all priests are diocesan priests.

Sharing the Iberian Peninsula, Spain and Portugal also share similar histories. Both emerged in the wake of the departure of the Moors from the Iberian peninsula. Both developed world empires based on seafaring skills in the fifteenth and sixteenth centuries, and both declined as world powers by the eighteenth century. In the early and mid-nineteenth century, both nations endured political violence, dictatorship, international conflicts, and near economic collapse. The Spanish Civil War of the 1930s profoundly affected the Church, with more than 6,600 men and women religious killed, amid terrible violence on all sides. During the ensuing dictatorship, the Church was intimately associated with the government. After the beginnings of democracy in 1976, the situation began to change. Mass attendance declined dramatically as Spain experienced a kind of rapid social change similar to that experienced elsewhere in Europe.

EASTERN EUROPE

Six countries in this region are 60 percent or more Catholic: Croatia, Hungary, Lithuania, Poland, Slovakia, and Slovenia. These countries were the heartland of the old Austro-Hungarian Empire, a fixture of Central Europe for centuries. Catholicism first came to Croatia in the seventh century, then to Slovenia and Slovakia in the eighth century, Poland in the ninth century, and Lithuania in the thirteenth century. The origins of Catholicism in Hungary are less clear, but it was planted by the tenth century.

The giant in Catholic life in Eastern Europe is Poland. Ninety-six percent of Poles are Catholic, and Polish missionaries are in 90 countries around the world. The massive preponderance of Latin Rite Catholicism in Poland, however, is new in Polish history. Between the two world wars,

Poland was 64 percent Catholics of the Latin Rite, 11 percent Catholics of the Byzantine Rite, 10 percent Greek Orthodox, 8 percent Jewish, and 4 percent Protestant. The level of Catholic identity was cemented further during Poland's long struggle under Soviet control. Priestly ordinations continued to increase throughout the 1980s after they had long begun to fall under the pressure of declining birth rates and religious practice in the rest of Europe. When the number of Polish priestly ordinations peaked in 1991, they were accounting for one-fourth of all such ordinations in Europe. Unlike the situation in the rest of Europe, growth in priests and parishes tended to outpace growth in Catholic population.

Table 7.7 Selected Church Statistics, Eastern Europe: 1975 and 2000			
	1975	**2000**	**Change**
Catholic Population	56,093,000	69,453,000	24%
% Catholic	17%	23%	35%
Ecclesiastical Territories	94	177	88%
Parishes per Territory	176	151	-14%
Dioceses	86	154	79%
Parishes	16,579	26,812	62%
Catholics per Parish	3,383	2,590	-23%
Total Catholic Schools	57	1,243	2,080%
Priests	30,312	44,608	47%
% Diocesan	81%	76%	-6%
Catholics per Priest	1,851	1,557	-16%
Women Religious	37,359	39,961	7%

These differences are a matter of both geography and history. The Catholic countries border the more affluent Western European nations, such as Germany and Austria, whereas the Orthodox countries are further to the east and south.

The Church in Eastern Europe faces the legacy of state control that dates back to the days of the Austro-Hungarian Empire, particularly the control exerted over the Church during the late eighteenth century. State control and patronage created ornate church buildings but so weakened the Church that priests were few and pastoral ministry weak. Only with the dissolution of the Austro-Hungarian Empire after World War I did the Church begin to renew itself. This was soon overshadowed by the experience of World War II and the totalitarian dictatorships that followed. State enforced atheism and destruction of Church institutions and personnel in the wake of communist rule was unparalleled to anything since the

French Revolution and far more prolonged. Church schools and institutions were almost entirely eliminated everywhere but Poland where resistance was strongest. Church property was confiscated. Men and women religious were imprisoned or disappeared.

After the fall of communism, many previous patterns and freedoms were restored for the Churches. This also presented some challenges, however, as old disputes and rivalries flared again. In many historically Orthodox countries, for example, legal frameworks were created that favored the Orthodox Church and hampered the free practice of religion by other faith traditions.

Table 7.8 The Catholic Church in Europe, by Region: 2000			
	Eastern	**Northwestern**	**Southwestern**
Total Population	297,732,000	270,242,000	117,521,000
% Catholic	23%	40%	88%
Ecclesiastical Territories	166	232	331
Parish per Territory	161	214	160
Dioceses	146	215	315
Parishes	26,742	49,758	53,018
Catholics per Parish	2,561	2,172	1,951
Total Catholic Schools	1,223	19,515	7,493
Priests	44,516	76,596	87,525
% Diocesan	76%	69%	67%
Women Religious	39,828	144,767	181,682
Catholics per Priest	1,538	1,411	1,182
Charitable Institutions			
Hospitals	111	941	271
Homes for Elderly	512	3,676	1,223
Orphanages	432	755	3,491
Other	4,026	9,453	5,883

In many countries, however, such institutional concerns diminish in importance compared to the more basic need of evangelization within societies where religious faith and socialization had been progressively attacked over generations. In the Czech Republic, for example, Catholicism predominates among those who profess a religious faith, but the percentage of the Czech population who are Catholics and the percentage who are atheists is the same (39 percent).

CHAPTER 8

Oceania

This chapter describes a single region within an area of ocean approximately the size of Europe. The countries and territories of Oceania range from an island continent to widely dispersed and very small islands, many of which are sovereign states and others that are dependencies of countries half a world away. Because Oceania is treated as a single region in itself, general trends related to the Church regarding population, institutions, and personnel are followed by a brief section identifying representative or contrasting countries and territories.

OVERVIEW

Oceania is the only part of the world named for a water mass rather than a land mass. Its roughly 25,000 islands are scattered across 8.5 million square kilometers. In spite of its considerable extent, just three countries, Australia, Papua New Guinea, and New Zealand, dominate the region and contain approximately 90 percent of the total population of Oceania. In every respect these countries dwarf the other countries or territories. A few territories are not included in this list due to their very small size.

Two-thirds of the 23 countries and territories of Oceania have minority Catholic populations. Only a little more than 10 percent of the 23 countries and territories of Oceania have Catholic populations in excess of 75 percent of the population. And more than three times as many countries have Catholic populations less than 25 percent of the population. Finally, as with the overall population, a little over 9 in 10 Catholics live in one of the three largest countries.

Table 8.1 Catholic Presence in the Countries of Oceania: 2000		
	Countries/ Territories	Percent of Countries
Less than 25 percent Catholic	11	48%
25 to 49 percent Catholic	5	22%
50 to 75 percent Catholic	4	17%
More than 75 percent Catholic	3	13%
Total	23	100%

POPULATION

In contrast to Asia, Oceania contains the smallest fraction of global population, just about half of 1 percent of total world population. About 1 percent of all the world's Catholics live in this part of the world. A little over 8 million of the total inhabitants are Catholic, a ratio of approximately one in four.

Table 8.2 Selected Church Population Statistics, Oceania: 1975 and 2000			
	1975	2000	Change
Total Population	21,094,000	30,566,000	45%
Catholic Population	5,227,000	8,202,000	57%
Percent Catholic	25%	27%	8%
Percent of Catholics Worldwide	1%	1%	7%*
Ecclesiastical Territories	63	77	22%
Parishes	2,223	2,384	7%
Parishes per Territory	35	31	-12%
Catholics per Territory	82,968	106,519	28%
All Baptisms	135,589	127,952	-6%
Baptisms under 7 years old (%)	89%	89%	0%
Confirmations	na	89,893	na
Marriages	39,054	27,023	-31%
*See notes to Chapter 8 at Appendix I.			

The Catholic population of Oceania grew some 57 percent between the years of 1975 and 2000, slightly faster than the 45 percent growth rate for the general population. The 77 ecclesiastical territories (72 dioceses and 5 other territories) are geographically dispersed and often quite small, and with small numbers of Catholics. As a result, Oceania averages 106,519 Catholics per ecclesiastical territory, the lowest number for any continental area in the world.

In Oceania, the decline in Catholic baptisms over the last quarter of the twentieth century (6 percent) is dwarfed by the decline in marriages recorded by the Church (31 percent). Both of these may reflect an aging of the population or other changing demographic realities. They could also suggest declining levels of commitment.

INSTITUTIONS

Oceania's 2,384 parishes in 2000 represented about 1 percent of all Catholic parishes in the world. Given the total Catholic population, however, there are only 3,440 Catholics per parish in Oceania, a figure lower than anywhere else in the world except Europe. These low numbers are explained by the traditionally strong parish structures of Australia and New Zealand and the need to have an institutional Catholic presence in the often isolated and low population island states.

During the last quarter century of the twentieth century, the number of parishes in Oceania rose 7 percent, and the number of ecclesiastical territories, including dioceses and eparchies, increased 22 percent. Australia is home to three eparchies of the Eastern Catholic Churches (Maronite, Melkite, and Ukrainian) as well as parishes that worship following the liturgy of five other Eastern Churches, although they are not formally constituted as separate ecclesiatical territories. Elsewhere, the ecclesiastical territories are all of the Western Church, or Latin Rite.

The unique history of Oceania has resulted in a particularly strong presence of Catholic schools as well as a relatively strong parish presence. Almost 3 percent of all Catholic schools in the world are located in Oceania, much higher than the proportion of Catholics or parishes represented by Oceania. The Church in Oceania has slightly more than one elementary school per parish, a result of the presence of schools founded by various religious institutes and operated independently of parishes.

As with the number of parishes and dioceses, the number of Catholic schools has long since stabilized and is unlikely to grow dramatically in coming years. From 1975 to 2000, the total number of schools increased by 1.4 percent, but the number of secondary schools declined by 8 percent. Following Catholic population distribution, the vast majority of the schools are located in Australia, Papua New Guinea, and New Zealand. The recently independent territories of Fiji and Vanuatu, as well as the French dependency of New Caledonia, all have large numbers of schools as well, over 50 per island.

In spite of the strong presence of Catholic schools, Oceania's 24 seminaries represent only 1.2 percent of all Catholic seminaries in the world and the number of Catholic universities are quite limited.

The Church reports 1,522 charitable institutions in Oceania. On a proportional basis, this comes to approximately two such institutions for every three parishes, an average of 20 charitable organizations per diocese or other ecclesiastical territory. The distribution of the Church's charitable infrastructure reflects the uneven distribution of social needs throughout Oceania. Australia has 65 percent of Oceania's Catholics, but 59 percent of charitable institutions. New Zealand has nearly 6 percent of Oceania's Catholics but 4 percent of its charitable institutions. On the other hand, Papua New Guinea has 29 percent of Oceania's officially Church-reported Catholic charitable institutions, but only 20 percent of Oceania's Catholics.

Table 8.3 Selected Church Institution Statistics, Oceania: 1975 and 2000			
	1975	**2000**	**Change**
Catholic Population	5,227,000	8,202,000	57%
Percent of Catholics Worldwide	1%	1%	7%
Ecclesiastical Territories	63	77	22%
Dioceses or Eparchies	59	72	22%
% of Territories Worldwide	3%	3%	1%
Total Pastoral Centers	4,281	3,653	-15%
Parishes	2,223	2,384	7%
Missions	1,546	839	-46%
Catholics per Parish	2,351	3,440	46%
Primary Schools	2,620	2,721	4%
Secondary Schools	707	651	-8%
Seminaries	43	24	-44%

PERSONNEL

As occurred elsewhere in certain other parts of the world during the last quarter of the twentieth century, the number of priests declined in Oceania, in this case by about 8 percent. Diocesan priests declined slightly less (by

7 percent) than religious priests (11 percent). Thus, Oceania had 967 Catholics per priest in 1975 and 1,658 Catholics per priest in 2000. As a result, although the number of Catholics per priest in Oceania is still the lowest in the world, the average number of Catholics per priest increased by 71 percent, a larger increase than anywhere else in the world.

Because changes in the total number of priests can be affected by a number of factors, including death and resignation rates as well as in-migration (incardination) and out-migration (excardination), the impact of changes in ordination trends is not always felt immediately. However, they serve to illustrate likely long-term trends. The number of ordinations to the diocesan priesthood decreased 7 percent from 1975 to 2000. Seminary enrollment figures suggest that even greater declines have occurred among vocations to religious priesthood. From 1975 to 2000, the number of theology-level seminarians preparing for diocesan priesthood increased by 5 percent–but those preparing for the religious clergy dropped 28 percent. In general, many of these overall trends are similar to those found in North America, not surprising given the relative similarities of the situation in Australia and New Zealand to the United States and Canada. The sheer size of the Church in Australia will always dominate overall figures for Oceania.

During the past quarter century, the number of deacons in Oceania increased by 374 percent, but overall numbers remain low. Interestingly, the proportion of Oceania's deacons located in Australia is lower than its proportion of total Catholic population might suggest. Oceania contains almost 1 percent of the world's deacons, approximately the same as the percentage of the world's Catholics who live in Oceania. Of the 180 deacons found in Oceania in 2000, Australia had 47, Micronesia 39, Samoa 24, French Polynesia 23, and the remaining countries and territories have fewer than 5 deacons each.

In 1975, nearly 17,000 women religious ministered in Oceania, but by 2000 the number had declined to 11,095, a drop of 35 percent. Again, this is generally comparable to the situation of decline in numbers of women religious characterizing the Americas (21 percent overall, but with a 41 percent decline in North America) and Europe (33 percent). The strongest contrasts on a continental basis are with Africa (increases of 56 percent), but especially neighboring Asia (increases of 83 percent). During the same period, the number of religious brothers declined by 39 percent, from 3,033 to 1,836. This compares to drops of 38 percent in Europe and 23 percent in the Americas. On the other hand, as in the case of women religious, it also contrasts to increases in Africa (47 percent) and Asia (34 percent).

These historic declines in the presence of religious have been acutely felt, particularly given the historical presence of religious in the rich network of Church institutions throughout Oceania, including their leadership in mission work.

Table 8.4 Selected Church Personnel Statistics, Oceania: 1975 and 2000			
	1975	2000	Change
Catholic Population	5,227,000	8,202,000	57%
Percent of Catholics Worldwide	1%	1%	7%
Bishops	na	121	na
Total Priests	5,403	4,947	-8%
Diocesan	2,908	2,714	-7%
Religious	2,495	2,233	-11%
Permanent Deacons	38	180	374%
Religious Brothers	3,033	1,836	-39%
Religious Women	16,950	11,095	-35%
Diocesan Priest Ordinations	71	66	-7%
Total Seminarians	1,019	923	-9%
Diocesan	573	604	5%
Religious	446	319	-28%
Catholics per Priest	967	1,658	71%
Catholics per Woman Religious	308	739	140%

A DIVERSE REGION

Oceania includes almost as many territories as countries, depending on how one counts the territories. For purposes of this book, the territories are as follows.

● French Territories: New Caledonia, Polynesia, Wallis and Futuna

● New Zealand Territories: Cook Islands, Niue, Tokelau, Samoa

● United States Territories: American Samoa, Guam, Northern Mariana Islands.

Countries may also be grouped by the country that administered the country prior to its independence. This is important because these ties continue to influence their social, economic, and religious context.

- Australian administration: Nauru, Papua New Guinea

- French administration: Vanuatu

- United Kingdom administration: Australia, Fiji, Kiribati, New Zealand, Solomon Islands, Tonga, Tuvalu

- United States administration: Marshall Islands, Micronesia, Palau

The history of the Catholic Church in Oceania can be split into three distinct periods over several centuries. During the first period from 1500 to the 1780s, Catholic missionaries sailed from Europe to the Pacific and established missionary outposts. In the second period, from the 1790s through the 1890s, the Church experienced rapid growth as the pace of European contact increased. By the late nineteenth century, European imperialism in Australasia and the Pacific islands had created a political climate that improved security and transportation, dramatically furthering evangelization. It was during this period that the Protestant missionary presence in Oceania began in earnest. The most recent period stretches throughout the twentieth century, and is marked by war, political violence, national independence, and the transition to more indigenous Church leadership.

The first Mass was celebrated in Guam in 1565 by Fr. Andrès de Urdaneta, an Augustinian friar. Catholicism came to Australia in 1795 with the arrival of Catholics in the form of Irish convicts exiled to the then-penal colony. Marist missionaries worked in Fiji and Papua New Guinea beginning in 1844. By 1896, Divine Word missionaries were in Papua New Guinea and French Missionaries of the Sacred Heart had begun evangelizing Kiribati by 1888. The romance of distant tropical islands and a newly settled island continent thrilled European missionaries, making them appealing destinations for the energetic, expanding European religious communities of the day. At the same time, the near-total political dominance of European powers made these distant shores accessible in spite of immense distances and relative isolation.

That sense of isolation was changed forever by the bloody Pacific campaigns of World War II. During the war, thousands died and whole islands and ethnic groups were destroyed or forever altered. After the war, many of the islands were administered by individual countries under United Nations' trusteeship, a trend that continued throughout the last half of the twentieth century.

The Church in Australia and New Zealand contrasts markedly with the Church in the rest of Oceania. These two countries are places of considerable European settlement and their population is largely drawn from the immigrants who arrived in the nineteenth and twentieth centuries. They have enjoyed dominion or near-equal status within the British Commonwealth since 1901 and 1840, respectively. No less importantly, their geographic location in the most southern portion of Oceania also means that they were not as directly affected by the horrors of the Second World War.

Because of the relatively large size of the Australian population (nearly 19 million, or 63 percent of the total population of Oceania), figures that reflect averages for Oceania as a whole may tend to reflect the reality of the Church in Australia more than the almost two dozen other countries or territories dotting the vast expanse of the South Pacific. The island continent is particularly exceptional in terms of population and sheer geographic size. About one-third of all Australians are Catholic, another third are Anglican, about 25 percent profess other Christian faiths, and the remaining 10 percent are non-Christians. It has the largest population, the highest per capita income, the lowest infant mortality rate (5 per 1,000 live births), a 100 percent literacy rate, and the second longest life expectancy in the region (80 years). Only the much smaller territory of American Samoa has a longer life expectancy (81 years).

Australia has eight times as many women religious and five and a half times more priests than any other country or territory in Oceania. However, it has only about one and a half times more catechists than the country with the next highest number.

Mass attendance among Catholics in Australia has declined from highs of perhaps 60 percent in the mid-twentieth century to current lows of between 15 and 25 percent, depending on the diocese. Nonetheless, more than half of all Catholic school-age children attend the approximately 1,700 Catholic elementary or secondary schools. Government grants cover about three-quarters of educational expenses. Most parishes have at least one elementary school and some larger parishes have more than one. About 3 percent of all Catholic school teachers are men or women religious.

As with other aspects of the Church in Oceania, Catholic education is intimately tied to the presence of religious women. Sisters of Mercy arrived in Australia from Ireland in 1831 and numbered about 2,100 in the mid-1990s. A community native to Australia, the Sisters of St. Joseph, or Josephites, were founded in the nineteenth century and numbered about 1,300 in the mid-1990s.

The Church in Australia increasingly has come to rely on lay ecclesial ministers. By the year 2000, there were perhaps as many as 1,000 paid lay ministers working on at least a half-time basis. Perhaps as many as three-quarters of these ministers are women religious. Almost all of the approximately 75 pastoral administrators of parishes where there is no resident pastor are women religious.

In addition to these personnel are the religious educators and catechists that are largely employed through parish elementary schools and less likely to be women religious. Each school employs a religious education coordinator, most of whom are also responsible for faith formation within the parish as a whole. In all, about 1,000 such religious education coordinators are employed in the country.

The Catholic Church in Australia began as largely Irish in its people and personnel during the nineteenth and early twentieth centuries. However, by the late twentieth century, the Catholic population had become very diverse, more diverse than most other religious bodies in the country. This happened first as a result of increasing mid-century immigrants from non-English-speaking European lands, and later through the large numbers of immigrants from Asia. Mass is celebrated in over 30 languages, more than eight Eastern Catholic Churches have priests or parishes where their liturgy is celebrated, and at least 25 percent of all Catholics in Australia are foreign born. About a million Catholics in Australia were born in non-English-speaking countries, a figure far higher than for any other religious group in Australia.

In 2000, the country was organized into 32 dioceses and 5 ecclesiastical provinces, a far more complex organization than elsewhere in Oceania. Other than Papua New Guinea, which has four provinces, no other country has more than one ecclesiastical province and most consist of a single diocese.

About 12 percent of all New Zealanders are Catholic, a proportion less than half that of Australia, which lies 1,200 miles to the west. There are five dioceses and one archdiocese. Like Australia, there is a large presence of Catholic schools, which are almost as numerous as parishes. The schools are government supported and have large enrollments relative to total Catholic school-age population. However, only about 10 percent of those who identify as Catholic regularly attend Mass, primarily those in older age groups. The largest religious affiliation in New Zealand is Anglican, but the largest single group are the approximately 25 percent of the population that indicate that they have "no religion," making New Zealand perhaps one of the least "religious" societies in the world. Reflecting this trend, between 1991 and 1996, the number of self-identified Catholics decreased by 5 percent and the number of self-identified Christians as a whole decreased by 10 percent. Other major Christian groups include the Presbyterians, Methodists, and Baptists, who collectively represent another fourth of the population. Finally, there is a strong and continued presence of non-Christian traditional religions among the Maori and other native peoples.

Directly to the north of Australia, just across the Coral Sea, lies Papua New Guinea. Rich in tribal tradition and anthropological significance, this unique country shares its main island with Indonesia's province of Irian Jaya and thus is the only island split between two continental-scale divisions of the world. There are more than 750 distinct language groups. In 1884, Britain claimed the southeastern portion of the island and Germany took the southwest. Britain turned its share of the island over to Australia in 1904, and Australia took control of the German side during World War I. Australia administered the country until its independence in 1975, but continues to provide substantial aid and other forms of assistance.

Nearly one-third of Papua New Guineans are Catholic thanks to the long-term presence of a variety of missionaries affiliated with the Church, particularly members of the Society of the Divine Word. Founded in Germany in 1837 and with a strong presence in the United States since 1875, this particular missionary society has contributed numerous bishops to the local Church and helped to form local vocations to priestly ministry for decades. In the year 2000, seven of the 29 bishops of Papua New Guinea were members of the Society of the Divine Word. Catholicism is the single largest religious body in Papua New Guinea. Most other Papua New Guineans are also Christian–the 2000 census found that 96 percent of Papua New Guineans self-identified in this way–but perhaps one-third of the population also practices religions that predate the arrival of Christianity.

Although larger than most of the island states of Oceania, Papua New Guinea is much more typical of these nations than Australia or New Zealand. Rich in natural resources, its per capita income is only about a tenth of Australia's. Literacy is about three-quarters of Australia's. Life expectancy is about 63 years, 17 years shorter than Australians' life expectancy. Almost 59 infants for every 1,000 Papua New Guineans die before they celebrate their first birthdays, 12 times the infant mortality rate of Australia, and the second highest infant mortality rate in Oceania.

The challenges posed by the geographical and topographical realities of Papua New Guinea are daunting. Fifteen percent of the country's territory is comprised of some 600 small islands in Melanesia. The main island is divided between relatively accessible lowland areas and very isolated highlands with rugged terrain, narrow rivers, and few roads. More than 80 percent of the country is covered by dense rain forest and most of the population lives on a subsistence level. However, Papua New Guinea has enormous mineral wealth, particularly copper, gold, oil, and natural gas.

In contrast to Papua New Guinea–the largest of the island nations of Oceania–Wallis and Futuna is among the smallest. These islands are one of France's three territories in Oceania, along with French Polynesia and New Caledonia. Total territory is only 274 square miles. The entire population was baptized Catholic in the 1840s, and the Church continues to count 100 percent of the population as Catholic.

Church personnel is entirely native. Ten priests minister to the 14,000 islanders, along with five brothers, 38 sisters, and 37 catechists. The islands form one diocese, which was established in 1966. The Church in these two islands maintains 14 Catholic primary schools and two secondary schools. Per capita income is $2,000, and the two main exports are handicrafts and copra, dried coconut kernels from which coconut oil is extracted. The islands have few natural resources, and only 5 percent of the land is arable. Literacy is about 50 percent.

Table 8.5 The Catholic Church in Oceania: 1975 and 2000			
	1975	**2000**	**Change**
Total Population	21,094,000	30,566,000	45%
% Catholic	25%	27%	8%
Ecclesiastical Territories	63	77	22%
Parishes per Territory	35	31	-12%
Dioceses	59	72	22%
Parishes	2,223	2,384	7%
Catholics per Parish	2,351	3,440	46%
Total Catholic Schools	3,327	3,372	1.40%
Priests	5,403	4,947	-8%
% Diocesan	54%	55%	2%
Women Religious	16,950	11,095	-35%
Catholics per Priest	967	1,658	71%
Charitable Institutions			
Hospital	na	174	na
Home	na	351	na
Orphanage	na	58	na
Other	na	939	na

Guam and the Northern Marianas are territories of the United States, and have the largest total population as well as the largest Catholic population of smaller island states of Oceania. Guam's relationship to the

United States has tended to produce a quality of life somewhat higher than that of other island territories, including a per capita income of $21,000. Infant mortality is just seven per 1,000, literacy is 99 percent, and life expectancy averages 78 years. Another contrast with elsewhere in Oceania is the relatively weak presence of key Church institutions and personnel. There are about 6,291 Catholics per parish and 3,212 Catholics per priest, more than double the regional average.

One reason for the weakness of the Church's presence has been the shifting fortunes of ecclesiastical administration. The first church on the island was established in 1699 by the Jesuit Father Diego Luis de San Vitores. However, after the suppression of the Jesuits in the following century, most missionary work was passed to the Augustinian Recollects. An independent mission of the Marianas was then established in 1807 under the Diocese of Cebu in the Philippines. The first native priest was educated at the San Carlos Seminary in Cebu and ordained in 1859. After the United States took possession of the island from Spain in 1898, however, Catholic missionaries were ordered off the island. The Church only slowly rebuilt itself in the twentieth century. The Church in Guam was established as a separate vicariate apostolic in 1911, and Agaña, the capital, became the see of a diocese established in 1965.

CHAPTER 9

Looking to the Future

This book is designed not to provide conclusions but to present information necessary for both sound analysis and effective pastoral decision-making. These final pages therefore offer only a few limited summaries of major themes presented in the main chapters. This is followed by a brief discussion of the more global Catholic presence that had emerged by the end of the twentieth century. The chapter ends with a summary review of selected worldwide patterns and trends in Church statistics. As has been the case throughout this book, the intent is not to lay claim to the future path of the Church or to identify the best path. That is not the mission of pastoral sociology and it is not the task of this book.

CONTRASTS BY CONTINENT

The Church has grown more rapidly in Africa than anywhere else, where it continues to have a particularly high proportion of adult baptisms. In some regions, the Church in Africa has experienced noteworthy increases in vocations to priesthood and religious life. In its pastoral life, catechists and mission stations have a wider role than elsewhere given the continuing relative absence of priests and parishes.

Africa has the lowest proportion of parishes relative to Catholic population of any continent. However, it also has a very strong presence of Catholic educational institutions, primarily primary schools, part of the legacy of the institution-building efforts of the missionaries and those who followed them. In spite of the large and growing numbers of Catholics, Church institutions, and personnel, inculturation of the Gospel within societies that have changed so rapidly and face such profound challenges in the years ahead will not be easy.

One of the greatest challenges Africa faces over the next few decades is AIDS, which has created over 13 million orphaned children and will reduce life expectancy and populations in many countries. Eight in ten AIDS deaths in the world are in Africa. The continent's very limited resources mean that advanced drugs and drug therapies are generally not available. Because those most threatened by the disease are typically at the most economically productive stage of their lives, AIDS and poverty rates will become increasingly interlinked.

Economic scarcity has only intensified struggles over control of resources, which have led to war and political instability. In the last decade of the twentieth century alone, civil wars or military coups have taken place in almost one in three African countries. Many of these struggles involve religion.

In a number of countries, tension with Islam is strongly felt. In part this is because the proselytizing impulses of both Christianity and Islam have had their greatest opportunities in this rapidly changing continent.

Over the last half of the twentieth century, the proportion of Muslims in the population of many African countries increased faster than anywhere in the world. In a number of African countries, the growth of Islam has far exceeded the growth of Christianity. This is particularly the case in those countries nearer the historically Muslim areas of North Africa and the Sahara.

Nonetheless, Asia is and remains the center of the Islamic world. Interestingly, however, the countries with the largest Muslim populations are outside the Arab world. Pakistan has 150 million Muslims, India 123 million, Indonesia 116 million, Bangladesh 111 million, and Iran 65 million. Asia is where the demand for dialogue with all the world's major religions is most urgent. Given the growing religious diversity in Europe and elsewhere, what the Church learns from its Asian context may serve it well elsewhere as globalization both homogenizes world culture and spreads greater diversity in culture and religion.

The marked minority status of the Church in Asia has clearly not hurt its growth or vibrancy. The proportion of women religious, priests, and parishes as a proportion of Catholic population worldwide is generally exceptionally large relative to other continents.

The Church in Latin America has very large parishes. There are an average of about five times more Catholics per parish in Latin America than in North America. Compared to the figures for Europe, Latin American parishes have about seven times more Catholics per parish. Thus, there are an average of 14,236 South American Catholics per parish, 14,236 Caribbean Catholics per parish, and 16,074 Mesoamerican Catholics per parish. With such a weak level of installed capacity, the remarkable increases in evangelical Christianity within recent years seem less surprising. In any case, as a result of the rapid growth of these new religious bodies, Latin American Catholicism is becoming a key place of encounter with pentecostal and evangelical Christianity.

Europeans increasingly express no formal religious preference. This is particularly the case in the more Protestant countries of Northern Europe and the formerly communist countries of Eastern Europe, but it is increasing throughout the continent. These are not the so-called cafeteria Christians who pick and choose what they believe from within their tradition–rather, this is a case of larger proportions of the population no longer identifying with any formal religious tradition. In spite of these overall trends, Europe remains a particularly strong center of Catholicism, particularly as measured by the presence of Catholic institutions and personnel.

The dominant religion in Oceania is Christianity. Although a number of islanders practice indigenous religions, and still others profess no religion, the majority are Catholic, Anglican, or other Protestant Christians. While English and French are widely understood, evangelization and catechesis in the vernacular remains a challenge. Over 715 distinct languages are spoken in Papua New Guinea, for example, and 120 in the Solomon Islands. Oceania's population is concentrated in a few places, but spreads over 25,000 islands. The Church therefore must navigate waters roiled by linguistic, religious, and cultural differences, from an increasing lack of identity with any tradition to the traditional animist faiths. The Church must also overcome a certain feeling that the rest of the world, including the Church itself, pays scant attention to the peoples of the Central and South Pacific. Oceania offers a rich opportunity to bring a certain freshness to Church life, and its many cultures and traditions can serve as a model for inclusiveness.

THE CHURCH AND THE WORLD ECONOMIC DIVIDE

Just as one may contrast the Church's position continent by continent, one may also contrast the Church in rich and poor parts of the world. This is a very important basis for comparison, since the Church looks vastly different in poor regions of the world than it does in wealthier ones. For purposes of comparison, the following table compares regions with an average gross national income per capita that place them among the wealthiest quarter of the global population with the rest of the world.

Table 9.1 The Economic Divide: 2000

	Rich World	% of World	Rest of the World	% of World
Total Population	730,623,000	12%	5,316,656,000	88%
Catholic Population	298,813,300	29%	746,244,800	71%
% Catholic	41%		14%	
Area (km²)	33,736,554	25%	102,052,974	75%
Ecclesiastical Territories	907	32%	1,939	68%
Parishes	129,640	59%	88,556	41%
Mission Stations	921	1%	103,443	99%
Permanent Deacons	22,618	81%	5,206	19%
Priests	249,815	62%	155,363	38%
Diocesan	151,020	57%	114,761	43%
Religious	76,177	55%	63,220	45%
Brothers	29,241	53%	25,816	47%
Women Religious	441,104	55%	360,081	45%
Catholics per Priest	1,196		4,803	
Catholics per Parish	2,305		8,427	
Hospitals	2,038	35%	3,815	65%
Orphanages	2,721	31%	5,974	69%
Homes for Elderly, Infirm	8,769	63%	5,164	37%
Other Charitable Institutions	20,761	28%	54,175	72%
Primary Schools	28,348	32%	61,109	68%
Secondary Schools	11,741	33%	23,818	67%

As a result of patterns of inequality in the world and in the regions constructed for this book, the wealthiest regions are North America, Northwestern Europe, Southwestern Europe, and all of Oceania. This masks a number of important countries or territories with wealthy economies that are nevertheless classified within much larger and poorer regions, such as Japan, South Korea, Taiwan, and Hong Kong. In the case of Oceania, this approach combines a number of very poor but also very small island economies with those of Australia and New Zealand. However, the purpose of this comparison is to consider broad differences between regions, not individual differences within countries or parts of countries. In any case, this only affects a relatively small number of Catholics.

The table above compares combined figures for Northwestern Europe, Southwestern Europe, North America, and Oceania, the so-called "Rich World," to ones for all the other regions of the world.

As the table shows, the wealthy side of the economic divide is more likely to be Catholic (41 percent compared to 14 percent). However, because the population is so much larger outside the rich regions of the world, the wealthy regions contain less than a third of the world's Catholics.

However, the wealthy side of the world economic divide with less than a third of all Catholics has more than half of all Church personnel—women religious, men religious, diocesan priests, and deacons. As an example, there are about 1,196 Catholics per priest in the richest regions and 4,803 Catholics per priest in the others.

The Church's installed capacity to meet the pastoral and sacramental needs of Catholics is much greater in the developed world. Many more parishes exist to serve the Catholic community in Western Europe, North America, and Oceania. Although these regions account for only about 25 percent of the world's inhabited land mass and 37 percent of the Church's dioceses and other ecclesiastical territories, they contain nearly 60 percent of all parishes. As a result, there are 2,305 Catholics per parish in these rich regions—compared to 8,427 Catholics per parish in the rest of the world.

Such differences in the distribution of Church personnel and parishes, however, are not reflected in the distribution of Catholic charitable and educational institutions, which are much more likely to parallel the distribution of Catholic population. The only exception found is that homes for the elderly tend to be more common in the wealthier regions, an interesting difference given the greater concentration of elderly there as a result of world demographic dynamics.

FROM CHRISTENDOM TO PLURALISM

The twentieth century saw enormous Catholic growth in Africa, significant personnel increases in South Asia, and a generally contrasting distribution of Church resources between rich and poor regions. Perhaps even more notably, the Church moved from being a strongly concentrated presence in a relatively few countries to becoming a significant minority presence in many countries. The ordinary experience of the Catholic Church around the world is thus less that of being a religion of the vast majority than one actor among many in a religiously pluralist environment.

For the foreseeable future, the Church is more likely to be a significant minority than a highly concentrated presence. Available Church statistics over the twentieth century suggest that the Church may be most effective in this situation. For example, Catholic institutional life is generally stronger in South Asia than in the two countries of Southeast Asia where it is most heavily concentrated. Being a minority, but not an insignificant minority, seems to make for much more vital parish, charitable, and educational structures.

As the most extensive organized religion in the world, the Church can also bring impressive resources to a situation through its transnational ties and internal organizational strengths. The case of Chad illustrates this. Catholics in Chad number only 623,000, or 8 percent of the population of this primarily Muslim land. There are 64 Catholic primary and secondary schools, nine hospitals, 102 parishes, and 237 priests. In spite of this relatively modest presence, Catholic leaders have played a very significant role in shaping public debate about the impact of globalization and the role that increasing oil revenues should play in this landlocked and very poor country's future.

In the United States and Canada, as well as a number of other countries long characterized by open, pluralist religious systems, Catholicism has flourished. In these cases, however, as well as in many countries of Africa, Asia, and Oceania, Catholicism is a significant but by no means majority form of Christianity. Nonetheless, the institutional strength of the Church in these countries is often strong, or stronger, than in more traditional centers of Catholicism.

In countries where the Church has long existed side by side with evangelical Protestants in an open, pluralist setting, Catholics have developed particularly strong forms of local parish life, commitment to practice and participation, and a sense of stewardship and relatively high Church giving. In other words, the Church has learned from the strengths characteristic of these other Christian traditions.

The European experience is different since it is based on institution-alized relationships between specific Churches and the State. The tradition of religious pluralism characteristic of the United States and other countries outside Europe has simply not been the experience of the Catholic Church in those countries where it has historically been most concentrated.

Throughout most of Christian history the State's support of religion and the rights of the Church has been crucial. Without it, Catholicism disappeared in North Africa in the seventh and eighth centuries. Similarly, the Church in France was nearly destroyed by the French Revolution and terribly affected by the Nazi and Soviet states in Central and Eastern

Europe. State support–or the lack of it–has made a big difference for the Church in Europe.

All of these experiences poorly prepare European Catholicism to understand religious pluralism. A "secular state" in European experience, after all, typically means an atheistic state that has secularized Church property and eliminated the Church's voice in civil society. Conversely, a state that respects religion often has translated as a state that controls religion through restrictive legislation, tax policy, or patronage and financial largesse. Whether a carrot or stick approach, the concept of religion as a fully respected part of civil society outside state interference is not a part of the European tradition. As a result, religious monopolies have long been dominant in Europe, correlating with low levels of commitment and practice, yet high levels of institutional development. In an increasingly globalized and pluralistic world, Catholicism may find that these long-established European patterns and expectations are more the exception than the rule.

A LOOK BACK TO LOOK FORWARD

The Catholic Church at the beginning of the twenty-first century is worldwide, far more so now than ever before. This new reality is illustrated in Figures 9.1 and 9.2, which include all the continental areas discussed in this book and for further nuance divide the Americas into North America and Latin America.

In 1950, the Churches in Africa and Asia were small, relatively insignificant parts of the Catholic Church. By 2000, those continents had become a major presence. In addition, Latin America and Europe shifted in their relative positions of dominance.

The numbers of all priests outside of Europe in 1950, particularly after subtracting those in North America, were insignificant compared to the proportion of priests in Europe. In 2000, the proportion of priests in North America was more than double North America's share of Catholic population. However, also in 2000, the distribution of likely future priests was just a few percentage points less than the proportion of Catholic population. This new reality was also the case in Europe, while Oceania continued to closely parallel its share of total Catholic population.

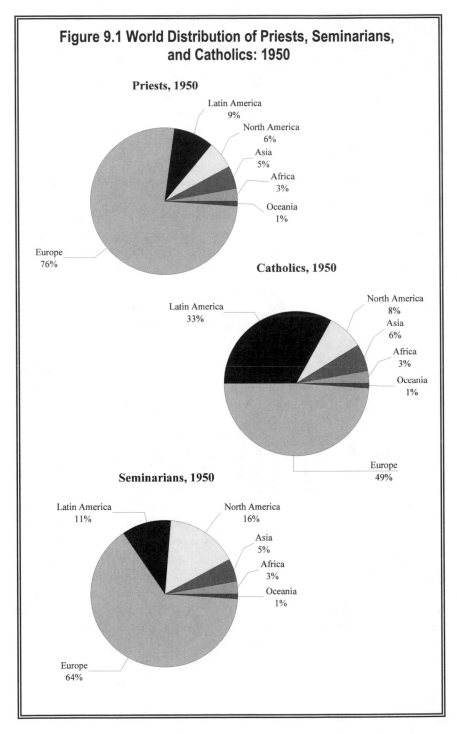

Figure 9.1 World Distribution of Priests, Seminarians, and Catholics: 1950

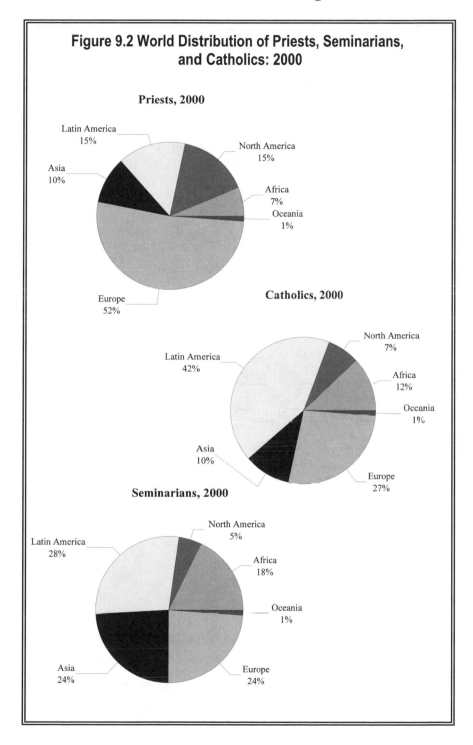

Figure 9.2 World Distribution of Priests, Seminarians, and Catholics: 2000

In 2000, the proportion of seminarians in Latin America more closely approached Latin America's share of global Catholic population. And two continents that before had hardly been present in the Catholic world, Asia and Africa, now had more than their share of seminarians relative to world Catholic population.

As these trends and other figures given in this book suggest, the Catholic Church in the twenty-first century is in a new situation, one likely to rapidly mature in the decades ahead. The twentieth century completed the emergence of a truly global Catholic Church.

Appendix I: Statistical Sources and Chapter Notes

MAJOR STATISTICAL SOURCES

The book is fundamentally based on statistics reported by each diocese or analogous Church territory around the world and released by the Vatican. There are two major sources released by the Vatican. One is the *Annuario Pontificio*, and includes information at the diocesan level. The other is the *Annuarium Statisticum Ecclesiae* and focuses on the country level.

The *Annuario Pontificio*, sometimes translated in English as the *Pontifical Yearbook* or the *Yearbook of the Holy See*, is annually issued by the Secretary of State of Vatican City in Italian. It has been issued in one form or another since 1716. Since 1946 it has included selected statistics for each diocese or other ecclesiatical territory listed in the publication.

From 1716 to 1849 it was published under the name *Notizie per l'anno,* and focused on the activities of the Papal States, along with information on the Holy See and the hierarchy worldwide. Publication was interrupted between 1798 until 1817 during the French occupation of Rome. In 1817, a publication was released called *Almanacco per i Dipartimenti di Roma e del Trasimeno*, which had some similar features. Publication of *Notizie* was resumed in 1818.

Publication under the title *Annuario Pontificio* began in 1850. Publication was halted in 1870 when the Papal States were forcibly included in the newly unified Italy. In 1872, a successor publication appeared entitled *Gerarchia Cattolica e la Famiglia Pontificia per l'anno con appendice di altre notizie riguardanti la S. Sede*. It contained information on the Holy See as well as the hierarchy worldwide and was published by a private firm for the Holy See. Beginning in 1885, *Gerarchia Cattolica* was produced and printed directly by the Holy See itself. Beginning in 1912, the name *Annuario Pontifico* was returned to the series.

In 1946 the information on dioceses and other ecclesiatical territories that had been a feature of the series since the beginning began to be accompanied with statistical information. Initially, the quality of the data varied widely and was often missing or based on statistics of widely varying years, due in part to the dislocations caused by the World War. By 1952, the dates to which the statistics referred had become more uniform and represented a two-year lag between publication year and the reporting year. Thus, the 1952 edition contains statistical information accurate as of December 31, 1950.

The *Annuarium Statisticum Ecclesiae*, or *Statistical Yearbook of the Church*, has been published since 1972. Typically there is a two- or three-year gap between the publication year and the year to which the statistics pertain. The first year of data in this series is 1969 and it is printed in a polyglot format using Latin and Italian. In that year the publication was simply called the *Raccolata da Tavola Statistiche* ("Collection of Statistical Tables"). In the edition containing 1970 data, both the title and format changed to its present style. As has been the case ever since, the languages used are Latin, English, and French.

GOING BEYOND AVAILABLE STATISTICS

Any source of statistics for a population, particularly one collected on a worldwide basis, has many sources for error. In any case, it is only accurate as of the moment it is completed. However, any effort to "correct" such figures may be only likely to introduce still more errors and be based on assumptions that may or may not be entirely accurate.

However, the figures given here should not be assumed to be exact. Even if they were exactly correct when supplied, they are subject to immediate change once recorded. Rather it may be best to use these figures to make comparisons across countries, regions, or time periods, assuming that whatever bias they may have is relatively randomly distributed.

In general, counts of the Catholic population are subject to a variety of problems. Very few counts are based on true annual head counts or a sophisticated calculation based on the numbers of Catholics who have been baptized, died, in-migrated, and out-migrated. In some cases, these figures are based on available government census data, where those censuses include questions on religious affiliation.

The most reliable figures tend to be those that depend on single counts conducted annually. For example, numbers of baptisms, confirmations, or marriages celebrated in the Church are counted each year and generally based on relatively firm figures provided by parishes. In addition, counts of available Church personnel, particularly priests, may for similar reasons be relatively more exacting.

While the figures provided in this book should be interpreted cautiously, they should also be respected for the insight they and other ratios that may be calculated from them might offer. The numbers of Catholics per parish, estimations of the proportion of infants baptized Catholic, or percent of priests who are diocesan all have their limitations. And yet, taken together, they and all the statistics presented in this book can offer considerable, if limited, insight into the lived pastoral reality of the Church around the world.

NOTES FOR CHAPTER 1

Calculations of global population over the course of human history are based on a United Nations report, "World Population for Year 0 to Stabilization." Issued in 1996, it is available at gopher://gopher.undp.org:70/00/ungophers/poppin/wdtrends/histor. Comparable efforts to estimate world population over time may be found at http://www.census.gov/ipc/www/worldhis.html. The Population Reference Bureau also has a number of resources, which may be accessed at www.cpb.org.

In Table 1.1 and all the tables and charts that follow, figures for 1900, 1950, and 2000 are based on three distinct but related sources. The 1900 data came from *The World Christian Encyclopedia* of 2001, issued by David Barrett and his collaborators. This source is referred to as Barrett 2001 for purposes of reference in these notes. The Catholic-related information in this massive work generally consists of extrapolations from diocesan-reported data as given in the *Annuario Pontificio*, although at times that source is supplemented by others. The 1950 data come directly from data on 1950 published in the *Annuario Pontificio* of 1952. The *Annuario Pontificio* is typically referred to as the "AP" for purposes of reference. Because it contains information at a diocesan level, the data were in turn summed at a country level. Figures for 2000 are based on the *Annuarium Statisticum Ecclesiae* 2000, which is in turn a more refined summary by country of the diocesan-level data provided to the Vatican and used for the creation of the *Annuario Pontificio*. The *Annuarium Statisticum Ecclesiae* ("Statistical Yearbook of the Church") is sometimes referred to as the "ASE" for purposes of citation in the text. All three sources provide information on both Church and secular population. These sources are used for both secular and Church population to ensure comparability. Wherever possible, information is taken exclusively from the *Annuarium Statisticum Ecclesiae* in order to provide for maximum comparability.

In Table 1.5, the percent of the world's Christians who are Catholic is based on Barrett 2001 since the ASE and other sources specific to the Catholic Church have figures only for Catholics. As noted earlier, Barrett's Catholic figures are generally based on AP figures, although sometimes they are projections or recalculated figures provided in the AP. For this reason, Barrett 2001 is used sparingly, to amplify points made in the text, or in reference to broader trends within the world Christian community. Discussions of the percent of the total population that is Catholic are based on the ASE or AP to ensure uniformity and comparability in statistical sources as much as possible.

Again, in Table 1.8 and all Church figures that follow, data are drawn from the ASE.

NOTES FOR CHAPTER 2

Table 2.5 is based on figures for the International Federation of Catholic Universities (www.fiuc.org) except in the case of the United States, where figures are based on a list provided by the Association of Catholic Colleges and Universities (www.accu.org). This list is designed to cover all Catholic institutions of general purpose, higher education in the United States, not only members of the association. This source is used because relatively few Catholic colleges and universities in the United States belong to the International Federation of Catholic Universities.

Table 2.6 is based on figures reported by the Vatican Congregation for Education in 1990.

NOTES FOR CHAPTER 3

In Table 3.1 "bishops" refers to anyone ordained a bishop, thus including bishops and archbishops, eparchies and archeparchs, patriarchs, and other roles within the Church.

NOTES FOR CHAPTER 4

The status of Sahara and Morocco's *de facto* control remains in dispute. To this day, there are two tiny Spanish outposts in North Africa, the cities of Melilla and Ceuta, with approximately 69,000 and 75,000 inhabitants, respectively, located on the coast of the Mediterranean Sea and established in the sixteenth century. Given their strong Spanish character and proximity to Spain, these two territories are included in the figures given for Spain.

In the text near Table 4.9 on the number of non-Catholic Christians in South Africa, figures from Barrett 2001 are used. As noted earlier, this is the single most comparable source for statistics on Christian religious bodies as a whole.

NOTES FOR CHAPTER 5

Table 5.1 is based on data from the ASE. However, the previous paragraph that compares proportions of the population of America and Europe that are Christian is based on Barrett 2001.

Generally understood as the part of America tied to Latin Europe, and most notably to Spain, "Latin America" is shorthand for an immense portion of the Western Hemisphere. This book defines "Latin America" as including the continental countries south of the United States except those granted independence by the British or Dutch (Belize, Guyana, and Surinam), as well as the island nations of Cuba, the Dominican Republic, and Haiti, together with the U.S. territory of Puerto Rico and the French territory of Cayenne, or French Guyana, on the north coast of South America. Given the strong historical presence of Catholicism in Latin Europe, these 25 countries or territories tend to have relatively larger proportions of Catholics than elsewhere.

After independence from Portugal in 1822, the government took a heavy hand to regulating Church actions and growth. This was not uncommon throughout Latin America. A century and a half later, during the dictatorships of the 1960s and 1970s, the Church in Brazil found itself at the forefront of leadership for change. Many bishops advocating land reform and defending democracy were threatened with violence. Again, similar trends could be observed throughout Latin America as a whole.

Table 5.2 uses ASE 2000 figures for Catholic baptisms and for the percent of baptized Catholics within the population. Figures for births used in the calculation of the percent of infants who are baptized is taken from the Population Reference

Bureau. These two measures are not in themselves precisely comparable. Catholic infant baptism figures refer to baptisms of anyone under the age of 7 during a one-year period. The number of births refer to those who were born in a twelve-month period. However, "infant" baptisms tend to be within the first year of life and, in any case, Catholic baptisms as well as births are one-time-only events. In the absence of other, more comparable figures these are the only tools available in understanding broader trends. In any case, baptism figures, as noted above, may be more precisely and accurately reported than counts of total Catholic population.

Finally, the estimates of those who were baptized Catholic but presently belong to evangelical religious bodies is taken from Barrett 2001. The category of so-called "doubly-affiliated" persons is only large in Latin America and a very few other countries outside of Latin America. In each case "doubly affiliated" refers to a calculation made in the national accounting of religious affiliation. It represents those who are counted by the Catholic Church as a baptized member but seem to also be counted by a non-Catholic Christian religious body as a member. When sources are available, Barrett also estimates the number of persons who are "disaffiliated," or baptized Catholic but no longer identify as religious. These estimates naturally share all the limitations of the data on which they are based. For this reason, they are best viewed comparatively and not treated as definitive in themselves.

Data regarding Catholic religious practice in Canada are taken from Bibby 1995 (pages 124-126).

Data on Catholic religious practice in the United States are taken from CARA surveys, particularly the CARA Catholic Poll, which has been annually conducted since 2000. One printed source that includes this information is the *CARA Working Paper #1* (page 19).

Uruguay separated Church and state in 1916 in imitation of the French model. There has been little major change since that time. Additional figures and specific sources on the historically low levels of Catholic affiliation and practice in Uruguay may be found in Barrett 2001 (pages 790-793).

NOTES FOR CHAPTER 6

Figures for the proportion of Armenian Orthodox within the population of Armenia are based on Barrett 2001 (pages 76-79).

Information on the proportion of Filipinos who were baptized Catholic but likely currently belong to another Christian religious body is in Barrett 2001 (page 594).

Information on the Church in China is reported in Barrett 2001 (page 193-194).

NOTES FOR CHAPTER 7

The themes in the overview to this chapter are also found in the documents relating to the Synod for Europe. See the General Secretariat of the Synod of

Bishops, *Instrumentum Laboris: Jesus Christ Alive in His Church, Source of Hope for Europe*. Prepared for the Synod of Bishops' Special Assembly for Europe 1–23 October 1999. http://www.vatican.va/roman_curia/synod/documents/rc_synod_doc_19071999_europe-instrlabor_en.html, accessed 10 October 2001.

Calculations on European population decline are taken from Joe Claude Harris, "A Demographic Revolution and the Future Church."

The declines suggested by Table 7.1 for the Catholic Church in Europe have been felt even more strongly in other established churches. In the Church of England, for example, 65 percent of all live births were baptized in the Church of England in 1902. The figure declined throughout the twentieth century from a high point of 71 percent in 1927. By 1960, the figure had dropped to 55 percent, by 1970 it was 47 percent, and by 1993 it was 27 percent. Similarly, around 1900, 70 percent of all English couples married in the Church of England. By 1990, only 30 percent of marriages were celebrated within the Church of England. During this period, other faith traditions did not win significant proportions of the English population; instead, participation in the established Church simply declined in salience. See Steve Bruce, *Religion in Modern Britain*, 1995 (pages 58-59) and Peter Brierley, *A Century of British Christianity: Historical Statistics 1900-1985*. See also Grace Davie 2000, *Religion in Modern Europe: A Memory Mutates* (pages 71-72).

The figures for Britain are taken from Streit 1929 (pages 12-13).

Catholic statistics for Belgium and France during the nineteenth and early twentieth centuries come from Streit 1929 (pages 12-13). Figures on Church attendance and other survey findings for the 1990s are drawn from Davie 2000 (page 9). The lack of formal religious practice in France has heightened tension regarding Muslim immigrants who insist on practicing Islam. More than one million North African Muslims moved to France in the 1960s and 1970s. By 1995, approximately five million of these immigrants and their descendants were living in France, making Islam the second most commonly reported religious affiliation. For more, see Barrett 2001 (page 281).

In France, the difference between the number of priests ordained and those lost to death or resignation in 2000 resulted in a net loss of 642 priests, the largest for any European country. These demographic changes have long been in the making and cannot be easily reversed. In 1965, 40 percent of priests in France were under 44. By the beginning of the 1990s, however, 5 percent of French priests were under 40 and 60 percent were over 60 years of age. See Davie 2000 (pages 43-46). See also Kerkhofs, *Europe without Priests*, 1995. Figures on declining numbers of priests for 2000 come from the ASE.

Figures on the large number of dioceses in Italy are from Streit 1929 (page 10). As a result of the elevated numbers of Church personnel in Rome, the country profile for Italy found in the appendix of this book subtracts figures for the Archdiocese of Rome from the corresponding figures for Italy. Those figures appear in the country profile for the Holy See. While the Vatican City state occupies only .44 square miles in the city of Rome, the Holy See is technically the entire Roman See. Since most of the clergy and institutions serving the Holy See are spread throughout the city of Rome, it is not possible to separate these Church personnel in any other way. Secular and Catholic population figures, however, are not reported under the Holy See and instead appear in the totals under Italy.

Figures on belief patterns, including atheism, and other trends within Eastern Europe during the 1990s come primarily from Barrett 2001.

NOTES FOR CHAPTER 8

In Table 8.2, the percentage change for the percent of worldwide Catholic population is 7 percent. The actual differences between the 1975 and 2000 are not shown due to rounding error. Note that Hawaii Islands, an island chain to the northeast of this area that is one of the 50 states of the United States, is not treated as part of Oceania. The Bishop of the Diocese of Honolulu belongs to the United States Conference of Catholic Bishops, not the Federation of Catholic Bishops' Conferences of Oceania.

Specific figures for Australia, including details on Catholic schools, numbers for specific communities of women religious, and others are from Robert E. Dixon, *The Catholics in Australia*, 1996 (pages 39 and 101). Dixon also supplied additional estimations of the number of lay ministers in 2000. Another source is Gary D. Bouma, ed., 1996, *Many Religions, One Australia: Religious Settlement, Identity and Cultural Diversity*.

Information on the Church in New Zealand comes from an unpublished paper "The Catholic Church in New Zealand–A Summary" supplied by the Bishops' Conference of that country. A final source for some of the figures is entitled "The Churches of Oceania amidst Peoples of the Past and the Future," published in the November 13, 1998, issue of *Fides*, an information service of the Vatican Office for the Propagation of the Faith.

NOTES FOR CHAPTER 9

Information about Oceania is taken from the sources named for Chapter 8. The observation about the fresh perspective offered by the experience of the Church in Oceania is taken from the document released by the Extraordinary Synod of Bishops for Oceania.

Statistics in Table 9.1 are from ASE 2000.

The number of countries with the largest concentrations of their population that is Catholic is low and likely to decline in the future. As the table below shows, the number of countries with populations that are more than 81 percent Catholic is 35. However, this figure declines considerably when one subtracts the best available estimates (from Barrett 2001) of those who were baptized Catholic but have left Catholicism to participate in other Christian religious bodies, principally evangelical and pentecostal congregations in Latin America. The greatest decline may be in the future as a result of lower baptism rates. This is particularly important since membership in the Catholic Church is ultimately measured by baptism, not by current practice. Only 15 countries are estimated to have 81 percent or more infants baptized Catholic. Twice as many countries have infant baptism figures of between 21 and 40 percent.

The table below is based on figures for 193 countries, including Taiwan and East Timor. Three separate kinds of figures are given for better estimation and understanding of long-term trends. The first column gives the proportion of the population estimated to be baptized Catholics and based on ASE 2000 figures. The second column uses estimates of current levels of Catholic self-identification. They are created by subtracting out the proportion of the population estimated to have been baptized Catholic but are currently a member of an evangelical religious body or have withdrawn altogether from the Christian tradition (as noted above, they are taken from Barrett 2001). The third column is based on the estimated proportion of infants who were baptized Catholic in the year 2000 using ASE 2000 figures for baptisms and the number of births reported or estimated for the most recent year. As noted earlier, because this figure is calculated from two different sources that are in turn not measured in comparable ways, it is not a definitive statistic so much as a suggestive one.

Table A.1 Number of Countries by Proportion Catholic: 2000			
Proportion of Each Country's Population	Percent Baptized Catholic	Subtracting Those Who Now Belong to Non-Catholic Religious Bodies	Percent Infants Baptized Catholic (estimate)
<3%	55	64	76
3-20%	56	51	46
21-40%	22	19	29
41-60%	11	17	9
61-80%	14	18	18
81-100%	35	24	15
Total	193	193	193

Figures 9.1 and 9.2 are based on AP 1950 and ASE 2000, respectively.

Appendix II: Definitions of Selected Terms

The Church-related definitions that follow are largely from the Code of Canon Law *(both Eastern and Western Churches) and* The Catholic Encyclopedia. *Demographics-related definitions are from the* Population Reference Bureau's Population Handbook, *4ᵗʰ International Edition, published in 1998.*

Abbot – The leader of a male monastic community, considered a supreme moderator of his religious institute in canon law. By tradition, also given the rank of prelate.

Apostolic Administration – A population or territory which for special and particularly serious reasons such as changes in boundaries, Church-State tensions, or internal disciplinary issues is not established yet as a diocese. Pastoral care is entrusted to an apostolic administrator who governs in the name of the Pope. The number of apostolic administrations is small and this type of structure is used only in exceptional circumstances.

Apostolic Exarchate – A population or territory of an Eastern Uniate Church not yet organized as a jurisdiction under a patriarch or eparch; an apostolic exarch usually is named by and rules in the name of the Holy See.

Church Council – An official gathering of Church leaders and representatives that assists in the process of decision-making within the Church. Councils of bishops have a particular role in the governance of the Church. Ecumenical councils are supreme exercises of the collegial authority of bishops. Current canon law allows only the Pope as head of the episcopal college to call an ecumenical council. The Pope also has the sole responsibility to set the council's agenda and to approve the decisions of the council. All members of the college of bishops (including auxiliary bishops and retired bishops) have the right to participate in an ecumenical council. In addition to the worldwide gathering of bishops in an ecumenical council, gatherings of bishops and ecclesiastical superiors may occur on a national (plenary) level or regional (provincial) level.

Demographic Transition – The historical shift of birth and death rates from high to low levels in a population. The decline of mortality usually precedes the decline in fertility. This results in rapid population growth during the transition period.

Demography – The scientific study of human populations, including their sizes, compositions, distributions, densities, growth, and other characteristics, as well as the causes and consequences of changes in these factors.

Dependency Ratio – The ratio of the economically dependent part of the population to the productive part; arbitrarily defined as the ratio of the elderly (ages 65 and older) plus the young (under age 15) to the population in the working ages (ages 15-64).

Diocese, Archdiocese – A portion of the people of God established by the Holy See and entrusted to the pastoral care of a bishop with the cooperation of the *presbyterium* that constitutes a particular Church. This is therefore not simply an administrative subdivision but a fully constituted Church in communion with other particular Churches. The boundaries are clearly delimited and ordinarily territorial in nature. The only exceptions are military ordinariates, Eastern Churches, which can overlap territory of Western Church dioceses, or of other Eastern Churches, and pastoral reasons or other exceptions made by the Holy See. An archdiocese is ordinarily a metropolitan see, or principal diocese in an ecclesiatical province. It is usually centered in a city important because of its size, history, or political status. A metropolitan archdiocese usually has some supervisory responsibility over the other suffragan dioceses of the province. Each diocese in turn is divided into parishes, which are also ordinarily territorially based.

Ecclesiastical Province – A grouping of a number of dioceses under the supervision of a metropolitan archbishop. The term "province" is also used for a major division, usually geographical, of some institutes of consecrated life under the governance of a provincial superior. The purpose is to promote, according to the circumstances of persons and place, a common pastoral action of various neighboring dioceses, as well as to foster closer relationships between the bishops of each diocese. Since the most recent revision of the Code of Canon Law for the Western Church (1983), there are to be no exempt dioceses. Churches that exist within the territory of an ecclesiastical province must be included in it. Only the Holy See can establish, suppress, or alter ecclesiastical provinces, although it is to consult with the local bishops' conference.

Ecclesiastical Territory – A general term for a designated geographical area or community (particularly in the case of the Eastern Churches) within the Church. This term is the most inclusive, in that it refers to dioceses (including patriarchal, metropolitan, archepiscopal, and episcopal sees) as well as territories that govern with ordinary jurisdiction but without being set up as dioceses (including territorial prelatures, apostolic administrations, vicariates, and prelatures apostolic).

Eparchy, Archeparchy – In Eastern canon law, a portion of the People of God under the pastoral care of a particular bishop (ordinarily termed an eparch within the Eastern Churches). This category is the equivalent of the diocese or archdiocese in the Western (Latin) Church. Eparchs or Eparchial Bishops are nominated by the Patriarch of their Church after candidates have been named by the respective synod of bishops, or by the Pope for those Churches without patriarchates. Some Eastern Churches have archeparchies, metropolitan archeparchies, or other particular Churches *sui iuris* that are subject directly to the Holy See rather than to a Patriarchate.

Episcopal Vicar – An office within a diocese held by a priest who functions as the bishop's vicar for people within a geographic segment of a diocese or for a specified group of the faithful. For that territory or group within the diocese, the episcopal vicar has authority comparable to that of a vicar general in that he may perform certain acts of executive power in the diocesan bishop's name. He is considered a local ordinary. This office is one of the innovations that emerged through the Second Vatican Council.

Fertility Rate – The average number of children born to a woman during her lifetime. The replacement rate for a population is 2.08. Numbers substantially higher reflect populations that are growing quickly, all things being equal. Numbers below 2.08 indicate a declining population with more deaths than births.

Gross National Income Adjusted by Purchasing Parity Power (GNI PPP) – The adjusted GNI provides an indicator of the economic welfare of people comparable across countries free of the price and exchange rate distortions that occur when GNI is converted using market exchange rates. GNI is the total value of all goods and services produced within a country plus net income earned abroad by nationals. GNI adjusted for purchasing power parity converts gross national income to international dollars using a purchasing power parity conversion factor based on the amount of goods or services one could buy in the United States with a given amount of money. In other words, GNI PPP provides the best measure to compare the relative standard of living of one country to another.

Immediately Subject to the Holy See – An ecclesiastical jurisdiction directly supervised by the Holy See rather than through an intermediary such as a metropolitan archbishop or patriarch.

Immigration – The process of entering one country from another to take up permanent or semi-permanent residence.

Immigration Rate – The number of immigrants arriving at a destination per 1,000 population at that destination in a given year.

Incardination – The process by which a diocesan priest is incorporated into the *presbyterium* of a diocese for which he was not originally ordained. This is particularly important, given the long term and stable relationship that is understood between a diocesan bishop, the diocesan presbyterium, and the people of the diocese.

Infant Mortality Rate – The number of deaths of infants under age one per 1,000 live births in a given year.

In-migration –The process of entering one administrative subdivision of a country (such as a province or state) from another subdivision to take up residence.

Less Developed Countries – The United Nations defines "less developed countries" (or regions) as consisting of all of Africa, Asia (except Japan), Latin America and the Caribbean, and Oceania (except Australia and New Zealand).

Life Expectancy – The average number of additional years a person could expect to live if current mortality trends were to continue for the rest of that person's life. The statistic is commonly given as life expectancy at birth.

Metropolitan – Adjective referring to the chief local Church of a region or to its bishop. A metropolitan see is based in a city important because of its size, history, or political status.

Migration – The movement of people across a specified boundary for the purpose of establishing a new or semi-permanent residence. There are two kinds of migration: international migration (migration between countries) and internal migration (migration within a country).

Military Ordinariate – A Church structure similar to a territorially based diocese and established to bring pastoral care to members of the military and their dependents. Membership is determined not on the basis of residence, but on the basis of membership in military service. A military ordinariate is headed by a bishop who is assisted by a staff comparable to that of a diocesan bishop. Priests who serve in it are drawn from dioceses and religious communities, but are released by their ecclesiastical superiors for such service.

Mission **sui iuris** – A territory that does not yet form part of a vicariate or prefecture apostolic but is placed under the guidance of missionaries or a missionary order, an ecclesiastical superior, and ultimately national mission secretariat and the Congregation for the Evangelization of Peoples (formerly call "Propaganda Fide"). It ordinarily has mission churches and mission stations within it. In the 1917 Code of Canon Law, no true parishes could be created in these areas until they had become dioceses.

More Developed Countries – According to the United Nations, definitions "more developed countries" (or "industrialized countries") include those of Europe (including all of Russia), the United States, Canada, Australia, New Zealand, and Japan.

Natural Increase (or Decrease) – The surplus (or deficit) of births over deaths in a population in a given time period.

Net Migration – The net effect of immigration and emigration on an area's population in a given time period, expressed as an increase or decrease.

Ordinary – The title for an individual who holds one of a certain class of offices within the Church. Although in common parlance the term often refers to the bishop of the diocese, canon law includes a greater number of officeholders under this title. The term includes the Pope, diocesan bishops, vicars general and episcopal vicars of a diocese, and many superiors in pontifical clerical institutes. All but those in the last category are also "local ordinaries." Canon law frequently uses the term "ordinary" and reserves certain powers to those who hold an office so designated. All of these officeholders have executive power of governance. Superiors in institutes that are classified as lay are not considered "ordinaries" because such superiors might be themselves laypersons, and canonical tradition excludes those who are not ordained from the power of governance in the strict meaning of that term.

Out-migration – The process of leaving one subdivision of a country to take up residence in another.

Parish – A defined, stable community of Christian faithful usually established locally within a geographical section of a diocese and ordinarily entrusted by the diocesan bishop to the pastoral care of a priest as its pastor. The diocesan bishop has the power to establish, suppress, or alter parishes, though he should not do so without consulting his presbyteral council. A "quasi-parish" is equivalent to a parish and is typically not distinguished from a parish. A quasi-parish is a certain community of Christ's faithful within a particular Church, entrusted to a priest as its proper pastor, but because of special circumstances not yet established as a parish. Not all communities can be established as parishes or quasi-parishes, and in those cases the diocesan bishop is to provide for their spiritual care in some other way. Ordinarily, parishes are to embrace all the faithful of a given territory. Where useful, however, "personal" parishes may be established, determined by reason of the rite, language, or nationality of Christ's faithful of a certain territory, or some other reason.

Particular Church – The canonical term for a local church. The Code of Canon Law identifies particular churches "first of all" as dioceses. Others include territorial prelatures and territorial abbacies, which are similar to dioceses for their permanency. Vicariates apostolic, prefectures apostolic, and permanently established apostolic administrations are also particular churches. In practice, they also includes missions *sui iuris*.

Pastoral Center – The pastoral center can be a parish, a quasi-parish, a mission station, or another center (such as a section of a parish or a chapel-of-ease) not canonically raised to the rank of parish or quasi-parish. A certain part of an ecclesiastical territory with its own church, people, and pastor or designated substitute for the care of souls. This term is used to group together all centers of Catholic worship including missionary churches or station and other non-parish centers such as chaplaincies, which do not have an established canonical status, with parishes and quasi-parishes.

Patriarchate – An autonomous, self-governing federation of dioceses under the jurisdiction of a patriarch (chief bishop) and his synod. In the Eastern Catholic Churches, a patriarch is canonically elected in the synod of bishops of the patriarchal church. Essentially a phenomenon of Eastern Churches. In Western Europe only a few were created as honorific titles (e.g. Lisbon, Venice) or to temporarily supervise missions (the West Indies in 1524 and East Indies in 1886). The Latin Patriarchate of Jerusalem, which had disappeared in earlier centuries, was reestablished in 1847.

Population Density – Population per unit of land area; for example, people per square mile or people per square kilometer of arable land.

Population Increase – The total population increase resulting from the interaction of births, deaths, and migration in a population in a given period of time.

Prelate – A priest who has the power of governance in the external (public) forum. There are also honorary prelates (monsignors).

Presbyterium – The union of all the priests secular and religious with the diocesan bishop, based upon ordination. They are represented by the presbyteral council or diocesan chapter, which is an advisory body to the bishop.

Provincial Council – A gathering of bishops of an ecclesiastical province for the purpose of deciding matters concerning the Church in that province. The term is also used to designate the group of advisors to the provincial superior of a religious institute required by canon law.

Synod of Bishops – A unique juridic institute whose membership varies according to the type of synod which is convened (ordinary, extraordinary, or special). In the case of ordinary sessions of the synod, the primary episcopal participation is regionally selected, while others are chosen by law, and still others appointed directly by the Roman Pontiff. The synod of bishops is primarily consultative but can be granted deliberative power by the Pope if he so chooses.

Territorial Abbacy or Prelature – A certain portion of the people of God which is established within certain territorial boundaries and whose care, due to special circumstances, is entrusted to some prelate or abbot who governs it as its proper pastor like a diocesan bishop. These were formerly called prelatures and abbacies *nullius dioceseos* because they were not dependent on any diocese. The prelate is ordinarily ordained a bishop. In 1976 the Holy See decreed that other territorial abbeys should not be established and that there should be an effort to transform those then existing into other jurisdictional forms and that episcopal ordination would not be conferred on abbots. In practice, this has meant that the territory of abbey *nullius* would be integrated into that of the diocese which surrounded it.

Vicar apostolic – A prelate who governs, in the name of the Pope, a territory that is equivalent to a diocese but has not become a diocese because of particular circumstances such as insufficient ministerial or material resources.

Vicariate or Prefecture Apostolic – These are geographic areas in which the local Church has not grown sufficiently to be a diocese. They are governed by a vicar or prefect apostolic in the name of the Pope. The Vicar Apostolic is usually a titular bishop (with the implied privileges and power) whereas the prefect apostolic does not usually receive episcopal ordination. They are in territories formerly called mission territories and which now depend on the Congregation for the Evangelization of Peoples. Both the vicar and the prefect apostolic govern their territory in the name of the Roman Pontiff, in other words, with ordinary power that is vicarious, not proper.

Appendix III: Country and Territory Listings

Table A.2   Dioceses (and Other Ecclesiastical Territories), Parishes, and Priests Listed in Descending Order by Catholic Population

Country	Catholics	Parishes	Priests
Brazil	143,900,000	8,732	16,598
Mexico	89,664,000	5,784	14,049
United States	63,347,000	19,356	48,288
Philippines	63,025,000	2,795	7,521
Italy	55,877,000	25,865	54,920
France	46,823,000	22,156	25,353
Colombia	37,723,000	3,614	7,851
Spain	37,152,000	22,618	27,281
Poland	37,002,000	9,966	27,458
Argentina	33,549,000	2,694	5,868
Germany	27,455,000	12,466	19,290
Congo, Democratic Republic of the	27,067,000	1,296	3,937
Peru	23,020,000	1,426	2,790
Venezuela	21,414,000	1,185	2,320
Nigeria	16,579,000	1,752	3,597
India	16,516,000	8,200	19,404
Canada	13,453,000	5,115	9,832
Ecuador	11,623,000	1,151	1,836
Chile	11,426,000	951	2,298
Uganda	10,057,000	424	1,590
Guatemala	9,471,000	434	970
Tanzania	9,470,000	792	2,067
Portugal	9,404,000	4,362	4,237
Belgium	8,105,000	3,939	8,070
Angola	7,737,000	239	543
Kenya	7,654,000	642	1,865
China	7,500,000	0	na
Dominican Republic	7,475,000	485	817
Bolivia	7,246,000	565	1,056
Haiti	6,778,000	266	611
Indonesia	6,284,000	1,044	2,883
Hungary	6,231,000	2,223	2,472
Cuba	6,179,000	264	296
Austria	6,027,000	3,063	4,487
Netherlands	5,365,000	1,492	3,876
Honduras	5,362,000	169	382
Australia	5,316,000	1,407	3,318
Vietnam	5,301,000	2,570	2,443

Country	Catholics	Parishes	Priests
United Kingdom of Great Britain and Northern Ireland	5,293,000	3,157	6,081
El Salvador	4,986,000	376	663
Paraguay	4,708,000	358	783
Ireland	4,666,000	1,367	5,642
Ukraine	4,611,000	3,676	2,522
Nicaragua	4,518,000	243	418
Czech Republic	4,307,000	3,135	1,959
Madagascar	4,147,000	310	1,111
South Korea	4,047,000	1,152	2,731
Burundi	3,991,000	144	351
Cameroon	3,920,000	630	1,270
Sudan	3,810,000	164	323
Croatia	3,745,000	1,533	2,259
Mozambique	3,737,000	271	447
Slovakia	3,659,000	1,480	2,508
Rwanda	3,628,000	132	485
Costa Rica	3,346,000	258	770
Switzerland	3,169,000	1,695	3,126
South Africa	3,081,000	729	1,077
Puerto Rico (United States)	3,045,000	354	761
Zambia	3,012,000	256	575
Lithuania	2,828,000	676	774
Malawi	2,680,000	150	398
Côte d'Ivoire	2,605,000	259	823
Uruguay	2,507,000	229	498
Panama	2,434,000	176	392
Ghana	2,242,000	318	918
Romania	2,032,000	1,770	1,686
Lebanon	1,819,000	1,029	1,370
Congo, Republic of	1,719,000	141	298
Papua New Guinea	1,630,000	342	547
Slovenia	1,622,000	805	1,150
Benin	1,493,000	185	418
Burkina Faso	1,324,000	123	624
Sri Lanka	1,300,000	376	941
Togo	1,259,000	133	377
Pakistan	1,237,000	112	266
Zimbabwe	1,172,000	152	414
Belarus	1,059,000	368	309
Russian Federation (in Asia)	1,049,000	197	96
Chad	905,000	110	223
Lesotho	894,000	81	146
Malaysia	752,000	140	244
East Timor	750,000	31	101

Country	Catholics	Parishes	Priests
Central African Republic	718,000	122	268
Gabon	643,000	62	111
Saudi Arabia	625,875	4	5
Myanmar	600,000	272	483
Réunion (France)	595,000	75	108
Yugoslavia	553,000	287	271
Albania	513,000	113	122
Japan	513,000	871	1,749
Senegal	483,000	98	396
Bosnia and Herzegovina	459,000	281	609
New Zealand	457,000	272	554
Ethiopia	443,000	216	439
Cape Verde	409,000	31	47
Latvia	408,000	243	116
Equatorial Guinea	385,000	66	94
Trinidad and Tobago	383,000	61	110
Luxembourg	378,000	275	279
China, Hong Kong SAR	371,000	55	325
Malta	364,000	79	931
Guadeloupe (France)	355,000	45	59
United Arab Emirates	336,000	5	17
Syria	335,000	203	253
China, Taiwan	310,000	459	699
Namibia	307,000	92	77
Martinique (France)	298,000	47	63
Mauritius	288,000	52	98
Iraq	281,000	92	135
Thailand	273,000	350	642
Bangladesh	264,000	78	276
Russia	255,000	109	213
Egypt	237,000	219	473
Mali	211,000	38	154
Kazakhstan	180,000	37	59
Kuwait	154,000	5	9
Netherlands Antilles (Netherlands)	152,000	28	30
Singapore	152,000	30	131
Guam (United States)	151,000	24	47
Armenia	150,000	18	4
French Guiana (France)	150,000	23	34
Liberia	142,000	48	52
Guinea-Bissau	136,000	22	66
Guinea	134,000	54	96
Belize	133,000	13	43
Eritrea	133,000	97	254
Israel	118,000	78	379

Country	Catholics	Parishes	Priests
Jamaica	116,000	87	90
Saint Lucia	116,000	22	29
New Caledonia (France)	110,000	27	57
São Tomé and Principe	109,000	12	12
Georgia	100,000	27	16
Suriname	100,000	31	20
Sweden	97,000	40	147
Polynesia (France)	91,000	91	37
Guyana	88,000	24	51
Fiji Islands	83,000	35	126
Solomon Islands	83,000	27	50
Bulgaria	80,000	54	51
Botswana	78,000	28	50
Libya	77,000	6	14
Aruba (Netherlands)	73,000	8	8
Jordan	72,000	62	75
Sierra Leone	72,000	38	121
Seychelles	69,000	17	15
Oman	66,000	4	8
Qatar	65,000	1	1
Andorra	64,000	7	18
Micronesia	62,000	23	23
Dominica	60,000	15	48
Greece	55,000	70	92
Grenada	55,000	20	22
North Korea	55,000	0	na
Northern Mariana Islands (United States)	53,000	11	17
Norway	53,000	32	69
Swaziland	53,000	15	40
Bahamas	48,000	30	27
Kiribati	46,000	23	26
Laos	38,000	111	13
Denmark	34,000	49	91
Turkey	32,000	52	59
Bahrain	30,000	1	3
China, Macau SAR	30,000	8	72
Gambia	30,000	56	24
Samoa	30,000	29	50
Virgin Islands (United States)	30,000	8	16
Monaco	29,000	6	22
Vanuatu	29,000	18	29
San Marino	26,000	12	31
Brunei Darussalem	25,000	3	3
Iran	25,000	18	18

Country	Catholics	Parishes	Priests
Liechtenstein	25,000	10	30
Morocco	24,000	35	62
Gibraltar (United Kingdom)	23,000	5	15
Tunisia	22,000	12	33
Cambodia	20,000	31	46
Moldova	20,000	11	15
Niger	20,000	22	48
Cyprus	17,000	13	22
Tonga	15,000	10	21
Wallis and Futuna Islands (France)	14,000	5	10
American Samoa (United States)	12,000	11	13
Barbados	10,000	6	8
Macedonia	10,000	7	13
Saint Vincent and the Grenadines	10,000	6	6
Bermuda (United Kingdom)	9,000	6	6
Antigua and Barbuda	8,000	2	6
Finland	8,000	7	21
Palau	8,000	3	5
Djibouti	7,000	5	6
Nepal	6,000	35	51
Saint Pierre and Miquelon (France)	6,000	2	2
Turks and Caicos Islands (United Kingdom)	6,000	2	3
Marshall Islands	5,000	4	6
Mauritania	5,000	6	10
Saint Kitts and Nevis	5,000	3	4
Cayman Islands (United Kingdom)	4,000	1	1
Estonia	4,000	5	9
Iceland	4,000	4	12
Yemen	4,000	4	4
Algeria	3,000	39	108
Cook Islands (New Zealand)	3,000	15	7
Nauru	3,000	1	1
Uzbekistan	3,000	3	9
Comoros	2,000	2	4
Montserrat (United Kingdom)	1,400	1	1
Falkland Islands (United Kingdom)	1,000	1	2
Tokelau (New Zealand)	1,000	2	1
Turkmenistan	1,000	1	3
Virgin Islands (United Kingdom)	1,000	3	3
Bhutan	400	1	0
Kyrgyzstan	300	7	6
Anguilla (United Kingdom)	200	1	1
Sahara (Morocco)	200	2	3
Tajikistan	200	2	4

Country	Catholics	Parishes	Priests
Azerbaijan	100	1	2
Faeroe Islands (Denmark)	100	1	0
Greenland (Denmark)	100	1	1
Mongolia	100	1	7
Niue (New Zealand)	100	3	1
Saint Helena (United Kingdom)	100	1	1
Somalia	100	1	4
Tuvalu	100	1	1
Afghanistan	na	0	0
Maldives	na	0	0
Svalbard and Jan Mayen Islands (Norway)	na	0	0

Appendix IV: Country and Territory Profiles

This appendix lists 192 countries. The Vatican City state, a sovereign territory consisting of about .44 square miles and administered by the Holy See, is not listed here. For Church purposes, its population of approximately 1,000 residents are part of the Archdiocese of Rome. However, East Timor is included in the profiles that follow, although it did not actually become a recognized independent country until 2002. Finally, Taiwan is given a separate entry even though it is not a member or observer of the United Nations.

The profiles that follow also include 31 territories. A few other territories are mentioned in the book but not given a separate profile entry due to very limited data, particularly regarding accurate Church statistics. These include Mayotte, a French island possession in the Indian Ocean, and the Palestinian Territories (East Jerusalem, West Bank, and the Gaza Strip).

Finally, the profiles that follow separately list contiguous parts of three countries in order to provide more accurate Church statistics. Thus, Russia in Asia and Russia in Europe are listed separately. Also, Hong Kong and Macau are listed as Separate Administrative Regions (SARs) within China.

Below are listed the numbers of countries and territories listed in the profiles that follow. Again, Hong Kong, Macau, and Russia in Asia are listed separately.

Table A.3 Count of Countries and Territories			
	Countries	Territories	Total
Africa	53	3	56
America	35	15	50
Asia	45		45
Europe	45	4	49
Oceania	14	9	23
World	192 *	31 **	223

*Note that Vatican City is not listed here. If it were, the number of countries in Europe would be 46.
**Excludes Palestine and Mayotte, a French island possession in the Indian Ocean.

Not all territories of the world are listed in the profiles. Some are too small to include and in other cases data are not available. What follows is a list of each territory given in the profiles, followed by the region of which it is a part and the country that has sovereignty over the territory. The sovereignty claimed by Morocco over Sahara, a territory formerly controlled by Spain, is disputed.

Table A.4 Territories of the World

Region	Territory	Sovereign Country
Oceania	American Samoa	United States
Caribbean	Anguilla	United Kingdom
Caribbean	Aruba	Netherlands
North America	Bermuda	United Kingdom
Caribbean	Cayman Islands	United Kingdom
Oceania	Cook Islands	New Zealand
NW Europe	Faeroe Islands	Denmark
South America	Falkland Islands	United Kingdom
South America	French Guiana	France
SW Europe	Gibraltar	United Kingdom
North America	Greenland	Denmark
Caribbean	Guadeloupe	France
Oceania	Guam	United States
Caribbean	Martinique	France
Caribbean	Montserrat	United Kingdom
Caribbean	Netherlands Antilles	Netherlands
Oceania	New Caledonia	France
Oceania	Niue	New Zealand
Oceania	Northern Marianas	United States
Oceania	Polynesia	France
Caribbean	Puerto Rico	United States
Africa	Reunion	France
Africa	St. Helena	United Kingdom
North America	St. Pierre et Miquelon	France
NW Europe	Svalbard and Jan Mayen Islands	Norway
Oceania	Tokelau	New Zealand
Caribbean	Turks and Caicos Islands	United Kingdom
Caribbean	Virgin Islands UK	United Kingdom
Caribbean	Virgin Islands USA	United States
Oceania	Wallis and Futuna Islands	France
North Africa	Sahara	Morocco

Afghanistan
Region: Western Asia
Oldest diocese: na (na)
Land mass: 647,500 km²
Primary language(s): Dari, Pashtu
Primary religion(s): Islam

Population: 21,770,000
Fertility rate: 6
Infant mortality per 1,000 births: 151.6
Life expectancy: 46
Literacy rate: 29.4 (1990 est.)
GNI per capita (PPP): $ na

Catholics; %: na; na
Dioceses; all territories: 0; 0
Parishes; pastoral centers: 0; 0
Catholics/parish; /priest: na; na

Baptisms; % infants: 0; na
% infants baptized Catholic (est.): na%
Confirmations: 0
Marriages; % both Catholic: 0; na

Hospitals: 0
Orphanages: 0
Homes for elderly, disabled: 0
Other charitable institutions: 0
Primary schools: 0
Secondary schools: 0
Colleges and universities: 0
Seminaries: 0

Permanent deacons: 0
Seminarians; % diocesan: 0; na
Diocesan priests: 0
Religious priests; brothers: 0; 0
Women religious: 0
Catechists: 0
Lay missionaries: 0

Albania
Region: Eastern Europe
Oldest diocese: Sapë (1062)
Land mass: 28,748 km²
Primary language(s): Albanian
Primary religion(s): Islam

Population: 3,130,000
Fertility rate: 2.8
Infant mortality per 1,000 births: 43.1
Life expectancy: 71
Literacy rate: 71.5 (1955 est.)
GNI per capita (PPP): $ 3,240

Catholics; %: 513,000; 16%
Dioceses; all territories: 6; 7
Parishes; pastoral centers: 113; 152
Catholics/parish; /priest: 4,540; 4,205

Baptisms; % infants: 5,792; 65%
% infants baptized Catholic (est.): 6%
Confirmations: 3,860
Marriages; % both Catholic: 563; 97%

Hospitals: 0
Orphanages: 9
Homes for elderly, disabled: 12
Other charitable institutions: 83
Primary schools: 42
Secondary schools: 20
Colleges and universities: 0
Seminaries: 1

Permanent deacons: 1
Seminarians; % diocesan: 57; 44%
Diocesan priests: 38
Religious priests; brothers: 84; 15
Women religious: 381
Catechists: 105
Lay missionaries: 0

Algeria Region: North Africa Oldest diocese: Alger (1838) Land mass: 2,381,741 km² Primary language(s): Arabic Primary religion(s): Islam	Population: 30,290,000 Fertility rate: 3.1 Infant mortality per 1,000 births: 43.6 Life expectancy: 69 Literacy rate: 57.4 (1990 est.) GNI per capita (PPP): $ 4,840
Catholics; %: 3,000; <1% Dioceses; all territories: 4; 4 Parishes; pastoral centers: 39; 62 Catholics/parish; /priest: 77; 28	Baptisms; % infants: 5; 20% % infants baptized Catholic (est.): <1% Confirmations: 2 Marriages; % both Catholic: 1; 100%
Hospitals: 1 Orphanages: 0 Homes for elderly, disabled: 2 Other charitable institutions: 17 Primary schools: 0 Secondary schools: 0 Colleges and universities: 0 Seminaries: 0	Permanent deacons: 1 Seminarians; % diocesan: 2; <1% Diocesan priests: 39 Religious priests; brothers: 69; 16 Women religious: 191 Catechists: 2 Lay missionaries: 9

American Samoa (United States) Region: Oceania Oldest diocese: Samoa-Pago (1982) Land mass: 199 km² Primary language(s): English Primary religion(s): Protestant	Population: 62,000 Fertility rate: na Infant mortality per 1,000 births: 6.5 Life expectancy: 81 Literacy rate: 97.34 (1980 est.) GNI per capita (PPP): $ na
Catholics; %: 12,000; 19% Dioceses; all territories: 1; 1 Parishes; pastoral centers: 11; 26 Catholics/parish; /priest: 1,091; 923	Baptisms; % infants: 481; 75% % infants baptized Catholic (est.): 14% Confirmations: 480 Marriages; % both Catholic: 45; 73%
Hospitals: 0 Orphanages: 0 Homes for elderly, disabled: 1 Other charitable institutions: 2 Primary schools: 2 Secondary schools: 1 Colleges and universities: 0 Seminaries: 0	Permanent deacons: 16 Seminarians; % diocesan: 13; 100% Diocesan priests: 10 Religious priests; brothers: 3; 0 Women religious: 14 Catechists: 21 Lay missionaries: 8

Andorra Region: Southwestern Europe Oldest diocese: na (na) Land mass: 453 km² Primary language(s): Catalan Primary religion(s): Catholic	Population: 68,000 Fertility rate: 1.2 Infant mortality per 1,000 births: 4.1 Life expectancy: 83 Literacy rate: 100 (na est.) GNI per capita (PPP): $ na
Catholics; %: 64,000; 94% Dioceses; all territories: 0; 0 Parishes; pastoral centers: 7; 7 Catholics/parish; /priest: 9,143; 3,556	Baptisms; % infants: 447; 97% % infants baptized Catholic (est.): 40% Confirmations: 211 Marriages; % both Catholic: 118; 98%
Hospitals: 0 Orphanages: 0 Homes for elderly, disabled: 0 Other charitable institutions: 0 Primary schools: 0 Secondary schools: 2 Colleges and universities: 0 Seminaries: 0	Permanent deacons: 0 Seminarians; % diocesan: 0; na Diocesan priests: 12 Religious priests; brothers: 6; 0 Women religious: 10 Catechists: 54 Lay missionaries: 0

Angola Region: Southern Africa Oldest diocese: Huambo (1940) Land mass: 1,246,700 km² Primary language(s): Portuguese Primary religion(s): Catholic, Indigenous religions	Population: 13,130,000 Fertility rate: 6.9 Infant mortality per 1,000 births: 197.8 Life expectancy: 38 Literacy rate: 41.7 (1990 est.) GNI per capita (PPP): $ 1,100
Catholics; %: 7,737,000; 59% Dioceses; all territories: 16; 16 Parishes; pastoral centers: 239; 3,211 Catholics/parish; /priest: 32,372; 14,249	Baptisms; % infants: 173,716; 64% % infants baptized Catholic (est.): 26% Confirmations: 47,757 Marriages; % both Catholic: 16,056; 98%
Hospitals: 13 Orphanages: 27 Homes for elderly, disabled: 6 Other charitable institutions: 339 Primary schools: 218 Secondary schools: 49 Colleges and universities: 0 Seminaries: 11	Permanent deacons: 1 Seminarians; % diocesan: 1,156; 69% Diocesan priests: 247 Religious priests; brothers: 296; 107 Women religious: 1,642 Catechists: 27,389 Lay missionaries: 21

Anguilla (United Kingdom)
Region: Caribbean
Oldest diocese: na (na)
Land mass: 96 km²
Primary language(s): English
Primary religion(s): Anglican, Methodist

Population: 7,000
Fertility rate: na
Infant mortality per 1,000 births: 25.9
Life expectancy: 76
Literacy rate: 95.05 (1984 est.)
GNI per capita (PPP): $ na

Catholics; %: 200; 3%
Dioceses; all territories: 0; 0
Parishes; pastoral centers: 1; 1
Catholics/parish; /priest: 200; 200

Baptisms; % infants: 5; 100%
% infants baptized Catholic (est.): 4%
Confirmations: 0
Marriages; % both Catholic: 6; 50%

Hospitals: 0
Orphanages: 0
Homes for elderly, disabled: 0
Other charitable institutions: 0
Primary schools: 0
Secondary schools: 0
Colleges and universities: 0
Seminaries: 0

Permanent deacons: 0
Seminarians; % diocesan: 0; na
Diocesan priests: 0
Religious priests; brothers: 1; 0
Women religious: 0
Catechists: 6
Lay missionaries: 0

Antigua and Barbuda
Region: Caribbean
Oldest diocese: Saint John's-Basseterre
(1971)
Land mass: 442 km²
Primary language(s): English
Primary religion(s): Anglican

Population: 64,000
Fertility rate: 2.4
Infant mortality per 1,000 births: 23.9
Life expectancy: 70
Literacy rate: 4 (1965 est.)
GNI per capita (PPP): $ 9,870

Catholics; %: 8,000; 12%
Dioceses; all territories: 1; 1
Parishes; pastoral centers: 2; 8
Catholics/parish; /priest: 4,000; 1,333

Baptisms; % infants: 99; 100%
% infants baptized Catholic (est.): 7%
Confirmations: 41
Marriages; % both Catholic: 13; 38%

Hospitals: 2
Orphanages: 1
Homes for elderly, disabled: 1
Other charitable institutions: 2
Primary schools: 1
Secondary schools: 2
Colleges and universities: 0
Seminaries: 0

Permanent deacons: 4
Seminarians; % diocesan: 1; 100%
Diocesan priests: 2
Religious priests; brothers: 4; 4
Women religious: 9
Catechists: 32
Lay missionaries: 0

Argentina Region: South America Oldest diocese: Buenos Aires (1620) Land mass: 2,766,889 km² Primary language(s): Spanish Primary religion(s): Catholic	Population: 37,030,000 Fertility rate: 2.6 Infant mortality per 1,000 births: 19.1 Life expectancy: 75 Literacy rate: 96.24 (1991 est.) GNI per capita (PPP): $ 11,940
Catholics; %: 33,549,000; 91% Dioceses; all territories: 64; 70 Parishes; pastoral centers: 2,694; 9,337 Catholics/parish; /priest: 12,453; 5,717	Baptisms; % infants: 554,190; 94% % infants baptized Catholic (est.): 74% Confirmations: 286,700 Marriages; % both Catholic: 92,036; 98%
Hospitals: 94 Orphanages: 280 Homes for elderly, disabled: 251 Other charitable institutions: 3,062 Primary schools: 1,652 Secondary schools: 1,458 Colleges and universities: 4 Seminaries: 49	Permanent deacons: 525 Seminarians; % diocesan: 2,003; 67% Diocesan priests: 3,608 Religious priests; brothers: 2,260; 822 Women religious: 9,829 Catechists: 83,173 Lay missionaries: 47,823

Armenia Region: Western Asia Oldest diocese: na (na) Land mass: 29,800 km² Primary language(s): Armenian Primary religion(s): Armenian Orthodox	Population: 3,800,000 Fertility rate: 1.1 Infant mortality per 1,000 births: 41.1 Life expectancy: 67 Literacy rate: 99 (1989 est.) GNI per capita (PPP): $ 2,360
Catholics; %: 150,000; 4% Dioceses; all territories: 0; 1 Parishes; pastoral centers: 18; 18 Catholics/parish; /priest: 8,333; 37,500	Baptisms; % Infants: 794; 49% % infants baptized Catholic (est.): 9% Confirmations: 794 Marriages; % both Catholic: 118; 93%
Hospitals: 1 Orphanages: 1 Homes for elderly, disabled: 0 Other charitable institutions: 24 Primary schools: 0 Secondary schools: 0 Colleges and universities: 0 Seminaries: 0	Permanent deacons: 0 Seminarians; % diocesan: 5; 100% Diocesan priests: 0 Religious priests; brothers: 4; 1 Women religious: 16 Catechists: 7 Lay missionaries: 0

Aruba (Netherlands)
Region: Caribbean
Oldest diocese: na (na)
Land mass: 193 km²
Primary language(s): Dutch
Primary religion(s): Catholic

Population: 91,000
Fertility rate: na
Infant mortality per 1,000 births: 6.7
Life expectancy: 78
Literacy rate: 97 (na est.)
GNI per capita (PPP): $ na

Catholics; %: 73,000; 80%
Dioceses; all territories: 0; 0
Parishes; pastoral centers: 8; 8
Catholics/parish; /priest: 9,125; 9,125

Baptisms; % infants: 952; 94%
% infants baptized Catholic (est.): 43%
Confirmations: 501
Marriages; % both Catholic: 91; 92%

Hospitals: 1
Orphanages: 1
Homes for elderly, disabled: 3
Other charitable institutions: 0
Primary schools: 26
Secondary schools: 14
Colleges and universities: 0
Seminaries: 0

Permanent deacons: 0
Seminarians; % diocesan: 0; na
Diocesan priests: 5
Religious priests; brothers: 3; 0
Women religious: 9
Catechists: 5
Lay missionaries: 0

Australia
Region: Oceania
Oldest diocese: Sydney (1842)
Land mass: 7,687,033 km²
Primary language(s): English
Primary religion(s): Protestant

Population: 19,160,000
Fertility rate: 1.7
Infant mortality per 1,000 births: 5.1
Life expectancy: 80
Literacy rate: 100 (1980 est.)
GNI per capita (PPP): $ 23,850

Catholics; %: 5,316,000; 28%
Dioceses; all territories: 31; 32
Parishes; pastoral centers: 1,407; 1,585
Catholics/parish; /priest: 3,778; 1,602

Baptisms; % infants: 66,789; 93%
% infants baptized Catholic (est.): 25%
Confirmations: 51,681
Marriages; % both Catholic: 17,710; 50%

Hospitals: 65
Orphanages: 54
Homes for elderly, disabled: 312
Other charitable institutions: 466
Primary schools: 1,307
Secondary schools: 420
Colleges and universities: 2
Seminaries: 11

Permanent deacons: 47
Seminarians; % diocesan: 272; 60%
Diocesan priests: 1,977
Religious priests; brothers: 1,341; 1,164
Women religious: 8,147
Catechists: 5,259
Lay missionaries: 0

Austria **Region: Northwestern Europe** Oldest diocese: Gurk (1071) Land mass: 83,853 km² Primary language(s): German Primary religion(s): Catholic	Population: 8,100,000 Fertility rate: 1.3 Infant mortality per 1,000 births: 4.5 Life expectancy: 78 Literacy rate: 99 (1974 est.) GNI per capita (PPP): $ 24,600
Catholics; %: 6,027,000; 74% Dioceses; all territories: 9; 12 Parishes; pastoral centers: 3,063; 4,068 Catholics/parish; /priest: 1,968; 1,343	Baptisms; % infants: 62,983; 89% % infants baptized Catholic (est.): 79% Confirmations: 64,665 Marriages; % both Catholic: 14,983; 89%
Hospitals: 33 Orphanages: 6 Homes for elderly, disabled: 70 Other charitable institutions: 706 Primary schools: 102 Secondary schools: 167 Colleges and universities: 0 Seminaries: 12	Permanent deacons: 428 Seminarians; % diocesan: 363; 47% Diocesan priests: 2,701 Religious priests; brothers: 1,786; 376 Women religious: 6,038 Catechists: 2,916 Lay missionaries: 0

Azerbaijan **Region: Western Asia** Oldest diocese: na (na) Land mass: 86,600 km² Primary language(s): Azeri Primary religion(s): Islam	Population: 8,050,000 Fertility rate: 2 Infant mortality per 1,000 births: 82.5 Life expectancy: 63 Literacy rate: 97 (1989 est.) GNI per capita (PPP): $ 2,450
Catholics; %: 100; <1% Dioceses; all territories: 0; 1 Parishes; pastoral centers: 1; 1 Catholics/parish; /priest: 100; 50	Baptisms; % infants: 0; na % infants baptized Catholic (est.): na% Confirmations: 0 Marriages; % both Catholic: 0; na
Hospitals: 0 Orphanages: 0 Homes for elderly, disabled: 0 Other charitable institutions: 1 Primary schools: 0 Secondary schools: 0 Colleges and universities: 0 Seminaries: 0	Permanent deacons: 0 Seminarians; % diocesan: 0; na Diocesan priests: 0 Religious priests; brothers: 2; 1 Women religious: 0 Catechists: 0 Lay missionaries: 0

Bahamas Region: Caribbean Oldest diocese: Nassau (1929) Land mass: 13,878 km² Primary language(s): English Primary religion(s): Baptist, Anglican	Population: 298,000 Fertility rate: 2.4 Infant mortality per 1,000 births: 16.9 Life expectancy: 72 Literacy rate: 89.7 (1963 est.) GNI per capita (PPP): $ 15,500
Catholics; %: 48,000; 16% Dioceses; all territories: 1; 1 Parishes; pastoral centers: 30; 56 Catholics/parish; /priest: 1,600; 1,778	Baptisms; % infants: 925; 51% % infants baptized Catholic (est.): 9% Confirmations: 188 Marriages; % both Catholic: 136; 57%
Hospitals: 0 Orphanages: 0 Homes for elderly, disabled: 0 Other charitable institutions: 4 Primary schools: 11 Secondary schools: 3 Colleges and universities: 0 Seminaries: 0	Permanent deacons: 14 Seminarians; % diocesan: 4; 100% Diocesan priests: 12 Religious priests; brothers: 15; 0 Women religious: 30 Catechists: 202 Lay missionaries: 0

Bahrain Region: Western Asia Oldest diocese: na (na) Land mass: 678 km² Primary language(s): Arabic, English Primary religion(s): Islam	Population: 690,000 Fertility rate: 2.8 Infant mortality per 1,000 births: 21.2 Life expectancy: 73 Literacy rate: 77.4 (1990 est.) GNI per capita (PPP): $ na
Catholics; %: 30,000; 4% Dioceses; all territories: 0; 0 Parishes; pastoral centers: 1; 4 Catholics/parish; /priest: 30,000; 10,000	Baptisms; % infants: 214; 96% % infants baptized Catholic (est.): 1% Confirmations: 137 Marriages; % both Catholic: 42; 83%
Hospitals: 0 Orphanages: 0 Homes for elderly, disabled: 0 Other charitable institutions: 0 Primary schools: 1 Secondary schools: 1 Colleges and universities: 0 Seminaries: 0	Permanent deacons: 0 Seminarians; % diocesan: 0; na Diocesan priests: 2 Religious priests; brothers: 1; 0 Women religious: 6 Catechists: 0 Lay missionaries: 0

Bangladesh **Region: South Asia** Oldest diocese: Dhaka (1886) Land mass: 143,998 km² Primary language(s): Bangla, English Primary religion(s): Islam	Population: 137,440,000 Fertility rate: 3.3 Infant mortality per 1,000 births: 73.3 Life expectancy: 60 Literacy rate: 36.13 (1991 est.) GNI per capita (PPP): $ 1,530
Catholics; %: 264,000; <1% Dioceses; all territories: 6; 6 Parishes; pastoral centers: 78; 239 Catholics/parish; /priest: 3,385; 957	Baptisms; % infants: 6,917; 74% % infants baptized Catholic (est.): <1% Confirmations: 4,432 Marriages; % both Catholic: 1,579; 88%
Hospitals: 11 Orphanages: 31 Homes for elderly, disabled: 11 Other charitable institutions: 146 Primary schools: 350 Secondary schools: 57 Colleges and universities: 0 Seminaries: 3	Permanent deacons: 0 Seminarians; % diocesan: 118; 58% Diocesan priests: 139 Religious priests; brothers: 137; 64 Women religious: 977 Catechists: 1,381 Lay missionaries: 0

Barbados **Region: Caribbean** Oldest diocese: Bridgetown (1970) Land mass: 430 km² Primary language(s): English Primary religion(s): Anglican	Population: 260,000 Fertility rate: 1.6 Infant mortality per 1,000 births: 12.8 Life expectancy: 73 Literacy rate: 99.2 (1970 est.) GNI per capita (PPP): $ 14,010
Catholics; %: 10,000; 4% Dioceses; all territories: 1; 1 Parishes; pastoral centers: 6; 6 Catholics/parish; /priest: 1,667; 1,250	Baptisms; % infants: 185; 95% % infants baptized Catholic (est.): 4% Confirmations: 62 Marriages; % both Catholic: 75; 56%
Hospitals: 1 Orphanages: 0 Homes for elderly, disabled: 0 Other charitable institutions: 0 Primary schools: 2 Secondary schools: 1 Colleges and universities: 0 Seminaries: 0	Permanent deacons: 1 Seminarians; % diocesan: 0; na Diocesan priests: 3 Religious priests; brothers: 5; 0 Women religious: 11 Catechists: 53 Lay missionaries: 0

Belarus
Region: Eastern Europe
Oldest diocese: Minsk-Mohilev (1783)
Land mass: 207,600 km²
Primary language(s): Russian
Primary religion(s): Orthodox

Population: 10,190,000
Fertility rate: 1.3
Infant mortality per 1,000 births: 14.4
Life expectancy: 68
Literacy rate: 99.9 (1979 est.)
GNI per capita (PPP): $ 6,880

Catholics; %: 1,059,000; 10%
Dioceses; all territories: 4; 4
Parishes; pastoral centers: 368; 368
Catholics/parish; /priest: 2,878; 3,427

Baptisms; % infants: 6,832; 92%
% infants baptized Catholic (est.): 66%
Confirmations: 6,050
Marriages; % both Catholic: 3,670; 76%

Hospitals: 0
Orphanages: 0
Homes for elderly, disabled: 0
Other charitable institutions: 0
Primary schools: 0
Secondary schools: 0
Colleges and universities: 0
Seminaries: 1

Permanent deacons: 0
Seminarians; % diocesan: 205; 83%
Diocesan priests: 162
Religious priests; brothers: 147; 15
Women religious: 327
Catechists: 40
Lay missionaries: 0

Belgium
Region: Northwestern Europe
Oldest diocese: Tournai, Doornik (1146)
Land mass: 30,514 km²
Primary language(s): Dutch, French, German
Primary religion(s): Catholic

Population: 10,250,000
Fertility rate: 1.6
Infant mortality per 1,000 births: 4.8
Life expectancy: 78
Literacy rate: 99 (1980 est.)
GNI per capita (PPP): $ 25,710

Catholics; %: 8,105,000; 79%
Dioceses; all territories: 8; 9
Parishes; pastoral centers: 3,939; 4,355
Catholics/parish; /priest: 2,058; 1,004

Baptisms; % infants: 77,355; 100%
% infants baptized Catholic (est.): 76%
Confirmations: 66,964
Marriages; % both Catholic: 21,176; 98%

Hospitals: 126
Orphanages: 154
Homes for elderly, disabled: 374
Other charitable institutions: 381
Primary schools: 2,304
Secondary schools: 1,148
Colleges and universities: 9
Seminaries: 12

Permanent deacons: 543
Seminarians; % diocesan: 259; 36%
Diocesan priests: 4,978
Religious priests; brothers: 3,092; 1,215
Women religious: 15,801
Catechists: 8,108
Lay missionaries: 0

Belize	Population: 250,000
Region: Mesoamerica	Fertility rate: 3.2
Oldest diocese: **Belize City-Belmopan** **(1893)**	Infant mortality per 1,000 births: 27.0
	Life expectancy: 71
Land mass: 22,965 km²	Literacy rate: 91 (1970 est.)
Primary language(s): **English**	GNI per capita (PPP): $ 4,750
Primary religion(s): **Catholic**	

Catholics; %: 133,000; 53%	Baptisms; % infants: 2,686; 86%
Dioceses; all territories: 1; 1	% infants baptized Catholic (est.): 35%
Parishes; pastoral centers: 13; 130	Confirmations: 1,932
Catholics/parish; /priest: 10,231; 3,093	Marriages; % both Catholic: 459; 92%

Hospitals: 0	Permanent deacons: 1
Orphanages: 1	Seminarians; % diocesan: 2; 100%
Homes for elderly, disabled: 1	Diocesan priests: 16
Other charitable institutions: 0	Religious priests; brothers: 27; 5
Primary schools: 134	Women religious: 66
Secondary schools: 12	Catechists: 608
Colleges and universities: 0	Lay missionaries: 0
Seminaries: 0	

Benin	Population: 6,170,000
Region: West Africa	Fertility rate: 6.3
Oldest diocese: **Cotonou (1883)**	Infant mortality per 1,000 births: 92.1
Land mass: 112,622 km²	Life expectancy: 50
Primary language(s): **French, tribal languages**	Literacy rate: 23.4 (1990 est.)
	GNI per capita (PPP): $ 920
Primary religion(s): **Indigenous religions**	

Catholics; %: 1,493,000; 24%	Baptisms; % infants: 46,864; 48%
Dioceses; all territories: 10; 10	% infants baptized Catholic (est.): 9%
Parishes; pastoral centers: 185; 867	Confirmations: 24,850
Catholics/parish; /priest: 8,070; 3,572	Marriages; % both Catholic: 2,536; 84%

Hospitals: 12	Permanent deacons: 0
Orphanages: 20	Seminarians; % diocesan: 384; 90%
Homes for elderly, disabled: 2	Diocesan priests: 305
Other charitable institutions: 88	Religious priests; brothers: 113; 73
Primary schools: 35	Women religious: 722
Secondary schools: 15	Catechists: 8,875
Colleges and universities: 0	Lay missionaries: 11
Seminaries: 2	

Bermuda (United Kingdom)
Region: North America
Oldest diocese: Hamilton in Bermuda (1953)
Land mass: 53 km²
Primary language(s): English
Primary religion(s): Anglican

Population: 62,000
Fertility rate: na
Infant mortality per 1,000 births: 10.0
Life expectancy: 77
Literacy rate: 98.4 (1970 est.)
GNI per capita (PPP): $ na

Catholics; %: 9,000; 15%
Dioceses; all territories: 1; 1
Parishes; pastoral centers: 6; 6
Catholics/parish; /priest: 1,500; 1,500

Baptisms; % infants: 96; 89%
% infants baptized Catholic (est.): 9%
Confirmations: 73
Marriages; % both Catholic: 47; 47%

Hospitals: 0
Orphanages: 0
Homes for elderly, disabled: 0
Other charitable institutions: 1
Primary schools: 1
Secondary schools: 1
Colleges and universities: 0
Seminaries: 0

Permanent deacons: 0
Seminarians; % diocesan: 0; na
Diocesan priests: 0
Religious priests; brothers: 6; 0
Women religious: 3
Catechists: 104
Lay missionaries: 0

Bhutan
Region: South Asia
Oldest diocese: na (na)
Land mass: 47,000 km²
Primary language(s): Dzongkha
Primary religion(s): Buddhism

Population: 2,090,000
Fertility rate: 5.6
Infant mortality per 1,000 births: 113.1
Life expectancy: 52
Literacy rate: 42.2 (1995 est.)
GNI per capita (PPP): $ 1,260

Catholics; %: 400; <1%
Dioceses; all territories: 0; 0
Parishes; pastoral centers: 1; 1
Catholics/parish; /priest: 400; na

Baptisms; % infants: 0; na
% infants baptized Catholic (est.): na%
Confirmations: 0
Marriages; % both Catholic: 0; na

Hospitals: 0
Orphanages: 0
Homes for elderly, disabled: 0
Other charitable institutions: 0
Primary schools: 0
Secondary schools: 0
Colleges and universities: 0
Seminaries: 0

Permanent deacons: 0
Seminarians; % diocesan: 0; na
Diocesan priests: 0
Religious priests; brothers: 0; 0
Women religious: 0
Catechists: 0
Lay missionaries: 0

Bolivia **Region: South America** Oldest diocese: Sucre (1552) Land mass: 1,098,581 km² Primary language(s): Spanish Primary religion(s): Catholic	Population: 8,330,000 Fertility rate: 4.2 Infant mortality per 1,000 births: 62.0 Life expectancy: 63 Literacy rate: 82.29 (1992 est.) GNI per capita (PPP): $ 2,300
Catholics; %: 7,246,000; 87% Dioceses; all territories: 10; 18 Parishes; pastoral centers: 565; 800 Catholics/parish; /priest: 12,825; 6,862	Baptisms; % infants: 119,131; 84% % infants baptized Catholic (est.): 64% Confirmations: 51,857 Marriages; % both Catholic: 28,031; 99%
Hospitals: 49 Orphanages: 70 Homes for elderly, disabled: 29 Other charitable institutions: 595 Primary schools: 642 Secondary schools: 292 Colleges and universities: 0 Seminaries: 22	Permanent deacons: 62 Seminarians; % diocesan: 697; 55% Diocesan priests: 453 Religious priests; brothers: 603; 212 Women religious: 2,463 Catechists: 10,243 Lay missionaries: 424

Bosnia and Herzegovina **Region: Eastern Europe** Oldest diocese: Mostar (1361) Land mass: 51,087 km² Primary language(s): Croatian, Serbian, Bosnian Primary religion(s): Islam, Orthodox	Population: 3,980,000 Fertility rate: 1.6 Infant mortality per 1,000 births: 26.4 Life expectancy: 70 Literacy rate: na (na est.) GNI per capita (PPP): $ na
Catholics; %: 459,000; 12% Dioceses; all territories: 3; 3 Parishes; pastoral centers: 281; 284 Catholics/parish; /priest: 1,633; 754	Baptisms; % infants: 6,186; 96% % infants baptized Catholic (est.): 22% Confirmations: 5,431 Marriages; % both Catholic: 2,484; 97%
Hospitals: 0 Orphanages: 0 Homes for elderly, disabled: 4 Other charitable institutions: 5 Primary schools: 5 Secondary schools: 5 Colleges and universities: 0 Seminaries: 1	Permanent deacons: 1 Seminarians; % diocesan: 137; 44% Diocesan priests: 258 Religious priests; brothers: 351; 16 Women religious: 501 Catechists: 5 Lay missionaries: 0

Botswana	Population: 1,650,000
Region: Southern Africa	Fertility rate: 3.9
Oldest diocese: Gaberone (1959)	Infant mortality per 1,000 births: 59.5
Land mass: 581,730 km²	Life expectancy: 41
Primary language(s): English	Literacy rate: 68.88 (1993 est.)
Primary religion(s): Protestant,	GNI per capita (PPP): $ 6,540
Indigenous religions	
Catholics; %: 78,000; 5%	Baptisms; % infants: 1,415; 47%
Dioceses; all territories: 1; 2	% infants baptized Catholic (est.): 2%
Parishes; pastoral centers: 28; 80	Confirmations: 1,438
Catholics/parish; /priest: 2,786; 1,560	Marriages; % both Catholic: 207; 45%
Hospitals: 0	Permanent deacons: 1
Orphanages: 1	Seminarians; % diocesan: 11; 91%
Homes for elderly, disabled: 0	Diocesan priests: 9
Other charitable institutions: 13	Religious priests; brothers: 41; 5
Primary schools: 9	Women religious: 69
Secondary schools: 4	Catechists: 376
Colleges and universities: 0	Lay missionaries: 0
Seminaries: 2	

Brazil	Population: 167,720,000
Region: South America	Fertility rate: 2.4
Oldest diocese: Sao Salvador (1551)	Infant mortality per 1,000 births: 39.3
Land mass: 8,511,965 km²	Life expectancy: 63
Primary language(s): Portuguese	Literacy rate: 81.1 (1990 est.)
Primary religion(s): Catholic	GNI per capita (PPP): $ 6,840
Catholics; %: 143,900,000; 86%	Baptisms; % infants: 2,163,086; 90%
Dioceses; all territories: 249; 267	% infants baptized Catholic (est.): 55%
Parishes; pastoral centers: 8,732; 42,812	Confirmations: 931,975
Catholics/parish; /priest: 16,480; 8,670	Marriages; % both Catholic: 368,672; 97%
Hospitals: 485	Permanent deacons: 1,157
Orphanages: 433	Seminarians; % diocesan: 8,831; 61%
Homes for elderly, disabled: 748	Diocesan priests: 9,240
Other charitable institutions: 6,863	Religious priests; brothers: 7,358; 2,421
Primary schools: 2,322	Women religious: 35,365
Secondary schools: 1,082	Catechists: 428,836
Colleges and universities: 15	Lay missionaries: 30,895
Seminaries: 196	

Brunei Darussalem Region: Southeast Asia Oldest diocese: na (na) Land mass: 5,765 km² Primary language(s): Malay, English Primary religion(s): Islam	Population: 331,000 Fertility rate: 2.7 Infant mortality per 1,000 births: 15.4 Life expectancy: 73 Literacy rate: 80 (1981 est.) GNI per capita (PPP): $ na
Catholics; %: 25,000; 8% Dioceses; all territories: 0; 1 Parishes; pastoral centers: 3; 3 Catholics/parish; /priest: 8,333; 8,333	Baptisms; % infants: 193; 56% % infants baptized Catholic (est.): <1% Confirmations: 38 Marriages; % both Catholic: 49; 67%
Hospitals: 0 Orphanages: 0 Homes for elderly, disabled: 1 Other charitable institutions: 0 Primary schools: 4 Secondary schools: 4 Colleges and universities: 0 Seminaries: 0	Permanent deacons: 0 Seminarians; % diocesan: 3; 100% Diocesan priests: 2 Religious priests; brothers: 1; 0 Women religious: 0 Catechists: 62 Lay missionaries: 0

Bulgaria Region: Eastern Europe Oldest diocese: Sofia e Plovdiv (1758) Land mass: 110,912 km² Primary language(s): Bulgarian Primary religion(s): Orthodox	Population: 7,950,000 Fertility rate: 1.2 Infant mortality per 1,000 births: 15.6 Life expectancy: 71 Literacy rate: 93 (1970 est.) GNI per capita (PPP): $ 5,070
Catholics; %: 80,000; 1% Dioceses; all territories: 2; 3 Parishes; pastoral centers: 54; 54 Catholics/parish; /priest: 1,481; 1,569	Baptisms; % infants: 444; 86% % infants baptized Catholic (est.): <1% Confirmations: 356 Marriages; % both Catholic: 190; 66%
Hospitals: 0 Orphanages: 1 Homes for elderly, disabled: 1 Other charitable institutions: 2 Primary schools: 0 Secondary schools: 0 Colleges and universities: 0 Seminaries: 0	Permanent deacons: 0 Seminarians; % diocesan: 8; 88% Diocesan priests: 17 Religious priests; brothers: 34; 2 Women religious: 86 Catechists: 68 Lay missionaries: 0

Burkina Faso	Population: 11,540,000
Region: West Africa	Fertility rate: 6.8
Oldest diocese: Ouagadougou (1901)	Infant mortality per 1,000 births: 110.3
Land mass: 274,200 km²	Life expectancy: 47
Primary language(s): French	Literacy rate: 18.2 (1990 est.)
Primary religion(s): Islam, Indigenous religions	GNI per capita (PPP): $ 960

Catholics; %: 1,324,000; 11%	Baptisms; % infants: 64,823; 46%
Dioceses; all territories: 12; 12	% infants baptized Catholic (est.): 4%
Parishes; pastoral centers: 123; 659	Confirmations: 40,595
Catholics/parish; /priest: 10,764; 2,122	Marriages; % both Catholic: 9,910; 65%

Hospitals: 3	Permanent deacons: 0
Orphanages: 4	Seminarians; % diocesan: 405; 84%
Homes for elderly, disabled: 7	Diocesan priests: 481
Other charitable institutions: 137	Religious priests; brothers: 143; 189
Primary schools: 56	Women religious: 1,078
Secondary schools: 28	Catechists: 9,584
Colleges and universities: 0	Lay missionaries: 23
Seminaries: 5	

Burundi	Population: 6,360,000
Region: Central Africa	Fertility rate: 6.5
Oldest diocese: Gitega (1949)	Infant mortality per 1,000 births: 72.3
Land mass: 27,834 km²	Life expectancy: 46
Primary language(s): French	Literacy rate: 41.32 (1990 est.)
Primary religion(s): Catholic	GNI per capita (PPP): $ 570

Catholics; %: 3,991,000; 63%	Baptisms; % infants: 157,660; 57%
Dioceses; all territories: 7; 7	% infants baptized Catholic (est.): 30%
Parishes; pastoral centers: 144; 1,271	Confirmations: 74,505
Catholics/parish; /priest: 27,715; 11,370	Marriages; % both Catholic: 24,827; 95%

Hospitals: 14	Permanent deacons: 1
Orphanages: 23	Seminarians; % diocesan: 400; 93%
Homes for elderly, disabled: 9	Diocesan priests: 270
Other charitable institutions: 280	Religious priests; brothers: 81; 137
Primary schools: 405	Women religious: 1,062
Secondary schools: 79	Catechists: 4,794
Colleges and universities: 0	Lay missionaries: 17
Seminaries: 3	

Cambodia Region: Southeast Asia Oldest diocese: na (na) Land mass: 181,035 km² Primary language(s): Khmer, French, English Primary religion(s): Buddhism	Population: 13,100,000 Fertility rate: 4 Infant mortality per 1,000 births: 68.3 Life expectancy: 56 Literacy rate: 68.7 (1996 est.) GNI per capita (PPP): $ 1,350
Catholics; %: 20,000; <1% Dioceses; all territories: 0; 3 Parishes; pastoral centers: 31; 63 Catholics/parish; /priest: 645; 435	Baptisms; % infants: 483; 57% % infants baptized Catholic (est.): <1% Confirmations: 194 Marriages; % both Catholic: 133; 20%
Hospitals: 1 Orphanages: 1 Homes for elderly, disabled: 2 Other charitable institutions: 14 Primary schools: 3 Secondary schools: 2 Colleges and universities: 0 Seminaries: 1	Permanent deacons: 0 Seminarians; % diocesan: 10; 40% Diocesan priests: 16 Religious priests; brothers: 30; 4 Women religious: 68 Catechists: 139 Lay missionaries: 0

Cameroon Region: Central Africa Oldest diocese: Yaoundé (1890) Land mass: 475,442 km² Primary language(s): English, French Primary religion(s): Protestant, Indigenous religions	Population: 14,880,000 Fertility rate: 5.2 Infant mortality per 1,000 births: 72.2 Life expectancy: 55 Literacy rate: 54.1 (1990 est.) GNI per capita (PPP): $ 1,490
Catholics; %: 3,920,000; 26% Dioceses; all territories: 23; 23 Parishes; pastoral centers: 630; 3,604 Catholics/parish; /priest: 6,222; 3,087	Baptisms; % infants: 85,158; 61% % infants baptized Catholic (est.): 7% Confirmations: 27,345 Marriages; % both Catholic: 5,601; 89%
Hospitals: 18 Orphanages: 21 Homes for elderly, disabled: 10 Other charitable institutions: 631 Primary schools: 991 Secondary schools: 129 Colleges and universities: 1 Seminaries: 8	Permanent deacons: 18 Seminarians; % diocesan: 1,049; 71% Diocesan priests: 787 Religious priests; brothers: 483; 205 Women religious: 1,581 Catechists: 15,512 Lay missionaries: 65

Canada **Region: North America** Oldest diocese: Québec (1674) Land mass: 9,976,139 km² Primary language(s): English, French Primary religion(s): Catholic, Anglican	Population: 30,750,000 Fertility rate: 1.4 Infant mortality per 1,000 births: 5.1 Life expectancy: 79 Literacy rate: 96 (1986 est.) GNI per capita (PPP): $ 25,440
Catholics; %: 13,453,000; 44% Dioceses; all territories: 71; 72 Parishes; pastoral centers: 5,115; 5,661 Catholics/parish; /priest: 2,630; 1,368	Baptisms; % infants: 138,057; 93% % infants baptized Catholic (est.): 37% Confirmations: 127,051 Marriages; % both Catholic: 35,626; 72%
Hospitals: 67 Orphanages: 21 Homes for elderly, disabled: 117 Other charitable institutions: 336 Primary schools: 1,340 Secondary schools: 273 Colleges and universities: 8 Seminaries: 12	Permanent deacons: 918 Seminarians; % diocesan: 537; 72% Diocesan priests: 5,766 Religious priests; brothers: 4,066; 2,254 Women religious: 23,917 Catechists: 12,025 Lay missionaries: 19

Cape Verde **Region: West Africa** Oldest diocese: Santiago (1533) Land mass: 4,033 km² Primary language(s): Portuguese Primary religion(s): Catholic	Population: 434,000 Fertility rate: 4 Infant mortality per 1,000 births: 55.6 Life expectancy: 69 Literacy rate: 66.5 (1989 est.) GNI per capita (PPP): $ 4,450
Catholics; %: 409,000; 94% Dioceses; all territories: 1; 1 Parishes; pastoral centers: 31; 51 Catholics/parish; /priest: 13,194; 8,702	Baptisms; % infants: 15,833; 60% % infants baptized Catholic (est.): 59% Confirmations: 2,465 Marriages; % both Catholic: 221; 100%
Hospitals: 0 Orphanages: 1 Homes for elderly, disabled: 0 Other charitable institutions: 18 Primary schools: 12 Secondary schools: 2 Colleges and universities: 0 Seminaries: 0	Permanent deacons: 0 Seminarians; % diocesan: 25; 64% Diocesan priests: 12 Religious priests; brothers: 35; 5 Women religious: 123 Catechists: 3,420 Lay missionaries: 22

Cayman Islands (United Kingdom) Region: Caribbean	Population: 33,000
Cayman Islands (United Kingdom) **Region: Caribbean** Oldest diocese: na (na) Land mass: 259 km² Primary language(s): English Primary religion(s): Protestant	Population: 33,000 Fertility rate: na Infant mortality per 1,000 births: 10.9 Life expectancy: 79 Literacy rate: 97.5 (1970 est.) GNI per capita (PPP): $ na
Catholics; %: 4,000; 12% Dioceses; all territories: 0; 1 Parishes; pastoral centers: 1; 1 Catholics/parish; /priest: 4,000; 4,000	Baptisms; % infants: 43; 84% % infants baptized Catholic (est.): 4% Confirmations: 35 Marriages; % both Catholic: 23; 52%
Hospitals: 0 Orphanages: 0 Homes for elderly, disabled: 0 Other charitable institutions: 0 Primary schools: 0 Secondary schools: 1 Colleges and universities: 0 Seminaries: 0	Permanent deacons: 1 Seminarians; % diocesan: 0; na Diocesan priests: 1 Religious priests; brothers: 0; 0 Women religious: 0 Catechists: 8 Lay missionaries: 0

Central African Republic **Region: Central Africa** Oldest diocese: Bangui (1909) Land mass: 622,984 km² Primary language(s): French Primary religion(s): Protestant, Indigenous religions	Population: 3,720,000 Fertility rate: 5.1 Infant mortality per 1,000 births: 108.2 Life expectancy: 44 Literacy rate: 37.7 (1990 est.) GNI per capita (PPP): $ 1,150
Catholics; %: 718,000; 19% Dioceses; all territories: 8; 8 Parishes; pastoral centers: 122; 1,732 Catholics/parish; /priest: 5,885; 2,679	Baptisms; % infants: 24,316; 34% % infants baptized Catholic (est.): 5% Confirmations: 9,146 Marriages; % both Catholic: 956; 86%
Hospitals: 1 Orphanages: 2 Homes for elderly, disabled: 11 Other charitable institutions: 102 Primary schools: 50 Secondary schools: 9 Colleges and universities: 0 Seminaries: 4	Permanent deacons: 0 Seminarians; % diocesan: 136; 76% Diocesan priests: 134 Religious priests; brothers: 134; 64 Women religious: 380 Catechists: 4,769 Lay missionaries: 51

Chad	Population: 7,890,000
Region: Central Africa	Fertility rate: 6.6
Oldest diocese: N'Djaména (1947)	Infant mortality per 1,000 births: 98.3
Land mass: 1,284,000 km²	Life expectancy: 50
Primary language(s): French, Arabic	Literacy rate: 29.8 (1990 est.)
Primary religion(s): Islam	GNI per capita (PPP): $ 840

Catholics; %: 905,000; 11%	Baptisms; % infants: 17,303; 17%
Dioceses; all territories: 7; 8	% infants baptized Catholic (est.): 1%
Parishes; pastoral centers: 110; 525	Confirmations: 4,953
Catholics/parish; /priest: 8,227; 4,058	Marriages; % both Catholic: 2,289; 74%

Hospitals: 3	Permanent deacons: 0
Orphanages: 1	Seminarians; % diocesan: 105; 97%
Homes for elderly, disabled: 3	Diocesan priests: 102
Other charitable institutions: 145	Religious priests; brothers: 121; 30
Primary schools: 58	Women religious: 302
Secondary schools: 9	Catechists: 8,076
Colleges and universities: 0	Lay missionaries: 9
Seminaries: 2	

Chile	Population: 15,210,000
Region: South America	Fertility rate: 2.3
Oldest diocese: Santiago (1561)	Infant mortality per 1,000 births: 9.9
Land mass: 756,945 km²	Life expectancy: 76
Primary language(s): Spanish	Literacy rate: 94.6 (1992 est.)
Primary religion(s): Catholic	GNI per capita (PPP): $ 8,410

Catholics; %: 11,426,000; 75%	Baptisms; % infants: 192,189; 85%
Dioceses; all territories: 23; 27	% infants baptized Catholic (est.): 63%
Parishes; pastoral centers: 951; 4,303	Confirmations: 95,855
Catholics/parish; /priest: 12,015; 4,972	Marriages; % both Catholic: 35,109; 94%

Hospitals: 37	Permanent deacons: 568
Orphanages: 105	Seminarians; % diocesan: 680; 52%
Homes for elderly, disabled: 195	Diocesan priests: 1,113
Other charitable institutions: 940	Religious priests; brothers: 1,185; 382
Primary schools: 708	Women religious: 5,574
Secondary schools: 447	Catechists: 53,143
Colleges and universities: 4	Lay missionaries: 703
Seminaries: 23	

China **Region: East Asia** Oldest diocese: Macau (1576) Land mass: 9,560,175 km² Primary language(s): Chinese Primary religion(s): Taoism, Buddhism	Population: 1,275,130,000 Fertility rate: 1.8 Infant mortality per 1,000 births: 30.2 Life expectancy: 71 Literacy rate: 83.52 (1995 est.) GNI per capita (PPP): $ 3,550
Catholics; %: 7,500,000; 1% Dioceses; all territories: 0; 0 Parishes; pastoral centers: 0; 0 Catholics/parish; /priest: na; na	Baptisms; % infants: na; na % infants baptized Catholic (est.): na% Confirmations: na Marriages; % both Catholic: na; na
Hospitals: 0 Orphanages: 0 Homes for elderly, disabled: 0 Other charitable institutions: 0 Primary schools: 0 Secondary schools: 0 Colleges and universities: 0 Seminaries: 0	Permanent deacons: na Seminarians; % diocesan: na; na Diocesan priests: na Religious priests; brothers: na; na Women religious: na Catechists: na Lay missionaries: na

China, Hong Kong SAR **Region: East Asia** Oldest diocese: Hong Kong (1946) Land mass: 1,045 km² Primary language(s): English, Chinese Primary religion(s): Protestant, Indigenous religions	Population: 6,800,000 Fertility rate: 1 Infant mortality per 1,000 births: 6.0 Life expectancy: 79 Literacy rate: 80.8 (1971 est.) GNI per capita (PPP): $ 22,570
Catholics; %: 371,000; 5% Dioceses; all territories: 1; 1 Parishes; pastoral centers: 55; 153 Catholics/parish; /priest: 6,745; 1,142	Baptisms; % infants: 4,116; 48% % infants baptized Catholic (est.): 3% Confirmations: 3,077 Marriages; % both Catholic: 929; 17%
Hospitals: 6 Orphanages: 15 Homes for elderly, disabled: 12 Other charitable institutions: 91 Primary schools: 151 Secondary schools: 121 Colleges and universities: 0 Seminaries: 2	Permanent deacons: 3 Seminarians; % diocesan: 15; 40% Diocesan priests: 70 Religious priests; brothers: 255; 67 Women religious: 532 Catechists: 981 Lay missionaries: 0

China, Macau SAR Region: East Asia Oldest diocese: Macau (1576) Land mass: 16 km² Primary language(s): Portuguese, Chinese Primary religion(s): Buddhism	Population: 440,000 Fertility rate: 1.2 Infant mortality per 1,000 births: 4.5 Life expectancy: 82 Literacy rate: 90.4 (1981 est.) GNI per capita (PPP): $ 16,940
Catholics; %: 30,000; 7% Dioceses; all territories: 1; 1 Parishes; pastoral centers: 8; 14 Catholics/parish; /priest: 3,750; 417	Baptisms; % infants: 437; 47% % infants baptized Catholic (est.): 4% Confirmations: 294 Marriages; % both Catholic: 103; 26%
Hospitals: 0 Orphanages: 1 Homes for elderly, disabled: 10 Other charitable institutions: 21 Primary schools: 26 Secondary schools: 16 Colleges and universities: 0 Seminaries: 0	Permanent deacons: 0 Seminarians; % diocesan: 0; na Diocesan priests: 27 Religious priests; brothers: 45; 17 Women religious: 176 Catechists: 5,273 Lay missionaries: 10

China, Taiwan Region: East Asia Oldest diocese: Kaohsiung (1913) Land mass: 35,961 km² Primary language(s): Chinese Primary religion(s): Taoism, Confucianism, Buddhism	Population: 21,910,000 Fertility rate: 1.7 Infant mortality per 1,000 births: 7.2 Life expectancy: 76 Literacy rate: 91.9 (1990 est.) GNI per capita (PPP): $ na
Catholics; %: 310,000; 1% Dioceses; all territories: 8; 8 Parishes; pastoral centers: 459; 623 Catholics/parish; /priest: 675; 443	Baptisms; % infants: 3,838; 51% % infants baptized Catholic (est.): 1% Confirmations: 1,859 Marriages; % both Catholic: 1,023; 30%
Hospitals: 10 Orphanages: 9 Homes for elderly, disabled: 21 Other charitable institutions: 53 Primary schools: 10 Secondary schools: 35 Colleges and universities: 2 Seminaries: 10	Permanent deacons: 0 Seminarians; % diocesan: 117; 47% Diocesan priests: 254 Religious priests; brothers: 445; 84 Women religious: 1,055 Catechists: 640 Lay missionaries: 9

Colombia Region: South America Oldest diocese: Santa Marta (1534) Land mass: 1,138,914 km² Primary language(s): Spanish Primary religion(s): Catholic	Population: 42,320,000 Fertility rate: 2.6 Infant mortality per 1,000 births: 25.6 Life expectancy: 70 Literacy rate: 86.7 (1990 est.) GNI per capita (PPP): $ 5,580
Catholics; %: 37,723,000; 89% Dioceses; all territories: 60; 71 Parishes; pastoral centers: 3,614; 4,730 Catholics/parish; /priest: 10,438; 4,805	Baptisms; % infants: 719,737; 92% % infants baptized Catholic (est.): 75% Confirmations: 347,049 Marriages; % both Catholic: 95,702; 100%
Hospitals: 84 Orphanages: 106 Homes for elderly, disabled: 284 Other charitable institutions: 1,121 Primary schools: 1,394 Secondary schools: 754 Colleges and universities: 11 Seminaries: 83	Permanent deacons: 161 Seminarians; % diocesan: 4,679; 68% Diocesan priests: 5,470 Religious priests; brothers: 2,381; 1,069 Women religious: 17,347 Catechists: 39,537 Lay missionaries: 21,699

Comoros Region: Indian Ocean Oldest diocese: na (na) Land mass: 2,235 km² Primary language(s): Arabic, French Primary religion(s): Islam	Population: 688,000 Fertility rate: 6.8 Infant mortality per 1,000 births: 88.8 Life expectancy: 60 Literacy rate: 47.9 (1980 est.) GNI per capita (PPP): $ 1,430
Catholics; %: 2,000; <1% Dioceses; all territories: 0; 1 Parishes; pastoral centers: 2; 7 Catholics/parish; /priest: 1,000; 500	Baptisms; % infants: 19; 84% % infants baptized Catholic (est.): <1% Confirmations: 7 Marriages; % both Catholic: 1; 100%
Hospitals: 1 Orphanages: 1 Homes for elderly, disabled: 0 Other charitable institutions: 13 Primary schools: 0 Secondary schools: 4 Colleges and universities: 0 Seminaries: 0	Permanent deacons: 0 Seminarians; % diocesan: 0; na Diocesan priests: 1 Religious priests; brothers: 3; 0 Women religious: 4 Catechists: 12 Lay missionaries: 0

Congo, Democratic Republic of the Congo Region: Central Africa Oldest diocese: Brazzaville (1955) Land mass: 2,345,409 km² Primary language(s): French Primary religion(s): Protestant, Indigenous religions	Population: 50,950,000 Fertility rate: 7 Infant mortality per 1,000 births: 103.3 Life expectancy: 48 Literacy rate: 56.6 (1990 est.) GNI per capita (PPP): $ na
Catholics; %: 27,067,000; 53% Dioceses; all territories: 47; 0 Parishes; pastoral centers: 1,296; 10,013 Catholics/parish; /priest: 20,885; 6,875	Baptisms; % infants: 439,512; 64% % infants baptized Catholic (est.): 7% Confirmations: 178,904 Marriages; % both Catholic: 30,412; 93%
Hospitals: 166 Orphanages: 97 Homes for elderly, disabled: 153 Other charitable institutions: 2,181 Primary schools: 6,929 Secondary schools: 2,295 Colleges and universities: 3 Seminaries: 38	Permanent deacons: 5 Seminarians; % diocesan: 2,734; 69% Diocesan priests: 2,685 Religious priests; brothers: 1,252; 1,442 Women religious: 6,652 Catechists: 64,883 Lay missionaries: 102

Congo, Republic of Region: Central Africa Oldest diocese: Kaiemie-Kirungu (1880) Land mass: 342,000 km² Primary language(s): French Primary religion(s): Catholic	Population: 3,020,000 Fertility rate: 6.3 Infant mortality per 1,000 births: 103.6 Life expectancy: 49 Literacy rate: 71.8 (1990 est.) GNI per capita (PPP): $ 540
Catholics; %: 1,719,000; 57% Dioceses; all territories: 6; 7 Parishes; pastoral centers: 141; 294 Catholics/parish; /priest: 12,191; 5,768	Baptisms; % infants: 13,456; 37% % infants baptized Catholic (est.): 9% Confirmations: 4,121 Marriages; % both Catholic: 651; 92%
Hospitals: 2 Orphanages: 5 Homes for elderly, disabled: 4 Other charitable institutions: 36 Primary schools: 16 Secondary schools: 8 Colleges and universities: 0 Seminaries: 3	Permanent deacons: 0 Seminarians; % diocesan: 216; 81% Diocesan priests: 213 Religious priests; brothers: 85; 49 Women religious: 227 Catechists: 2,957 Lay missionaries: 2

Cook Islands (New Zealand) Region: Oceania Oldest diocese: Rarotonga (1922) Land mass: 236 km² Primary language(s): English Primary religion(s): Protestant	Population: 15,000 Fertility rate: na Infant mortality per 1,000 births: 24.7 Life expectancy: 71 Literacy rate: na (na est.) GNI per capita (PPP): $ na
Catholics; %: 3,000; 20% Dioceses; all territories: 1; 1 Parishes; pastoral centers: 15; 16 Catholics/parish; /priest: 200; 429	Baptisms; % infants: 100; 89% % infants baptized Catholic (est.): 17% Confirmations: 70 Marriages; % both Catholic: 11; 73%
Hospitals: 0 Orphanages: 0 Homes for elderly, disabled: 1 Other charitable Institutions: 0 Primary schools: 2 Secondary schools: 1 Colleges and universities: 0 Seminaries: 0	Permanent deacons: 0 Seminarians; % diocesan: 0; na Diocesan priests: 1 Religious priests; brothers: 6; 5 Women religious: 6 Catechists: 23 Lay missionaries: 0

Costa Rica Region: Mesoamerica Oldest diocese: San José de Costa Rica (1850) Land mass: 51,100 km² Primary language(s): Spanish Primary religion(s): Catholic	Population: 3,820,000 Fertility rate: 2.6 Infant mortality per 1,000 births: 11.8 LIfe expectancy: 76 Literacy rate: 92.8 (1990 est.) GNI per capita (PPP): $ 7,880
Catholics; %: 3,346,000; 88% Dioceses; all territories: 7; 7 Parishes; pastoral centers: 258; 328 Catholics/parish; /priest: 12,969; 4,345	Baptisms; % infants: 63,056; 98% % infants baptized Catholic (est.): 98% Confirmations: 40,496 Marriages; % both Catholic: 16,437; 99%
Hospitals: 10 Orphanages: 15 Homes for elderly, disabled: 40 Other charitable institutions: 96 Primary schools: 43 Secondary schools: 37 Colleges and universities: 0 Seminaries: 5	Permanent deacons: 2 Seminarians; % diocesan: 252; 63% Diocesan priests: 547 Religious priests; brothers: 223; 47 Women religious: 888 Catechists: 25,945 Lay missionaries: 13

Côte d'Ivoire **Region: West Africa** Oldest diocese: Abidjan (1895) Land mass: 322,463 km² Primary language(s): French Primary religion(s): Islam	Population: 16,400,000 Fertility rate: 5.2 Infant mortality per 1,000 births: 96.6 Life expectancy: 45 Literacy rate: 53.8 (1990 est.) GNI per capita (PPP): $ 1,540
Catholics; %: 2,605,000; 16% Dioceses; all territories: 14; 14 Parishes; pastoral centers: 259; 914 Catholics/parish; /priest: 10,058; 3,165	Baptisms; % infants: 54,424; 32% % infants baptized Catholic (est.): 3% Confirmations: 32,225 Marriages; % both Catholic: 4,276; 81%
Hospitals: 8 Orphanages: 3 Homes for elderly, disabled: 1 Other charitable institutions: 60 Primary schools: 279 Secondary schools: 35 Colleges and universities: 1 Seminaries: 4	Permanent deacons: 6 Seminarians; % diocesan: 635; 87% Diocesan priests: 570 Religious priests; brothers: 253; 317 Women religious: 938 Catechists: 14,939 Lay missionaries: 63

Croatia **Region: Eastern Europe** Oldest diocese: Dubrovnik (990) Land mass: 62,206 km² Primary language(s): Croatian Primary religion(s): Catholic	Population: 4,650,000 Fertility rate: 1.4 Infant mortality per 1,000 births: 7.7 Life expectancy: 73 Literacy rate: 97 (1991 est.) GNI per capita (PPP): $ 7,260
Catholics; %: 3,745,000; 81% Dioceses; all territories: 14; 15 Parishes; pastoral centers: 1,533; 1,551 Catholics/parish; /priest: 2,443; 1,658	Baptisms; % infants: 41,984; 92% % infants baptized Catholic (est.): 92% Confirmations: 43,736 Marriages; % both Catholic: 17,189; 93%
Hospitals: 0 Orphanages: 29 Homes for elderly, disabled: 33 Other charitable institutions: 58 Primary schools: 0 Secondary schools: 8 Colleges and universities: 0 Seminaries: 15	Permanent deacons: 0 Seminarians; % diocesan: 385; 65% Diocesan priests: 1,449 Religious priests; brothers: 810; 98 Women religious: 3,464 Catechists: 1,512 Lay missionaries: 0

Cuba	Population: 11,190,000
Region: Caribbean	Fertility rate: 1.6
Oldest diocese: Santiago de Cuba (1522)	Infant mortality per 1,000 births: 7.6
Land mass: 110,861 km²	Life expectancy: 76
Primary language(s): Spanish	Literacy rate: 94 (1990 est.)
Primary religion(s): Catholic	GNI per capita (PPP): $ na

Catholics; %: 6,179,000; 55%	Baptisms; % infants: 74,164; 89%
Dioceses; all territories: 11; 11	% infants baptized Catholic (est.): 52%
Parishes; pastoral centers: 264; 930	Confirmations: 2,368
Catholics/parish; /priest: 23,405; 20,875	Marriages; % both Catholic: 1,430; 93%

Hospitals: 1	Permanent deacons: 48
Orphanages: 5	Seminarians; % diocesan: 105; 65%
Homes for elderly, disabled: 8	Diocesan priests: 166
Other charitable institutions: 11	Religious priests; brothers: 130; 36
Primary schools: 0	Women religious: 500
Secondary schools: 2	Catechists: 4,577
Colleges and universities: 0	Lay missionaries: 796
Seminaries: 3	

Cyprus	Population: 780,000
Region: Western Asia	Fertility rate: 1.8
Oldest diocese: Cipro (1357)	Infant mortality per 1,000 births: 8.2
Land mass: 9,251 km²	Life expectancy: 77
Primary language(s): Greek, Turkish, English	Literacy rate: 94 (1987 est.)
	GNI per capita (PPP): $ 19,080
Primary religion(s): Greek Orthodox	

Catholics; %: 17,000; 2%	Baptisms; % infants: 82; 100%
Dioceses; all territories: 1; 1	% infants baptized Catholic (est.): 1%
Parishes; pastoral centers: 13; 17	Confirmations: 102
Catholics/parish; /priest: 1,308; 773	Marriages; % both Catholic: 40; 65%

Hospitals: 0	Permanent deacons: 0
Orphanages: 0	Seminarians; % diocesan: 1; 100%
Homes for elderly, disabled: 0	Diocesan priests: 11
Other charitable institutions: 0	Religious priests; brothers: 11; 7
Primary schools: 2	Women religious: 43
Secondary schools: 2	Catechists: 15
Colleges and universities: 0	Lay missionaries: 0
Seminaries: 0	

Czech Republic Region: Eastern Europe Oldest diocese: Olomouc (1063) Land mass: 78,426 km² Primary language(s): Czech Primary religion(s): Catholic, Indigenous religions	Population: 10,270,000 Fertility rate: 1.1 Infant mortality per 1,000 births: 5.7 Life expectancy: 74 Literacy rate: 99.9 (1999 est.) GNI per capita (PPP): $ 12,840
Catholics; %: 4,307,000; 42% Dioceses; all territories: 8; 9 Parishes; pastoral centers: 3,135; 3,156 Catholics/parish; /priest: 1,374; 2,199	Baptisms; % infants: 26,321; 90% % infants baptized Catholic (est.): 27% Confirmations: 7,890 Marriages; % both Catholic: 7,544; 74%
Hospitals: 20 Orphanages: 20 Homes for elderly, disabled: 38 Other charitable institutions: 145 Primary schools: 21 Secondary schools: 31 Colleges and universities: 1 Seminaries: 6	Permanent deacons: 141 Seminarians; % diocesan: 324; 68% Diocesan priests: 1,364 Religious priests; brothers: 595; 101 Women religious: 2,297 Catechists: 1,364 Lay missionaries: 0

Denmark Region: Northwestern Europe Oldest diocese: Kobenhavn (1868) Land mass: 43,077 km² Primary language(s): Danish Primary religion(s): Lutheran	Population: 5,340,000 Fertility rate: 1.7 Infant mortality per 1,000 births: 5.1 Life expectancy: 76 Literacy rate: 99 (1980 est.) GNI per capita (PPP): $ 25,600
Catholics; %: 34,000; 1% Dioceses; all territories: 1; 1 Parishes; pastoral centers: 49; 49 Catholics/parish; /priest: 694; 374	Baptisms; % infants: 656; 96% % infants baptized Catholic (est.): 1% Confirmations: 211 Marriages; % both Catholic: 147; 39%
Hospitals: 0 Orphanages: 0 Homes for elderly, disabled: 6 Other charitable institutions: 0 Primary schools: 23 Secondary schools: 1 Colleges and universities: 0 Seminaries: 1	Permanent deacons: 3 Seminarians; % diocesan: 6; 83% Diocesan priests: 41 Religious priests; brothers: 50; 3 Women religious: 229 Catechists: 116 Lay missionaries: 0

Djibouti **Region: East Africa** Oldest diocese: Mogadishu (1904) Land mass: 23,200 km² Primary language(s): Arabic, French Primary religion(s): Islam	Population: 630,000 Fertility rate: 6.1 Infant mortality per 1,000 births: 105.2 Life expectancy: 50 Literacy rate: 46.2 (1995 est.) GNI per capita (PPP): $ na
Catholics; %: 7,000; 1% Dioceses; all territories: 1; 1 Parishes; pastoral centers: 5; 11 Catholics/parish; /priest: 1,400; 1,167	Baptisms; % infants: 15; 93% % infants baptized Catholic (est.): <1% Confirmations: 15 Marriages; % both Catholic: 2; 100%
Hospitals: 0 Orphanages: 0 Homes for elderly, disabled: 0 Other charitable institutions: 0 Primary schools: 9 Secondary schools: 1 Colleges and universities: 0 Seminaries: 0	Permanent deacons: 0 Seminarians; % diocesan: 0; na Diocesan priests: 2 Religious priests; brothers: 4; 5 Women religious: 19 Catechists: 16 Lay missionaries: 27

Dominica **Region: Caribbean** Oldest diocese: Roseau (1850) Land mass: 751 km² Primary language(s): English Primary religion(s): Catholic	Population: 75,000 Fertility rate: 1.8 Infant mortality per 1,000 births: 17.7 Life expectancy: 73 Literacy rate: 94.1 (1970 est.) GNI per capita (PPP): $ 5,040
Catholics; %: 60,000; 80% Dioceses; all territories: 1; 1 Parishes; pastoral centers: 15; 54 Catholics/parish; /priest: 4,000; 1,250	Baptisms; % infants: 923; 100% % infants baptized Catholic (est.): 74% Confirmations: 513 Marriages; % both Catholic: 143; 92%
Hospitals: 0 Orphanages: 0 Homes for elderly, disabled: 0 Other charitable institutions: 3 Primary schools: 5 Secondary schools: 3 Colleges and universities: 0 Seminaries: 0	Permanent deacons: 0 Seminarians; % diocesan: 9; 22% Diocesan priests: 6 Religious priests; brothers: 42; 8 Women religious: 27 Catechists: 485 Lay missionaries: 0

Dominican Republic Region: Caribbean Oldest diocese: Santo Domingo (1511) Land mass: 48,734 km² Primary language(s): Spanish Primary religion(s): Catholic	Population: 8,520,000 Fertility rate: 3.1 Infant mortality per 1,000 births: 37.4 Life expectancy: 73 Literacy rate: 83.5 (1990 est.) GNI per capita (PPP): $ 5,210
Catholics; %: 7,475,000; 88% Dioceses; all territories: 11; 12 Parishes; pastoral centers: 485; 1,442 Catholics/parish; /priest: 15,412; 9,149	Baptisms; % infants: 108,702; 61% % infants baptized Catholic (est.): 35% Confirmations: 36,882 Marriages; % both Catholic: 9,498; 97%
Hospitals: 20 Orphanages: 26 Homes for elderly, disabled: 28 Other charitable institutions: 1,505 Primary schools: 236 Secondary schools: 137 Colleges and universities: 1 Seminaries: 4	Permanent deacons: 231 Seminarians; % diocesan: 516; 71% Diocesan priests: 390 Religious priests; brothers: 427; 78 Women religious: 1,644 Catechists: 27,721 Lay missionaries: 9

East Timor Region: Southeast Asia Oldest diocese: Dili (1940) Land mass: 14,874 km² Primary language(s): Timorese Primary religion(s): Catholic	Population: 794,000 Fertility rate: 4.4 Infant mortality per 1,000 births: na Life expectancy: na Literacy rate: na (na est.) GNI per capita (PPP): $ na
Catholics; %: 750,000; 94% Dioceses; all territories: 2; 2 Parishes; pastoral centers: 31; 105 Catholics/parish; /priest: 24,194; 7,426	Baptisms; % infants: 22,910; 82% % infants baptized Catholic (est.): na% Confirmations: 9,710 Marriages; % both Catholic: 4,757; 100%
Hospitals: 1 Orphanages: 11 Homes for elderly, disabled: 0 Other charitable institutions: 37 Primary schools: 178 Secondary schools: 61 Colleges and universities: 0 Seminaries: 5	Permanent deacons: 1 Seminarians; % diocesan: 174; 41% Diocesan priests: 44 Religious priests; brothers: 57; 15 Women religious: 284 Catechists: 1,513 Lay missionaries: 0

Ecuador **Region: South America** Oldest diocese: **Quito (1546)** Land mass: **283,561 km²** Primary language(s): **Spanish** Primary religion(s): **Catholic**	Population: 12,650,000 Fertility rate: 3.3 Infant mortality per 1,000 births: 36.4 Life expectancy: 71 Literacy rate: 89.75 (1990 est.) GNI per capita (PPP): $ 2,820
Catholics; %: 11,623,000; 92% Dioceses; all territories: 15; 24 Parishes; pastoral centers: 1,151; 4,503 Catholics/parish; /priest: 10,098; 6,331	Baptisms; % infants: 272,350; 90% % infants baptized Catholic (est.): 72% Confirmations: 123,814 Marriages; % both Catholic: 34,038; 99%
Hospitals: 35 Orphanages: 93 Homes for elderly, disabled: 48 Other charitable institutions: 1,386 Primary schools: 830 Secondary schools: 385 Colleges and universities: 3 Seminaries: 37	Permanent deacons: 69 Seminarians; % diocesan: 795; 68% Diocesan priests: 1,019 Religious priests; brothers: 817; 339 Women religious: 4,894 Catechists: 34,985 Lay missionaries: 529

Egypt **Region: North Africa** Oldest diocese: **Alexandria Coptic Rite (1824)** Land mass: **1,001,449 km²** Primary language(s): **Arabic** Primary religion(s): **Islam**	Population: 63,980,000 Fertility rate: 3.5 Infant mortality per 1,000 births: 64.7 Life expectancy: 63 Literacy rate: 48.4 (1990 est.) GNI per capita (PPP): $ 3,460
Catholics; %: 237,000; <1% Dioceses; all territories: 12; 14 Parishes; pastoral centers: 219; 425 Catholics/parish; /priest: 1,082; 501	Baptisms; % infants: 3,006; 90% % infants baptized Catholic (est.): <1% Confirmations: 2,433 Marriages; % both Catholic: 1,070; 92%
Hospitals: 13 Orphanages: 17 Homes for elderly, disabled: 21 Other charitable institutions: 235 Primary schools: 167 Secondary schools: 70 Colleges and universities: 0 Seminaries: 4	Permanent deacons: 12 Seminarians; % diocesan: 90; 59% Diocesan priests: 210 Religious priests; brothers: 263; 50 Women religious: 1,413 Catechists: 1,586 Lay missionaries: 1

El Salvador Region: Mesoamerica Oldest diocese: San Salvador (1842) Land mass: 21,041 km² Primary language(s): Spanish Primary religion(s): Catholic	Population: 6,280,000 Fertility rate: 3.5 Infant mortality per 1,000 births: 30.2 Life expectancy: 69 Literacy rate: 73 (1990 est.) GNI per capita (PPP): $ 4,260
Catholics; %: 4,986,000; 79% Dioceses; all territories: 8; 9 Parishes; pastoral centers: 376; 787 Catholics/parish; /priest: 13,261; 7,520	Baptisms; % infants: 97,023; 97% % infants baptized Catholic (est.): 62% Confirmations: 50,305 Marriages; % both Catholic: 10,040; 100%
Hospitals: 15 Orphanages: 14 Homes for elderly, disabled: 24 Other charitable institutions: 105 Primary schools: 110 Secondary schools: 38 Colleges and universities: 0 Seminaries: 17	Permanent deacons: 3 Seminarians; % diocesan: 390; 74% Diocesan priests: 430 Religious priests; brothers: 233; 82 Women religious: 1,542 Catechists: 5,247 Lay missionaries: 2

Equatorial Guinea Region: Central Africa Oldest diocese: Malabo (1855) Land mass: 28,051 km² Primary language(s): Spanish Primary religion(s): Catholic	Population: 407,000 Fertility rate: 5.9 Infant mortality per 1,000 births: 96.8 Life expectancy: 53 Literacy rate: 50.2 (1990 est.) GNI per capita (PPP): $ 3,910
Catholics; %: 385,000; 95% Dioceses; all territories: 3; 3 Parishes; pastoral centers: 66; 860 Catholics/parish; /priest: 5,833; 4,096	Baptisms; % infants: 9,832; 99% % infants baptized Catholic (est.): 47% Confirmations: 2,446 Marriages; % both Catholic: 363; 96%
Hospitals: 0 Orphanages: 0 Homes for elderly, disabled: 3 Other charitable institutions: 8 Primary schools: 38 Secondary schools: 8 Colleges and universities: 0 Seminaries: 1	Permanent deacons: 1 Seminarians; % diocesan: 65; 62% Diocesan priests: 45 Religious priests; brothers: 49; 29 Women religious: 237 Catechists: 1,934 Lay missionaries: 4

Eritrea **Region: East Africa** Oldest diocese: Asmara (1930) Land mass: 134,700 km² Primary language(s): Afar, Amharic Primary religion(s): Protestant, Islam	Population: 3,670,000 Fertility rate: 6 Infant mortality per 1,000 births: 78.2 Life expectancy: 55 Literacy rate: 25 (na est.) GNI per capita (PPP): $ 1,040
Catholics; %: 133,000; 4% Dioceses; all territories: 3; 3 Parishes; pastoral centers: 97; 217 Catholics/parish; /priest: 1,371; 524	Baptisms; % infants: 4,036; 92% % infants baptized Catholic (est.): 3% Confirmations: 1,307 Marriages; % both Catholic: 533; 93%
Hospitals: 1 Orphanages: 4 Homes for elderly, disabled: 0 Other charitable institutions: 64 Primary schools: 39 Secondary schools: 5 Colleges and universities: 0 Seminaries: 2	Permanent deacons: 0 Seminarians; % diocesan: 104; 38% Diocesan priests: 52 Religious priests; brothers: 202; 27 Women religious: 460 Catechists: 139 Lay missionaries: 4

Estonia **Region: Eastern Europe** Oldest diocese: na (na) Land mass: 45,215 km² Primary language(s): Estonian, Russian Primary religion(s): Orthodox	Population: 1,390,000 Fertility rate: 1.3 Infant mortality per 1,000 births: 13.3 Life expectancy: 69 Literacy rate: 99.7 (1989 est.) GNI per capita (PPP): $ 8,190
Catholics; %: 4,000; <1% Dioceses; all territories: 0; 1 Parishes; pastoral centers: 5; 5 Catholics/parish; /priest: 800; 444	Baptisms; % infants: 84; 50% % infants baptized Catholic (est.): <1% Confirmations: 18 Marriages; % both Catholic: 16; 25%
Hospitals: 0 Orphanages: 1 Homes for elderly, disabled: 1 Other charitable institutions: 2 Primary schools: 1 Secondary schools: 0 Colleges and universities: 0 Seminaries: 0	Permanent deacons: 0 Seminarians; % diocesan: 1; 100% Diocesan priests: 5 Religious priests; brothers: 4; 0 Women religious: 19 Catechists: 7 Lay missionaries: 0

Ethiopia Region: East Africa Oldest diocese: Adigrat (1937) Land mass: 1,087,200 km² Primary language(s): Amharic, Tigrinya Primary religion(s): Islam, Orthodox	Population: 63,490,000 Fertility rate: 5.9 Infant mortality per 1,000 births: 102.8 Life expectancy: 45 Literacy rate: 27.66 (1984 est.) GNI per capita (PPP): $ 620
Catholics; %: 443,000; 1% Dioceses; all territories: 2; 9 Parishes; pastoral centers: 216; 812 Catholics/parish; /priest: 2,051; 1,009	Baptisms; % infants: 17,528; 53% % infants baptized Catholic (est.): <1% Confirmations: 11,902 Marriages; % both Catholic: 1,928; 94%
Hospitals: 12 Orphanages: 18 Homes for elderly, disabled: 12 Other charitable institutions: 111 Primary schools: 128 Secondary schools: 56 Colleges and universities: 0 Seminaries: 2	Permanent deacons: 1 Seminarians; % diocesan: 329; 41% Diocesan priests: 162 Religious priests; brothers: 277; 69 Women religious: 696 Catechists: 1,756 Lay missionaries: 8

Faeroe Islands (Denmark) Region: Northwestern Europe Oldest diocese: na (na) Land mass: 1,399 km² Primary language(s): Faroese, Danish Primary religion(s): Lutheran	Population: 46,000 Fertility rate: na Infant mortality per 1,000 births: 7.1 Life expectancy: 78 Literacy rate: na (na est.) GNI per capita (PPP): $ na
Catholics; %: 100; <1% Dioceses; all territories: 0; 0 Parishes; pastoral centers: 1; 1 Catholics/parish; /priest: 100; na	Baptisms; % infants: 0; na % infants baptized Catholic (est.): <1% Confirmations: 0 Marriages; % both Catholic: 0; na
Hospitals: 0 Orphanages: 0 Homes for elderly, disabled: 0 Other charitable institutions: 0 Primary schools: 1 Secondary schools: 0 Colleges and universities: 0 Seminaries: 0	Permanent deacons: 1 Seminarians; % diocesan: 0; na Diocesan priests: 0 Religious priests; brothers: 0; 0 Women religious: 6 Catechists: 1 Lay missionaries: 0

Falkland Islands (United Kingdom) Region: South America Oldest diocese: na (na) Land mass: 12,173 km² Primary language(s): English Primary religion(s): Anglican	Population: 4,000 Fertility rate: na Infant mortality per 1,000 births: na Life expectancy: na Literacy rate: na (na est.) GNI per capita (PPP): $ na
Catholics; %: 1,000; 25% Dioceses; all territories: 0; 1 Parishes; pastoral centers: 1; 1 Catholics/parish; /priest: 1,000; 500	Baptisms; % infants: 3; 100% % infants baptized Catholic (est.): na% Confirmations: 0 Marriages; % both Catholic: 2; 50%
Hospitals: 0 Orphanages: 0 Homes for elderly, disabled: 0 Other charitable institutions: 0 Primary schools: 0 Secondary schools: 0 Colleges and universities: 0 Seminaries: 0	Permanent deacons: 0 Seminarians; % diocesan: 0; na Diocesan priests: 0 Religious priests; brothers: 2; 1 Women religious: 1 Catechists: 0 Lay missionaries: 0

Fiji Islands Region: Oceania Oldest diocese: Suva (1863) Land mass: 18,274 km² Primary language(s): English Primary religion(s): Methodist, Hinduism	Population: 816,000 Fertility rate: 3.3 Infant mortality per 1,000 births: 14.9 Life expectancy: 68 Literacy rate: 79 (1976 est.) GNI per capita (PPP): $ 4,780
Catholics; %: 83,000; 10% Dioceses; all territories: 1; 1 Parishes; pastoral centers: 35; 38 Catholics/parish; /priest: 2,371; 659	Baptisms; % infants: 1,372; 87% % infants baptized Catholic (est.): 10% Confirmations: 1,369 Marriages; % both Catholic: 404; 61%
Hospitals: 1 Orphanages: 0 Homes for elderly, disabled: 2 Other charitable institutions: 3 Primary schools: 43 Secondary schools: 18 Colleges and universities: 0 Seminaries: 2	Permanent deacons: 0 Seminarians; % diocesan: 53; 28% Diocesan priests: 29 Religious priests; brothers: 97; 61 Women religious: 172 Catechists: 466 Lay missionaries: 6

Finland
Region: Northwestern Europe
Oldest diocese: Helsinki (1955)
Land mass: 338,127 km²
Primary language(s): Finnish
Primary religion(s): Lutheran

Population: 5,180,000
Fertility rate: 1.7
Infant mortality per 1,000 births: 3.8
Life expectancy: 77
Literacy rate: 100 (1980 est.)
GNI per capita (PPP): $ 22,600

Catholics; %: 8,000; <1%
Dioceses; all territories: 1; 1
Parishes; pastoral centers: 7; 11
Catholics/parish; /priest: 1,143; 381

Baptisms; % infants: 158; 95%
% infants baptized Catholic (est.): <1%
Confirmations: 102
Marriages; % both Catholic: 48; 23%

Hospitals: 0
Orphanages: 0
Homes for elderly, disabled: 0
Other charitable institutions: 2
Primary schools: 1
Secondary schools: 1
Colleges and universities: 0
Seminaries: 0

Permanent deacons: 3
Seminarians; % diocesan: 2; 50%
Diocesan priests: 6
Religious priests; brothers: 15; 0
Women religious: 49
Catechists: 0
Lay missionaries: 0

France
Region: Northwestern Europe
Oldest diocese: Auch (879)
Land mass: 551,500 km²
Primary language(s): French
Primary religion(s): Catholic

Population: 58,890,000
Fertility rate: 1.9
Infant mortality per 1,000 births: 4.6
Life expectancy: 79
Literacy rate: 99 (1980 est.)
GNI per capita (PPP): $ 23,020

Catholics; %: 46,823,000; 80%
Dioceses; all territories: 94; 98
Parishes; pastoral centers: 22,156;
22,924
Catholics/parish; /priest: 2,113; 1,847

Baptisms; % infants: 401,054; 95%
% infants baptized Catholic (est.): 55%
Confirmations: 62,003
Marriages; % both Catholic: 122,580;
88%

Hospitals: 103
Orphanages: 98
Homes for elderly, disabled: 534
Other charitable institutions: 643
Primary schools: 4,865
Secondary schools: 2,602
Colleges and universities: 6
Seminaries: 48

Permanent deacons: 1,622
Seminarians; % diocesan: 1,537; 61%
Diocesan priests: 19,234
Religious priests; brothers: 6,119; 3,456
Women religious: 48,499
Catechists: 74,769
Lay missionaries: 0

French Guiana (France) Region: South America Oldest diocese: Cayenne (1651) Land mass: 90,000 km² Primary language(s): French Primary religion(s): Catholic	Population: 200,000 Fertility rate: 3.4 Infant mortality per 1,000 births: 14.5 Life expectancy: 76 Literacy rate: 80.26 (1982 est.) GNI per capita (PPP): $ na
Catholics; %: 150,000; 75% Dioceses; all territories: 1; 1 Parishes; pastoral centers: 23; 28 Catholics/parish; /priest: 6,522; 4,412	Baptisms; % infants: 1,959; 94% % infants baptized Catholic (est.): 37% Confirmations: 943 Marriages; % both Catholic: 121; 98%
Hospitals: 1 Orphanages: 1 Homes for elderly, disabled: 1 Other charitable institutions: 6 Primary schools: 7 Secondary schools: 5 Colleges and universities: 0 Seminaries: 0	Permanent deacons: 5 Seminarians; % diocesan: 4; 25% Diocesan priests: 7 Religious priests; brothers: 27; 3 Women religious: 73 Catechists: 614 Lay missionaries: 0

Gabon Region: Central Africa Oldest diocese: Libreville (1842) Land mass: 267,667 km² Primary language(s): French Primary religion(s): Catholic	Population: 1,210,000 Fertility rate: 4.3 Infant mortality per 1,000 births: 97.7 Life expectancy: 50 Literacy rate: 60.7 (1990 est.) GNI per capita (PPP): $ 5,280
Catholics; %: 643,000; 53% Dioceses; all territories: 4; 4 Parishes; pastoral centers: 62; 124 Catholics/parish; /priest: 10,371; 5,793	Baptisms; % infants: 7,623; 72% % infants baptized Catholic (est.): 10% Confirmations: 4,284 Marriages; % both Catholic: 346; 86%
Hospitals: 0 Orphanages: 2 Homes for elderly, disabled: 4 Other charitable institutions: 16 Primary schools: 227 Secondary schools: 22 Colleges and universities: 0 Seminaries: 2	Permanent deacons: 1 Seminarians; % diocesan: 91; 55% Diocesan priests: 47 Religious priests; brothers: 64; 31 Women religious: 168 Catechists: 855 Lay missionaries: 8

Gambia **Region: West Africa** Oldest diocese: Banjul (1974) Land mass: 11,295 km² Primary language(s): English Primary religion(s): Islam	Population: 1,390,000 Fertility rate: 5.9 Infant mortality per 1,000 births: 80.8 Life expectancy: 53 Literacy rate: 27.2 (1990 est.) GNI per capita (PPP): $ 1,550
Catholics; %: 30,000; 2% Dioceses; all territories: 1; 1 Parishes; pastoral centers: 56; 62 Catholics/parish; /priest: 536; 1,250	Baptisms; % infants: 1,844; 94% % infants baptized Catholic (est.): 3% Confirmations: 510 Marriages; % both Catholic: 38; 76%
Hospitals: 0 Orphanages: 2 Homes for elderly, disabled: 1 Other charitable institutions: 6 Primary schools: 22 Secondary schools: 13 Colleges and universities: 0 Seminaries: 0	Permanent deacons: 0 Seminarians; % diocesan: 9; 44% Diocesan priests: 12 Religious priests; brothers: 12; 13 Women religious: 53 Catechists: 49 Lay missionaries: 0

Georgia **Region: Eastern Europe** Oldest diocese: na (na) Land mass: 69,700 km² Primary language(s): Georgian, Russian Primary religion(s): Orthodox	Population: 5,270,000 Fertility rate: 1.2 Infant mortality per 1,000 births: 52.0 Life expectancy: 65 Literacy rate: 99 (1989 est.) GNI per capita (PPP): $ 2,540
Catholics; %: 100,000; 2% Dioceses; all territories: 0; 1 Parishes; pastoral centers: 27; 27 Catholics/parish; /priest: 3,704; 6,250	Baptisms; % infants: 192; 41% % infants baptized Catholic (est.): <1% Confirmations: 99 Marriages; % both Catholic: 80; 66%
Hospitals: 6 Orphanages: 0 Homes for elderly, disabled: 0 Other charitable institutions: 1 Primary schools: 0 Secondary schools: 0 Colleges and universities: 0 Seminaries: 0	Permanent deacons: 0 Seminarians; % diocesan: 11; 45% Diocesan priests: 3 Religious priests; brothers: 13; 0 Women religious: 27 Catechists: 44 Lay missionaries: 3

Germany Region: Northwestern Europe Oldest diocese: Passau (737) Land mass: 356,910 km² Primary language(s): German Primary religion(s): Protestant, Catholic	Population: 82,020,000 Fertility rate: 1.3 Infant mortality per 1,000 births: 4.8 Life expectancy: 77 Literacy rate: 99 (1977 est.) GNI per capita (PPP): $ 23,510
Catholics; %: 27,455,000; 33% Dioceses; all territories: 27; 29 Parishes; pastoral centers: 12,466; 13,728 Catholics/parish; /priest: 2,202; 1,423	Baptisms; % infants: 234,010; 96% % infants baptized Catholic (est.): 33% Confirmations: 211,264 Marriages; % both Catholic: 65,627; 67%
Hospitals: 573 Orphanages: 386 Homes for elderly, disabled: 2,304 Other charitable institutions: 7,052 Primary schools: 171 Secondary schools: 797 Colleges and universities: 1 Seminaries: 37	Permanent deacons: 2,235 Seminarians; % diocesan: 1,330; 76% Diocesan priests: 14,682 Religious priests; brothers: 4,608; 1,606 Women religious: 38,400 Catechists: 23,524 Lay missionaries: 745

Ghana Region: West Africa Oldest diocese: Cape Coast (1879) Land mass: 238,537 km² Primary language(s): English Primary religion(s): Islam, Indigenous religions	Population: 18,410,000 Fertility rate: 4.3 Infant mortality per 1,000 births: 58.3 Life expectancy: 58 Literacy rate: 60.3 (1990 est.) GNI per capita (PPP): $ 1,850
Catholics; %: 2,242,000; 12% Dioceses; all territories: 18; 18 Parishes; pastoral centers: 318; 3,069 Catholics/parish; /priest: 7,050; 2,442	Baptisms; % infants: 75,138; 64% % infants baptized Catholic (est.): 5% Confirmations: 35,472 Marriages; % both Catholic: 5,942; 84%
Hospitals: 31 Orphanages: 12 Homes for elderly, disabled: 7 Other charitable institutions: 193 Primary schools: 1,809 Secondary schools: 856 Colleges and universities: 0 Seminaries: 4	Permanent deacons: 2 Seminarians; % diocesan: 603; 90% Diocesan priests: 747 Religious priests; brothers: 171; 169 Women religious: 774 Catechists: 5,715 Lay missionaries: 19

Gibraltar (United Kingdom) Region: Southwestern Europe Oldest diocese: Gibraltar (1910) Land mass: 6 km² Primary language(s): English, Spanish Primary religion(s): Catholic	Population: 27,000 Fertility rate: na Infant mortality per 1,000 births: 5.8 Life expectancy: 79 Literacy rate: 80 (na est.) GNI per capita (PPP): $ na
Catholics; %: 23,000; 85% Dioceses; all territories: 1; 1 Parishes; pastoral centers: 5; 5 Catholics/parish; /priest: 4,600; 1,533	Baptisms; % infants: 361; 96% % infants baptized Catholic (est.): 78% Confirmations: 299 Marriages; % both Catholic: 99; 89%
Hospitals: 0 Orphanages: 0 Homes for elderly, disabled: 0 Other charitable institutions: 1 Primary schools: 1 Secondary schools: 0 Colleges and universities: 0 Seminaries: 0	Permanent deacons: 0 Seminarians; % diocesan: 1; 100% Diocesan priests: 14 Religious priests; brothers: 1; 0 Women religious: 5 Catechists: 0 Lay missionaries: 0

Greece Region: Southwestern Europe Oldest diocese: Santorini, Thira (1204) Land mass: 131,990 km² Primary language(s): Greek Primary religion(s): Greek Orthodox	Population: 10,010,000 Fertility rate: 1.3 Infant mortality per 1,000 births: 6.7 Life expectancy: 78 Literacy rate: 93.2 (1990 est.) GNI per capita (PPP): $ 15,800
Catholics; %: 55,000; 1% Dioceses; all territories: 8; 11 Parishes; pastoral centers: 70; 109 Catholics/parish; /priest: 786; 598	Baptisms; % infants: 640; 95% % infants baptized Catholic (est.): 1% Confirmations: 316 Marriages; % both Catholic: 378; 56%
Hospitals: 2 Orphanages: 0 Homes for elderly, disabled: 5 Other charitable institutions: 12 Primary schools: 10 Secondary schools: 10 Colleges and universities: 0 Seminaries: 0	Permanent deacons: 2 Seminarians; % diocesan: 7; 57% Diocesan priests: 50 Religious priests; brothers: 42; 31 Women religious: 133 Catechists: 106 Lay missionaries: 0

Greenland (Denmark) Region: North America Oldest diocese: () Land mass: 2,175,600 km² Primary language(s): Greenlandic, Danish, English Primary religion(s): Lutheran	Population: 56,000 Fertility rate: na Infant mortality per 1,000 births: 18.8 Life expectancy: 68 Literacy rate: na (na est.) GNI per capita (PPP): $ na
Catholics; %: 100; <1% Dioceses; all territories: 0; 0 Parishes; pastoral centers: 1; 1 Catholics/parish; /priest: 100; 100	Baptisms; % infants: 1; 100% % infants baptized Catholic (est.): <1% Confirmations: 1 Marriages; % both Catholic: 0; na
Hospitals: 0 Orphanages: 0 Homes for elderly, disabled: 0 Other charitable institutions: 0 Primary schools: 0 Secondary schools: 0 Colleges and universities: 0 Seminaries: 0	Permanent deacons: 0 Seminarians; % diocesan: 0; na Diocesan priests: 0 Religious priests; brothers: 1; 0 Women religious: 3 Catechists: 0 Lay missionaries: 0

Grenada Region: Caribbean Oldest diocese: Saint George (1956) Land mass: 344 km² Primary language(s): English Primary religion(s): Catholic	Population: 93,000 Fertility rate: 2.4 Infant mortality per 1,000 births: 14.6 Life expectancy: 65 Literacy rate: 97.8 (1970 est.) GNI per capita (PPP): $ 6,330
Catholics; %: 55,000; 59% Dioceses; all territories: 1; 1 Parishes; pastoral centers: 20; 59 Catholics/parish; /priest: 2,750; 2,500	Baptisms; % infants: 553; 92% % infants baptized Catholic (est.): 21% Confirmations: 324 Marriages; % both Catholic: 105; 81%
Hospitals: 0 Orphanages: 2 Homes for elderly, disabled: 3 Other charitable institutions: 1 Primary schools: 25 Secondary schools: 5 Colleges and universities: 0 Seminaries: 0	Permanent deacons: 5 Seminarians; % diocesan: 7; 43% Diocesan priests: 5 Religious priests; brothers: 17; 5 Women religious: 31 Catechists: 123 Lay missionaries: 1

Guadeloupe (France)
Region: Caribbean
Oldest diocese: Basse-Terre (1951)
Land mass: 1,705 km²
Primary language(s): French
Primary religion(s): Catholic

Population: 436,000
Fertility rate: 1.9
Infant mortality per 1,000 births: 10.0
Life expectancy: 77
Literacy rate: 91.32 (1982 est.)
GNI per capita (PPP): $ na

Catholics; %: 355,000; 81%
Dioceses; all territories: 1; 1
Parishes; pastoral centers: 45; 105
Catholics/parish; /priest: 7,889; 6,017

Baptisms; % infants: 7,360; 96%
% infants baptized Catholic (est.): 73%
Confirmations: 2,978
Marriages; % both Catholic: 945; 96%

Hospitals: 1
Orphanages: 2
Homes for elderly, disabled: 1
Other charitable institutions: 12
Primary schools: 13
Secondary schools: 4
Colleges and universities: 0
Seminaries: 0

Permanent deacons: 3
Seminarians; % diocesan: 12; 100%
Diocesan priests: 41
Religious priests; brothers: 18; 1
Women religious: 165
Catechists: 3,746
Lay missionaries: 0

Guam (United States)
Region: Oceania
Oldest diocese: Agaña (1902)
Land mass: 549 km²
Primary language(s): English,
Chamorro, Japanese
Primary religion(s): Catholic

Population: 167,000
Fertility rate: 4.2
Infant mortality per 1,000 births: 7.0
Life expectancy: 78
Literacy rate: 96.42 (1980 est.)
GNI per capita (PPP): $ na

Catholics; %: 151,000; 90%
Dioceses; all territories: 1; 1
Parishes; pastoral centers: 24; 24
Catholics/parish; /priest: 6,292; 3,213

Baptisms; % infants: 2,272; 98%
% infants baptized Catholic (est.): 74%
Confirmations: 873
Marriages; % both Catholic: 264; 96%

Hospitals: 0
Orphanages: 0
Homes for elderly, disabled: 1
Other charitable institutions: 15
Primary schools: 7
Secondary schools: 3
Colleges and universities: 0
Seminaries: 1

Permanent deacons: 7
Seminarians; % diocesan: 19; 74%
Diocesan priests: 31
Religious priests; brothers: 16; 1
Women religious: 125
Catechists: 471
Lay missionaries: 0

Guatemala Region: Mesoamerica Oldest diocese: Guatemala (1534) Land mass: 108,889 km² Primary language(s): Spanish Primary religion(s): Catholic	Population: 11,390,000 Fertility rate: 4.8 Infant mortality per 1,000 births: 48.4 Life expectancy: 66 Literacy rate: 55.1 (1990 est.) GNI per capita (PPP): $ 3,630
Catholics; %: 9,471,000; 83% Dioceses; all territories: 12; 15 Parishes; pastoral centers: 434; 2,085 Catholics/parish; /priest: 21,823; 9,764	Baptisms; % infants: 518,310; 98% % infants baptized Catholic (est.): 91% Confirmations: 173,104 Marriages; % both Catholic: 76,931; 100%
Hospitals: 19 Orphanages: 20 Homes for elderly, disabled: 24 Other charitable institutions: 692 Primary schools: 838 Secondary schools: 104 Colleges and universities: 1 Seminaries: 14	Permanent deacons: 6 Seminarians; % diocesan: 366; 55% Diocesan priests: 360 Religious priests; brothers: 610; 172 Women religious: 2,070 Catechists: 43,318 Lay missionaries: 94

Guinea Region: West Africa Oldest diocese: N'Zerékoré (1937) Land mass: 245,857 km² Primary language(s): French Primary religion(s): Islam	Population: 8,150,000 Fertility rate: 5.5 Infant mortality per 1,000 births: 132.9 Life expectancy: 45 Literacy rate: 24 (1990 est.) GNI per capita (PPP): $ 1,870
Catholics; %: 134,000; 2% Dioceses; all territories: 3; 3 Parishes; pastoral centers: 54; 177 Catholics/parish; /priest: 2,481; 1,396	Baptisms; % infants: 2,384; 23% % infants baptized Catholic (est.): <1% Confirmations: 762 Marriages; % both Catholic: 193; 73%
Hospitals: 0 Orphanages: 1 Homes for elderly, disabled: 4 Other charitable institutions: 9 Primary schools: 16 Secondary schools: 2 Colleges and universities: 0 Seminaries: 0	Permanent deacons: 0 Seminarians; % diocesan: 25; 100% Diocesan priests: 70 Religious priests; brothers: 26; 27 Women religious: 100 Catechists: 563 Lay missionaries: 15

Guinea-Bissau Region: West Africa Oldest diocese: Bissau (1955) Land mass: 36,125 km² Primary language(s): Portuguese Primary religion(s): Islam, Indigenous religions	Population: 1,140,000 Fertility rate: 5.8 Infant mortality per 1,000 births: 114.1 Life expectancy: 49 Literacy rate: 36.5 (1990 est.) GNI per capita (PPP): $ 630
Catholics; %: 136,000; 12% Dioceses; all territories: 2; 2 Parishes; pastoral centers: 22; 22 Catholics/parish; /priest: 6,182; 2,061	Baptisms; % infants: 1,500; 100% % infants baptized Catholic (est.): 3% Confirmations: 500 Marriages; % both Catholic: 130; 100%
Hospitals: 3 Orphanages: 0 Homes for elderly, disabled: 0 Other charitable institutions: 15 Primary schools: 24 Secondary schools: 3 Colleges and universities: 0 Seminaries: 0	Permanent deacons: 0 Seminarians; % diocesan: 15; 80% Diocesan priests: 13 Religious priests; brothers: 53; 8 Women religious: 94 Catechists: 615 Lay missionaries: 12

Guyana Region: South America Oldest diocese: Georgetown (1837) Land mass: 214,969 km² Primary language(s): English Primary religion(s): Protestant and Hinduism	Population: 800,000 Fertility rate: 2.5 Infant mortality per 1,000 births: 39.8 Life expectancy: 64 Literacy rate: 96.4 (1990 est.) GNI per capita (PPP): $ 3,330
Catholics; %: 88,000; 11% Dioceses; all territories: 1; 1 Parishes; pastoral centers: 24; 125 Catholics/parish; /priest: 3,667; 1,725	Baptisms; % infants: 1,323; 92% % infants baptized Catholic (est.): 12% Confirmations: 987 Marriages; % both Catholic: 201; 65%
Hospitals: 1 Orphanages: 2 Homes for elderly, disabled: 9 Other charitable institutions: 55 Primary schools: 0 Secondary schools: 0 Colleges and universities: 0 Seminaries: 0	Permanent deacons: 0 Seminarians; % diocesan: 5; 0% Diocesan priests: 5 Religious priests; brothers: 46; 5 Women religious: 49 Catechists: 571 Lay missionaries: 2

Haiti Region: Caribbean Oldest diocese: Port-au-Prince (1861) Land mass: 27,750 km² Primary language(s): French Primary religion(s): Catholic	Population: 7,960,000 Fertility rate: 4.7 Infant mortality per 1,000 births: 98.9 Life expectancy: 49 Literacy rate: 53 (1990 est.) GNI per capita (PPP): $ 1,470
Catholics; %: 6,778,000; 85% Dioceses; all territories: 9; 9 Parishes; pastoral centers: 266; 1,124 Catholics/parish; /priest: 25,481; 11,093	Baptisms; % infants: 143,381; 91% % infants baptized Catholic (est.): 53% Confirmations: 22,780 Marriages; % both Catholic: 19,163; 99%
Hospitals: 20 Orphanages: 38 Homes for elderly, disabled: 29 Other charitable institutions: 674 Primary schools: 1,420 Secondary schools: 156 Colleges and universities: 0 Seminaries: 4	Permanent deacons: 5 Seminarians; % diocesan: 362; 55% Diocesan priests: 340 Religious priests; brothers: 271; 295 Women religious: 1,037 Catechists: 5,607 Lay missionaries: 19

Honduras Region: Mesoamerica Oldest diocese: Tegucigalpa (1561) Land mass: 112,088 km² Primary language(s): Spanish Primary religion(s): Catholic	Population: 6,420,000 Fertility rate: 4.4 Infant mortality per 1,000 births: 32.0 Life expectancy: 70 Literacy rate: 73.1 (1990 est.) GNI per capita (PPP): $ 2,270
Catholics; %: 5,362,000; 84% Dioceses; all territories: 7; 7 Parishes; pastoral centers: 169; 1,012 Catholics/parish; /priest: 31,728; 14,037	Baptisms; % infants: 83,403; 88% % infants baptized Catholic (est.): 34% Confirmations: 31,196 Marriages; % both Catholic: 14,473; 100%
Hospitals: 28 Orphanages: 16 Homes for elderly, disabled: 16 Other charitable institutions: 442 Primary schools: 27 Secondary schools: 35 Colleges and universities: 1 Seminaries: 2	Permanent deacons: 1 Seminarians; % diocesan: 128; 90% Diocesan priests: 168 Religious priests; brothers: 214; 35 Women religious: 561 Catechists: 13,092 Lay missionaries: 360

Hungary Region: Eastern Europe Oldest diocese: Kalocsa-Kecskemét (1000) Land mass: 93,032 km² Primary language(s): Hungarian Primary religion(s): Catholic	Population: 10,020,000 Fertility rate: 1.3 Infant mortality per 1,000 births: 9.4 Life expectancy: 71 Literacy rate: 98.3 (1980 est.) GNI per capita (PPP): $ 11,050
Catholics; %: 6,231,000; 62% Dioceses; all territories: 13; 16 Parishes; pastoral centers: 2,223; 2,416 Catholics/parish; /priest: 2,803; 2,521	Baptisms; % infants: 55,084; 91% % infants baptized Catholic (est.): 47% Confirmations: 23,299 Marriages; % both Catholic: 16,158; 78%
Hospitals: 5 Orphanages: 6 Homes for elderly, disabled: 45 Other charitable institutions: 141 Primary schools: 90 Secondary schools: 57 Colleges and universities: 1 Seminaries: 13	Permanent deacons: 46 Seminarians; % diocesan: 566; 69% Diocesan priests: 1,915 Religious priests; brothers: 557; 81 Women religious: 1,515 Catechists: 3,444 Lay missionaries: 0

Iceland Region: Northwestern Europe Oldest diocese: Reykjavik (1854) Land mass: 103,000 km² Primary language(s): Icelandic Primary religion(s): Lutheran	Population: 283,000 Fertility rate: 2 Infant mortality per 1,000 births: 3.6 Life expectancy: 79 Literacy rate: 100 (1976 est.) GNI per capita (PPP): $ 27,210
Catholics; %: 4,000; 1% Dioceses; all territories: 1; 1 Parishes; pastoral centers: 4; 9 Catholics/parish; /priest: 1,000; 333	Baptisms; % infants: 82; 96% % infants baptized Catholic (est.): 1% Confirmations: 39 Marriages; % both Catholic: 28; 43%
Hospitals: 1 Orphanages: 0 Homes for elderly, disabled: 0 Other charitable institutions: 0 Primary schools: 1 Secondary schools: 0 Colleges and universities: 0 Seminaries: 0	Permanent deacons: 0 Seminarians; % diocesan: 0; na Diocesan priests: 6 Religious priests; brothers: 6; 1 Women religious: 37 Catechists: 0 Lay missionaries: 0

India Region: South Asia Oldest diocese: Goa (1533) Land mass: 3,287,590 km² Primary language(s): English, Hindi Primary religion(s): Hinduism	Population: 1,002,140,000 Fertility rate: 3.2 Infant mortality per 1,000 births: 66.8 Life expectancy: 62 Literacy rate: 52.21 (1991 est.) GNI per capita (PPP): $ 2,230
Catholics; %: 16,516,000; 2% Dioceses; all territories: 145; 145 Parishes; pastoral centers: 8,200; 24,540 Catholics/parish; /priest: 2,014; 851	Baptisms; % infants: 352,474; 80% % infants baptized Catholic (est.): 1% Confirmations: 222,356 Marriages; % both Catholic: 118,325; 94%
Hospitals: 1,220 Orphanages: 1,938 Homes for elderly, disabled: 818 Other charitable institutions: 11,114 Primary schools: 9,480 Secondary schools: 4,350 Colleges and universities: 17 Seminaries: 124	Permanent deacons: 21 Seminarians; % diocesan: 10,537; 45% Diocesan priests: 11,004 Religious priests; brothers: 8,400; 2,471 Women religious: 81,551 Catechists: 59,963 Lay missionaries: 537

Indonesia Region: Southeast Asia Oldest diocese: Jakarta (1841) Land mass: 1,904,569 km² Primary language(s): Malay, English, Dutch Primary religion(s): Islam	Population: 210,490,000 Fertility rate: 2.7 Infant mortality per 1,000 births: 43.7 Life expectancy: 68 Literacy rate: 84.06 (1990 est.) GNI per capita (PPP): $ 2,660
Catholics; %: 6,284,000; 3% Dioceses; all territories: 34; 35 Parishes; pastoral centers: 1,044; 7,983 Catholics/parish; /priest: 6,019; 2,180	Baptisms; % infants: 196,559; 72% % infants baptized Catholic (est.): 3% Confirmations: 69,301 Marriages; % both Catholic: 44,865; 76%
Hospitals: 106 Orphanages: 116 Homes for elderly, disabled: 45 Other charitable institutions: 454 Primary schools: 2,445 Secondary schools: 1,283 Colleges and universities: 3 Seminaries: 28	Permanent deacons: 14 Seminarians; % diocesan: 2,803; 43% Diocesan priests: 1,114 Religious priests; brothers: 1,769; 874 Women religious: 6,889 Catechists: 21,763 Lay missionaries: 2,584

Iran	Population: 63,660,000
Region: Western Asia	Fertility rate: 2.6
Oldest diocese: Espahan (1629)	Infant mortality per 1,000 births: 31.2
Land mass: 1,648,000 km²	Life expectancy: 69
Primary language(s): Farsi	Literacy rate: 54 (1990 est.)
Primary religion(s): Islam	GNI per capita (PPP): $ 5,520

Catholics; %: 25,000; <1%	Baptisms; % infants: 68; 96%
Dioceses; all territories: 6; 6	% infants baptized Catholic (est.): <1%
Parishes; pastoral centers: 18; 19	Confirmations: 65
Catholics/parish; /priest: 1,389; 1,389	Marriages; % both Catholic: 31; 97%

Hospitals: 0	Permanent deacons: 5
Orphanages: 0	Seminarians; % diocesan: 5; 40%
Homes for elderly, disabled: 4	Diocesan priests: 7
Other charitable institutions: 3	Religious priests; brothers: 11; 0
Primary schools: 3	Women religious: 31
Secondary schools: 3	Catechists: 30
Colleges and universities: 0	Lay missionaries: 0
Seminaries: 0	

Iraq	Population: 22,950,000
Region: Western Asia	Fertility rate: 5.3
Oldest diocese: Baghdad (1632)	Infant mortality per 1,000 births: 62.5
Land mass: 438,317 km²	Life expectancy: 67
Primary language(s): Arabic	Literacy rate: 59.7 (1990 est.)
Primary religion(s): Islam	GNI per capita (PPP): $ na

Catholics; %: 281,000; 1%	Baptisms; % infants: 3,543; 100%
Dioceses; all territories: 15; 17	% infants baptized Catholic (est.): <1%
Parishes; pastoral centers: 92; 125	Confirmations: 3,535
Catholics/parish; /priest: 3,054; 2,081	Marriages; % both Catholic: 1,046; 99%

Hospitals: 2	Permanent deacons: 7
Orphanages: 6	Seminarians; % diocesan: 108; 94%
Homes for elderly, disabled: 9	Diocesan priests: 115
Other charitable institutions: 23	Religious priests; brothers: 20; 9
Primary schools: 11	Women religious: 283
Secondary schools: 11	Catechists: 1,041
Colleges and universities: 0	Lay missionaries: 0
Seminaries: 2	

Ireland Region: Northwestern Europe Oldest diocese: **Armagh (445)** Land mass: **84,405 km²** Primary language(s): **English, Gaelic** Primary religion(s): **Catholic**	Population: **6,121,000** Fertility rate: **1.9** Infant mortality per 1,000 births: **5.7** Life expectancy: **77** Literacy rate: **98 (1981 est.)** GNI per capita (PPP): **$ 22,460**
Catholics; %: **4,666,000; 76%** Dioceses; all territories: **26; 26** Parishes; pastoral centers: **1,367; 1,403** Catholics/parish; /priest: **3,413; 827**	Baptisms; % infants: **62,600; 100%** % infants baptized Catholic (est.): **na%** Confirmations: **68,852** Marriages; % both Catholic: **17,866; 91%**
Hospitals: **66** Orphanages: **19** Homes for elderly, disabled: **103** Other charitable institutions: **193** Primary schools: **3,356** Secondary schools: **705** Colleges and universities: **1** Seminaries: **9**	Permanent deacons: **2** Seminarians; % diocesan: **253; 58%** Diocesan priests: **3,336** Religious priests; brothers: **2,306; 950** Women religious: **9,254** Catechists: **1,397** Lay missionaries: **0**

Israel Region: Western Asia Oldest diocese: **Acre (1753)** Land mass: **20,770 km²** Primary language(s): **Hebrew** Primary religion(s): **Judaism**	Population: **6,040,000** Fertility rate: **3** Infant mortality per 1,000 births: **8.1** Life expectancy: **78** Literacy rate: **91.8 (1983 est.)** GNI per capita (PPP): **$ 18,070**
Catholics; %: **118,000; 2%** Dioceses; all territories: **4; 9** Parishes; pastoral centers: **78; 88** Catholics/parish; /priest: **1,513; 311**	Baptisms; % infants: **1,558; 93%** % infants baptized Catholic (est.): **1%** Confirmations: **1,578** Marriages; % both Catholic: **655; 81%**
Hospitals: **10** Orphanages: **11** Homes for elderly, disabled: **10** Other charitable institutions: **14** Primary schools: **31** Secondary schools: **26** Colleges and universities: **1** Seminaries: **6**	Permanent deacons: **6** Seminarians; % diocesan: **125; 32%** Diocesan priests: **78** Religious priests; brothers: **301; 162** Women religious: **1,038** Catechists: **1** Lay missionaries: **0**

Italy	Population: 57,530,000
Region: Southwestern Europe	Fertility rate: 1.3
Oldest diocese: Mantova (804)	Infant mortality per 1,000 births: 6.0
Land mass: 301,268 km²	Life expectancy: 79
Primary language(s): Italian	Literacy rate: 97.1 (1990 est.)
Primary religion(s): Catholic	GNI per capita (PPP): $ 22,000

Catholics; %: 55,877,000; 97%	Baptisms; % infants: 487,935; 97%
Dioceses; all territories: 217; 228	% infants baptized Catholic (est.): 93%
Parishes; pastoral centers: 25,865; 31,775	Confirmations: 490,828
Catholics/parish; /priest: 2,160; 1,017	Marriages; % both Catholic: 248,920; 99%

Hospitals: 137	Permanent deacons: 2,439
Orphanages: 799	Seminarians; % diocesan: 6,433; 57%
Homes for elderly, disabled: 1,895	Diocesan priests: 36,117
Other charitable institutions: 2,767	Religious priests; brothers: 18,803; 3,947
Primary schools: 1,346	Women religious: 113,295
Secondary schools: 1,206	Catechists: 182,552
Colleges and universities: 10	Lay missionaries: 959
Seminaries: 236	

Jamaica	Population: 2,590,000
Region: Caribbean	Fertility rate: 2.4
Oldest diocese: Kingston in Jamaica (1956)	Infant mortality per 1,000 births: 15.2
	Life expectancy: 75
Land mass: 10,990 km²	Literacy rate: 98.4 (1990 est.)
Primary language(s): English, Creole	GNI per capita (PPP): $ 3,390
Primary religion(s): Protestant	

Catholics; %: 116,000; 4%	Baptisms; % infants: 1,369; 67%
Dioceses; all territories: 3; 3	% infants baptized Catholic (est.): 1%
Parishes; pastoral centers: 87; 88	Confirmations: 564
Catholics/parish; /priest: 1,333; 1,289	Marriages; % both Catholic: 207; 33%

Hospitals: 1	Permanent deacons: 32
Orphanages: 9	Seminarians; % diocesan: 16; 69%
Homes for elderly, disabled: 7	Diocesan priests: 49
Other charitable institutions: 27	Religious priests; brothers: 41; 51
Primary schools: 38	Women religious: 177
Secondary schools: 24	Catechists: 436
Colleges and universities: 0	Lay missionaries: 21
Seminaries: 1	

Japan **Region: East Asia** Oldest diocese: Sendai (1891) Land mass: 377,801 km² Primary language(s): Japanese Primary religion(s): Buddhism	Population: 126,870,000 Fertility rate: 1.3 Infant mortality per 1,000 births: 4.0 Life expectancy: 81 Literacy rate: 99 (1970 est.) GNI per capita (PPP): $ 25,170
Catholics; %: 513,000; <1% Dioceses; all territories: 16; 17 Parishes; pastoral centers: 871; 910 Catholics/parish; /priest: 589; 293	Baptisms; % infants: 9,838; 50% % infants baptized Catholic (est.): <1% Confirmations: 5,913 Marriages; % both Catholic: 3,094; 25%
Hospitals: 25 Orphanages: 103 Homes for elderly, disabled: 159 Other charitable institutions: 171 Primary schools: 56 Secondary schools: 159 Colleges and universities: 4 Seminaries: 5	Permanent deacons: 8 Seminarians; % diocesan: 202; 45% Diocesan priests: 549 Religious priests; brothers: 1,200; 253 Women religious: 6,488 Catechists: 1,294 Lay missionaries: 10

Jordan **Region: Western Asia** Oldest diocese: Petra (1932) Land mass: 97,740 km² Primary language(s): Arabic Primary religion(s): Islam	Population: 4,910,000 Fertility rate: 3.6 Infant mortality per 1,000 births: 22.0 Life expectancy: 77 Literacy rate: 85.85 (1994 est.) GNI per capita (PPP): $ 3,880
Catholics; %: 72,000; 1% Dioceses; all territories: 1; 2 Parishes; pastoral centers: 62; 65 Catholics/parish; /priest: 1,161; 960	Baptisms; % infants: 1,100; 99% % infants baptized Catholic (est.): 1% Confirmations: 1,195 Marriages; % both Catholic: 516; 90%
Hospitals: 1 Orphanages: 0 Homes for elderly, disabled: 0 Other charitable institutions: 5 Primary schools: 29 Secondary schools: 20 Colleges and universities: 0 Seminaries: 0	Permanent deacons: 1 Seminarians; % diocesan: 3; 100% Diocesan priests: 59 Religious priests; brothers: 16; 9 Women religious: 256 Catechists: 1 Lay missionaries: 0

Kazakhstan	Population: 16,170,000
Region: Western Asia	Fertility rate: 1.8
Oldest diocese: Karaganda (1991)	Infant mortality per 1,000 births: 58.8
Land mass: 2,717,300 km²	Life expectancy: 63
Primary language(s): Kazakh, Russian	Literacy rate: 97.78 (1989 est.)
Primary religion(s): Islam, Orthodox	GNI per capita (PPP): $ 4,790

Catholics; %: 180,000; 1%	Baptisms; % infants: 1,116; 35%
Dioceses; all territories: 1; 4	% infants baptized Catholic (est.): <1%
Parishes; pastoral centers: 37; 227	Confirmations: 201
Catholics/parish; /priest: 4,865; 3,051	Marriages; % both Catholic: 191; 87%

Hospitals: 0	Permanent deacons: 2
Orphanages: 6	Seminarians; % diocesan: 14; 86%
Homes for elderly, disabled: 4	Diocesan priests: 37
Other charitable institutions: 23	Religious priests; brothers: 22; 7
Primary schools: 0	Women religious: 62
Secondary schools: 1	Catechists: 50
Colleges and universities: 0	Lay missionaries: 11
Seminaries: 1	

Kenya	Population: 30,670,000
Region: East Africa	Fertility rate: 4.4
Oldest diocese: Nairobi (1860)	Infant mortality per 1,000 births: 69.6
Land mass: 580,367 km²	Life expectancy: 48
Primary language(s): English, Kiswahili	Literacy rate: 69 (1990 est.)
Primary religion(s): Protestant, Catholic, Indigenous religions	GNI per capita (PPP): $ 1,010

Catholics; %: 7,654,000; 25%	Baptisms; % infants: 258,302; 51%
Dioceses; all territories: 23; 25	% infants baptized Catholic (est.): 14%
Parishes; pastoral centers: 642; 4,625	Confirmations: 115,729
Catholics/parish; /priest: 11,922; 4,104	Marriages; % both Catholic: 27,548; 94%

Hospitals: 63	Permanent deacons: 2
Orphanages: 73	Seminarians; % diocesan: 1,504; 54%
Homes for elderly, disabled: 365	Diocesan priests: 989
Other charitable institutions: 2,040	Religious priests; brothers: 876; 690
Primary schools: 5,303	Women religious: 4,082
Secondary schools: 1,268	Catechists: 9,582
Colleges and universities: 0	Lay missionaries: 76
Seminaries: 7	

Kiribati Region: Oceania Oldest diocese: Tarawa and Nauru (1897) Land mass: 798 km² Primary language(s): English Primary religion(s): Catholic	Population: 83,000 Fertility rate: 4.5 Infant mortality per 1,000 births: 56.8 Life expectancy: 59 Literacy rate: na (na est.) GNI per capita (PPP): $ na
Catholics; %: 46,000; 55% Dioceses; all territories: 1; 1 Parishes; pastoral centers: 23; 24 Catholics/parish; /priest: 2,000; 1,769	Baptisms; % infants: 1,679; 93% % infants baptized Catholic (est.): 91% Confirmations: 376 Marriages; % both Catholic: 299; 82%
Hospitals: 0 Orphanages: 0 Homes for elderly, disabled: 1 Other charitable institutions: 4 Primary schools: 0 Secondary schools: 5 Colleges and universities: 0 Seminaries: 0	Permanent deacons: 1 Seminarians; % diocesan: 19; 68% Diocesan priests: 12 Religious priests; brothers: 14; 23 Women religious: 92 Catechists: 222 Lay missionaries: 10

Kuwait Region: Western Asia Oldest diocese: na (na) Land mass: 17,818 km² Primary language(s): Arabic, English Primary religion(s): Islam	Population: 2,190,000 Fertility rate: 4.2 Infant mortality per 1,000 births: 11.9 Life expectancy: 76 Literacy rate: 73 (1990 est.) GNI per capita (PPP): $ na
Catholics; %: 154,000; 7% Dioceses; all territories: 0; 2 Parishes; pastoral centers: 5; 5 Catholics/parish; /priest: 30,800; 17,111	Baptisms; % Infants: 571; 99% % infants baptized Catholic (est.): 1% Confirmations: 125 Marriages; % both Catholic: 100; 95%
Hospitals: 0 Orphanages: 0 Homes for elderly, disabled: 0 Other charitable institutions: 0 Primary schools: 2 Secondary schools: 2 Colleges and universities: 0 Seminaries: 0	Permanent deacons: 1 Seminarians; % diocesan: 0; na Diocesan priests: 3 Religious priests; brothers: 6; 0 Women religious: 13 Catechists: 0 Lay missionaries: 0

Kyrgyzstan Region: Western Asia Oldest diocese: na (na) Land mass: 198,500 km² Primary language(s): Kirghiz, Russian Primary religion(s): Islam	Population: 4,900,000 Fertility rate: 2.4 Infant mortality per 1,000 births: 75.9 Life expectancy: 64 Literacy rate: 97 (1989 est.) GNI per capita (PPP): $ 2,420
Catholics; %: 300; <1% Dioceses; all territories: 0; 1 Parishes; pastoral centers: 7; 9 Catholics/parish; /priest: 43; 50	Baptisms; % infants: 8; 75% % infants baptized Catholic (est.): <1% Confirmations: 11 Marriages; % both Catholic: 10; 70%
Hospitals: 0 Orphanages: 1 Homes for elderly, disabled: 1 Other charitable institutions: 0 Primary schools: 0 Secondary schools: 0 Colleges and universities: 0 Seminaries: 0	Permanent deacons: 0 Seminarians; % diocesan: 1; 0% Diocesan priests: 0 Religious priests; brothers: 6; 0 Women religious: 4 Catechists: 1 Lay missionaries: 0

Laos Region: Southeast Asia Oldest diocese: na (na) Land mass: 236,800 km² Primary language(s): Lao, French, English Primary religion(s): Buddhism	Population: 5,280,000 Fertility rate: 5.4 Infant mortality per 1,000 births: 96.8 Life expectancy: 53 Literacy rate: 45 (1988 est.) GNI per capita (PPP): $ 1,430
Catholics; %: 38,000; 1% Dioceses; all territories: 0; 4 Parishes; pastoral centers: 111; 140 Catholics/parish; /priest: 342; 2,923	Baptisms; % infants: 1,060; 72% % infants baptized Catholic (est.): <1% Confirmations: 683 Marriages; % both Catholic: 209; 77%
Hospitals: 0 Orphanages: 0 Homes for elderly, disabled: 0 Other charitable institutions: 0 Primary schools: 0 Secondary schools: 0 Colleges and universities: 0 Seminaries: 1	Permanent deacons: 0 Seminarians; % diocesan: 20; 100% Diocesan priests: 12 Religious priests; brothers: 1; 0 Women religious: 149 Catechists: 278 Lay missionaries: 0

Latvia Region: Eastern Europe Oldest diocese: Riga (1918) Land mass: 63,700 km² Primary language(s): Lettish Primary religion(s): Lutheran	Population: 2,430,000 Fertility rate: 1.2 Infant mortality per 1,000 births: 16.2 Life expectancy: 68 Literacy rate: 99.45 (1989 est.) GNI per capita (PPP): $ 6,220
Catholics; %: 408,000; 17% Dioceses; all territories: 4; 4 Parishes; pastoral centers: 243; 264 Catholics/parish; /priest: 1,679; 3,517	Baptisms; % infants: 5,894; 66% % infants baptized Catholic (est.): 21% Confirmations: 3,978 Marriages; % both Catholic: 1,379; 78%
Hospitals: 0 Orphanages: 1 Homes for elderly, disabled: 1 Other charitable institutions: 2 Primary schools: 5 Secondary schools: 2 Colleges and universities: 0 Seminaries: 1	Permanent deacons: 1 Seminarians; % diocesan: 52; 98% Diocesan priests: 95 Religious priests; brothers: 21; 0 Women religious: 86 Catechists: 284 Lay missionaries: 0

Lebanon Region: Western Asia Oldest diocese: Beirut - Maronite Rite (1577) Land mass: 10,400 km² Primary language(s): Arabic Primary religion(s): Islam	Population: 3,500,000 Fertility rate: 2.5 Infant mortality per 1,000 births: 30.4 Life expectancy: 71 Literacy rate: 80.1 (1990 est.) GNI per capita (PPP): $ na
Catholics; %: 1,819,000; 52% Dioceses; all territories: 23; 24 Parishes; pastoral centers: 1,029; 1,041 Catholics/parish; /priest: 1,768; 1,328	Baptisms; % infants: 11,975; 99% % infants baptized Catholic (est.): 20% Confirmations: 11,104 Marriages; % both Catholic: 6,539; 83%
Hospitals: 66 Orphanages: 49 Homes for elderly, disabled: 41 Other charitable institutions: 288 Primary schools: 335 Secondary schools: 209 Colleges and universities: 3 Seminaries: 9	Permanent deacons: 4 Seminarians; % diocesan: 497; 58% Diocesan priests: 730 Religious priests; brothers: 640; 210 Women religious: 2,625 Catechists: 585 Lay missionaries: 0

Lesotho Region: Southern Africa Oldest diocese: Maseru (1894) Land mass: 30,355 km² Primary language(s): Sesotho, English Primary religion(s): Protestant	Population: 2,040,000 Fertility rate: 4.3 Infant mortality per 1,000 births: 83.3 Life expectancy: 52 Literacy rate: 56.27 (1966 est.) GNI per capita (PPP): $ 2,350
Catholics; %: 894,000; 44% Dioceses; all territories: 4; 4 Parishes; pastoral centers: 81; 445 Catholics/parish; /priest: 11,037; 6,123	Baptisms; % infants: 24,914; 84% % infants baptized Catholic (est.): 25% Confirmations: 16,642 Marriages; % both Catholic: 2,562; 71%
Hospitals: 5 Orphanages: 0 Homes for elderly, disabled: 2 Other charitable institutions: 96 Primary schools: 505 Secondary schools: 82 Colleges and universities: 0 Seminaries: 1	Permanent deacons: 0 Seminarians; % diocesan: 91; 46% Diocesan priests: 61 Religious priests; brothers: 85; 41 Women religious: 676 Catechists: 1,627 Lay missionaries: 0

Liberia Region: West Africa Oldest diocese: Monrovia (1903) Land mass: 111,369 km² Primary language(s): English Primary religion(s): Protestant, Indigenous religions	Population: 2,910,000 Fertility rate: 6.6 Infant mortality per 1,000 births: 136.9 Life expectancy: 51 Literacy rate: 39.5 (1990 est.) GNI per capita (PPP): $ na
Catholics; %: 142,000; 5% Dioceses; all territories: 3; 3 Parishes; pastoral centers: 48; 49 Catholics/parish; /priest: 2,958; 2,731	Baptisms; % infants: 10,205; 50% % infants baptized Catholic (est.): 5% Confirmations: 5,518 Marriages; % both Catholic: 282; 71%
Hospitals: 4 Orphanages: 1 Homes for elderly, disabled: 0 Other charitable institutions: 27 Primary schools: 76 Secondary schools: 24 Colleges and universities: 0 Seminaries: 1	Permanent deacons: 3 Seminarians; % diocesan: 31; 90% Diocesan priests: 31 Religious priests; brothers: 21; 18 Women religious: 48 Catechists: 433 Lay missionaries: 4

Libya **Region: North Africa** Oldest diocese: na (na) Land mass: 1,759,540 km² Primary language(s): Arabic Primary religion(s): Islam	Population: 5,290,000 Fertility rate: 3.9 Infant mortality per 1,000 births: 31.4 Life expectancy: 75 Literacy rate: 63.8 (1990 est.) GNI per capita (PPP): $ na
Catholics; %: 77,000; 1% Dioceses; all territories: 0; 4 Parishes; pastoral centers: 6; 30 Catholics/parish; /priest: 12,833; 5,500	Baptisms; % infants: 112; 57% % infants baptized Catholic (est.): <1% Confirmations: 121 Marriages; % both Catholic: 20; 80%
Hospitals: 0 Orphanages: 0 Homes for elderly, disabled: 0 Other charitable institutions: 4 Primary schools: 0 Secondary schools: Colleges and universities: 0 Seminaries: 0	Permanent deacons: 0 Seminarians; % diocesan: 2; 100% Diocesan priests: 4 Religious priests; brothers: 10; 0 Women religious: 62 Catechists: 71 Lay missionaries: 2

Liechtenstein **Region: Northwestern Europe** Oldest diocese: Vaduz (1997) Land mass: 160 km² Primary language(s): German Primary religion(s): Catholic	Population: 32,000 Fertility rate: 1.4 Infant mortality per 1,000 births: 5.3 Life expectancy: 78 Literacy rate: 99.69 (1981 est.) GNI per capita (PPP): $ na
Catholics; %: 25,000; 78% Dioceses; all territories: 1; 1 Parishes; pastoral centers: 10; 12 Catholics/parish; /priest: 2,500; 833	Baptisms; % infants: 322; 99% % infants baptized Catholic (est.): 82% Confirmations: 345 Marriages; % both Catholic: 92; 72%
Hospitals: 0 Orphanages: 0 Homes for elderly, disabled: 0 Other charitable institutions: 0 Primary schools: 0 Secondary schools: 0 Colleges and universities: 0 Seminaries: 0	Permanent deacons: 1 Seminarians; % diocesan: 14; 100% Diocesan priests: 19 Religious priests; brothers: 11; 0 Women religious: 69 Catechists: 25 Lay missionaries: 0

Lithuania Region: Eastern Europe Oldest diocese: Kaunas (1417) Land mass: 65,200 km² Primary language(s): Lithuanian Primary religion(s): Catholic	Population: 3,690,000 Fertility rate: 1.3 Infant mortality per 1,000 births: 14.7 Life expectancy: 69 Literacy rate: 98.4 (1989 est.) GNI per capita (PPP): $ 6,490
Catholics; %: 2,828,000; 77% Dioceses; all territories: 7; 8 Parishes; pastoral centers: 676; 824 Catholics/parish; /priest: 4,183; 3,654	Baptisms; % infants: 32,072; 91% % infants baptized Catholic (est.): 83% Confirmations: 25,645 Marriages; % both Catholic: 10,579; 95%
Hospitals: 3 Orphanages: 15 Homes for elderly, disabled: 24 Other charitable institutions: 113 Primary schools: 171 Secondary schools: 320 Colleges and universities: 0 Seminaries: 4	Permanent deacons: 3 Seminarians; % diocesan: 247; 93% Diocesan priests: 670 Religious priests; brothers: 104; 28 Women religious: 743 Catechists: 2,077 Lay missionaries: 0

Luxembourg Region: Northwestern Europe Oldest diocese: Luxembourg, Luxemburg (1840) Land mass: 2,586 km² Primary language(s): German, French Primary religion(s): Catholic	Population: 436,000 Fertility rate: 1.7 Infant mortality per 1,000 births: 5.0 Life expectancy: 77 Literacy rate: 100 (1980 est.) GNI per capita (PPP): $ 41,230
Catholics; %: 378,000; 87% Dioceses; all territories: 1; 1 Parishes; pastoral centers: 275; 275 Catholics/parish; /priest: 1,375; 1,355	Baptisms; % infants: 3,185; 100% % infants baptized Catholic (est.): 69% Confirmations: 4,168 Marriages; % both Catholic: 676; 91%
Hospitals: 7 Orphanages: 4 Homes for elderly, disabled: 24 Other charitable institutions: 8 Primary schools: 1 Secondary schools: 5 Colleges and universities: 0 Seminaries: 2	Permanent deacons: 7 Seminarians; % diocesan: 4; 50% Diocesan priests: 207 Religious priests; brothers: 72; 20 Women religious: 650 Catechists: 460 Lay missionaries: 0

Macedonia Region: Eastern Europe Oldest diocese: Skopje (1924) Land mass: 40,887 km² Primary language(s): Macedonian, Albanian Primary religion(s): Orthodox	Population: 2,030,000 Fertility rate: 1.9 Infant mortality per 1,000 births: 14.4 Life expectancy: 73 Literacy rate: na (na est.) GNI per capita (PPP): $ 4,590
Catholics; %: 10,000; <1% Dioceses; all territories: 1; 2 Parishes; pastoral centers: 7; 8 Catholics/parish; /priest: 1,429; 769	Baptisms; % infants: 128; 88% % infants baptized Catholic (est.): <1% Confirmations: 82 Marriages; % both Catholic: 77; 86%
Hospitals: 0 Orphanages: 0 Homes for elderly, disabled: 1 Other charitable institutions: 4 Primary schools: 0 Secondary schools: 0 Colleges and universities: 0 Seminaries: 0	Permanent deacons: 0 Seminarians; % diocesan: 42; 100% Diocesan priests: 12 Religious priests; brothers: 1; 0 Women religious: 32 Catechists: 3 Lay missionaries: 0

Madagascar Region: Indian Ocean Oldest diocese: Antananarivo (1643) Land mass: 587,041 km² Primary language(s): French, Malagasy Primary religion(s): Protestant, Indigenous religions	Population: 15,970,000 Fertility rate: 5.8 Infant mortality per 1,000 births: 87.0 Life expectancy: 55 Literacy rate: 80.2 (1990 est.) GNI per capita (PPP): $ 790
Catholics; %: 4,147,000; 26% Dioceses; all territories: 20; 20 Parishes; pastoral centers: 310; 7,547 Catholics/parish; /priest: 13,377; 3,733	Baptisms; % infants: 153,941; 77% % infants baptized Catholic (est.): 17% Confirmations: 55,116 Marriages; % both Catholic: 21,312; 86%
Hospitals: 9 Orphanages: 25 Homes for elderly, disabled: 18 Other charitable institutions: 324 Primary schools: 2,479 Secondary schools: 426 Colleges and universities: 0 Seminaries: 6	Permanent deacons: 0 Seminarians; % diocesan: 894; 52% Diocesan priests: 436 Religious priests; brothers: 675; 467 Women religious: 3,584 Catechists: 16,382 Lay missionaries: 30

Malawi **Region: East Africa** Oldest diocese: Lilongwe (1889) Land mass: 118,484 km² Primary language(s): **English, Chichewa** Primary religion(s): **Protestant**	Population: 11,310,000 Fertility rate: 6.4 Infant mortality per 1,000 births: 123.4 Life expectancy: 38 Literacy rate: 48.63 (1987 est.) GNI per capita (PPP): $ 570
Catholics; %: 2,680,000; 24% Dioceses; all territories: 7; 7 Parishes; pastoral centers: 150; 925 Catholics/parish; /priest: 17,867; 6,734	Baptisms; % infants: 112,491; 59% % infants baptized Catholic (est.): 23% Confirmations: 101,240 Marriages; % both Catholic: 17,899; 53%
Hospitals: 31 Orphanages: 82 Homes for elderly, disabled: 2 Other charitable institutions: 79 Primary schools: 1,146 Secondary schools: 49 Colleges and universities: 0 Seminaries: 4	Permanent deacons: 0 Seminarians; % diocesan: 256; 86% Diocesan priests: 269 Religious priests; brothers: 129; 82 Women religious: 725 Catechists: 7,174 Lay missionaries: 9

Malaysia **Region: Southeast Asia** Oldest diocese: Kuching (1855) Land mass: 329,749 km² Primary language(s): **Bahasa Melayu, English** Primary religion(s): **Islam, Buddhism**	Population: 23,260,000 Fertility rate: 3.2 Infant mortality per 1,000 births: 21.7 Life expectancy: 71 Literacy rate: 78.4 (1990 est.) GNI per capita (PPP): $ 7,640
Catholics; %: 752,000; 3% Dioceses; all territories: 8; 8 Parishes; pastoral centers: 140; 1,160 Catholics/parish; /priest: 5,371; 3,082	Baptisms; % infants: 24,098; 52% % infants baptized Catholic (est.): 2% Confirmations: 12,700 Marriages; % both Catholic: 5,331; 68%
Hospitals: 3 Orphanages: 2 Homes for elderly, disabled: 7 Other charitable institutions: 15 Primary schools: 191 Secondary schools: 95 Colleges and universities: 0 Seminaries: 3	Permanent deacons: 1 Seminarians; % diocesan: 60; 88% Diocesan priests: 188 Religious priests; brothers: 56; 68 Women religious: 540 Catechists: 2,841 Lay missionaries: 0

Maldives Region: South Asia Oldest diocese: na (na) Land mass: 298 km² Primary language(s): Maldivian Dhivehi, English Primary religion(s): Islam	Population: 290,000 Fertility rate: 5.8 Infant mortality per 1,000 births: 67.5 Life expectancy: 62 Literacy rate: 91.3 (1985 est.) GNI per capita (PPP): $ na
Catholics; %: na; na Dioceses; all territories: 0; 0 Parishes; pastoral centers: 0; 0 Catholics/parish; /priest: na; na	Baptisms; % infants: 0; na % infants baptized Catholic (est.): na% Confirmations: 0 Marriages; % both Catholic: 0; na
Hospitals: 0 Orphanages: 0 Homes for elderly, disabled: 0 Other charitable institutions: 0 Primary schools: 0 Secondary schools: 0 Colleges and universities: 0 Seminaries: 0	Permanent deacons: 0 Seminarians; % diocesan: 0; na Diocesan priests: 0 Religious priests; brothers: 0; 0 Women religious: 0 Catechists: 0 Lay missionaries: 0

Mali Region: West Africa Oldest diocese: Mopti (1942) Land mass: 1,240,192 km² Primary language(s): French Primary religion(s): Islam	Population: 11,350,000 Fertility rate: 7 Infant mortality per 1,000 births: 125.1 Life expectancy: 46 Literacy rate: 32 (1990 est.) GNI per capita (PPP): $ 740
Catholics; %: 211,000; 2% Dioceses; all territories: 6; 6 Parishes; pastoral centers: 38; 168 Catholics/parish; /priest: 5,553; 1,370	Baptisms; % infants: 4,041; 65% % infants baptized Catholic (est.): <1% Confirmations: 2,658 Marriages; % both Catholic: 496; 80%
Hospitals: 0 Orphanages: 7 Homes for elderly, disabled: 0 Other charitable institutions: 68 Primary schools: 51 Secondary schools: 13 Colleges and universities: 0 Seminaries: 1	Permanent deacons: 0 Seminarians; % diocesan: 27; 93% Diocesan priests: 74 Religious priests; brothers: 80; 22 Women religious: 264 Catechists: 958 Lay missionaries: 1

Malta	Population: 380,000
Region: Southwestern Europe	Fertility rate: 1.7
Oldest diocese: Gozo (1864)	Infant mortality per 1,000 births: 6.1
Land mass: 316 km²	Life expectancy: 78
Primary language(s): Maltese, English	Literacy rate: 87.98 (1985 est.)
Primary religion(s): Catholic	GNI per capita (PPP): $ na

Catholics; %: 364,000; 96%	Baptisms; % infants: 4,177; 100%
Dioceses; all territories: 2; 2	% infants baptized Catholic (est.): 99%
Parishes; pastoral centers: 79; 82	Confirmations: 5,733
Catholics/parish; /priest: 4,608; 391	Marriages; % both Catholic: 1,887; 98%

Hospitals: 0	Permanent deacons: 0
Orphanages: 13	Seminarians; % diocesan: 97; 51%
Homes for elderly, disabled: 21	Diocesan priests: 496
Other charitable institutions: 24	Religious priests; brothers: 435; 77
Primary schools: 32	Women religious: 1,248
Secondary schools: 22	Catechists: 1,215
Colleges and universities: 1	Lay missionaries: 0
Seminaries: 5	

Marshall Islands	Population: 51,000
Region: Oceania	Fertility rate: 6.6
Oldest diocese: na (na)	Infant mortality per 1,000 births: 42.2
Land mass: 181 km²	Life expectancy: 65
Primary language(s): English	Literacy rate: 90.84 (1980 est.)
Primary religion(s): Protestant	GNI per capita (PPP): $ na

Catholics; %: 5,000; 10%	Baptisms; % infants: 537; 28%
Dioceses; all territories: 0; 1	% infants baptized Catholic (est.): 2%
Parishes; pastoral centers: 4; 4	Confirmations: 36
Catholics/parish; /priest: 1,250; 833	Marriages; % both Catholic: 29; 21%

Hospitals: 0	Permanent deacons: 2
Orphanages: 0	Seminarians; % diocesan: 1; 0%
Homes for elderly, disabled: 0	Diocesan priests: 0
Other charitable institutions: 0	Religious priests; brothers: 6; 0
Primary schools: 5	Women religious: 17
Secondary schools: 2	Catechists: 35
Colleges and universities: 0	Lay missionaries: 0
Seminaries: 0	

Martinique (France) Region: Caribbean Oldest diocese: Fort-de-France (1850) Land mass: 1,102 km² Primary language(s): French Primary religion(s): Catholic	Population: 381,000 Fertility rate: 1.8 Infant mortality per 1,000 births: 8.2 Life expectancy: 78 Literacy rate: 102.33 (1983 est.) GNI per capita (PPP): $ na
Catholics; %: 298,000; 78% Dioceses; all territories: 1; 1 Parishes; pastoral centers: 47; 49 Catholics/parish; /priest: 6,340; 4,730	Baptisms; % infants: 4,403; 100% % infants baptized Catholic (est.): 62% Confirmations: 1,610 Marriages; % both Catholic: 972; 100%
Hospitals: 0 Orphanages: 2 Homes for elderly, disabled: 2 Other charitable institutions: 18 Primary schools: 8 Secondary schools: 4 Colleges and universities: 0 Seminaries: 0	Permanent deacons: 0 Seminarians; % diocesan: 19; 100% Diocesan priests: 38 Religious priests; brothers: 25; 11 Women religious: 229 Catechists: 2,207 Lay missionaries: 0

Mauritania Region: West Africa Oldest diocese: Nouakchott (1965) Land mass: 1,025,520 km² Primary language(s): Arabic, Wolof Primary religion(s): Islam	Population: 2,670,000 Fertility rate: 6 Infant mortality per 1,000 births: 79.6 Life expectancy: 50 Literacy rate: 34 (1990 est.) GNI per capita (PPP): $ 1,550
Catholics; %: 5,000; <1% Dioceses; all territories: 1; 1 Parishes; pastoral centers: 6; 7 Catholics/parish; /priest: 833; 500	Baptisms; % infants: 34; 65% % infants baptized Catholic (est.): <1% Confirmations: 20 Marriages; % both Catholic: 3; 100%
Hospitals: 0 Orphanages: 0 Homes for elderly, disabled: 0 Other charitable institutions: 0 Primary schools: 0 Secondary schools: 0 Colleges and universities: 0 Seminaries: 0	Permanent deacons: 0 Seminarians; % diocesan: 0; na Diocesan priests: 1 Religious priests; brothers: 9; 0 Women religious: 32 Catechists: 10 Lay missionaries: 5

Mauritius Region: Indian Ocean Oldest diocese: Port-Louis (1847) Land mass: 1,865 km² Primary language(s): English Primary religion(s): Hinduism	Population: 1,180,000 Fertility rate: 2 Infant mortality per 1,000 births: 18.4 Life expectancy: 71 Literacy rate: 80.84 (1990 est.) GNI per capita (PPP): $ 8,950
Catholics; %: 288,000; 24% Dioceses; all territories: 1; 1 Parishes; pastoral centers: 52; 52 Catholics/parish; /priest: 5,538; 2,939	Baptisms; % infants: 4,236; 94% % infants baptized Catholic (est.): 22% Confirmations: 4,635 Marriages; % both Catholic: 1,467; 88%
Hospitals: 2 Orphanages: 2 Homes for elderly, disabled: 9 Other charitable institutions: 21 Primary schools: 51 Secondary schools: 28 Colleges and universities: 0 Seminaries: 0	Permanent deacons: 0 Seminarians; % diocesan: 11; 64% Diocesan priests: 59 Religious priests; brothers: 39; 30 Women religious: 249 Catechists: 807 Lay missionaries: 0

Mexico Region: Mesoamerica Oldest diocese: Puebla de los Angeles, Puebla (1525) Land mass: 1,958,201 km² Primary language(s): Spanish Primary religion(s): Catholic	Population: 97,020,000 Fertility rate: 2.8 Infant mortality per 1,000 births: 27.2 Life expectancy: 71 Literacy rate: 87.39 (1990 est.) GNI per capita (PPP): $ 8,070
Catholics; %: 89,664,000; 92% Dioceses; all territories: 80; 85 Parishes; pastoral centers: 5,784; 9,515 Catholics/parish; /priest: 15,502; 6,382	Baptisms; % infants: 2,002,515; 94% % infants baptized Catholic (est.): 78% Confirmations: 990,724 Marriages; % both Catholic: 396,019; 99%
Hospitals: 262 Orphanages: 209 Homes for elderly, disabled: 228 Other charitable institutions: 3,054 Primary schools: 2,544 Secondary schools: 1,290 Colleges and universities: 7 Seminaries: 94	Permanent deacons: 670 Seminarians; % diocesan: 7,059; 74% Diocesan priests: 10,421 Religious priests; brothers: 3,628; 1,270 Women religious: 29,050 Catechists: 171,719 Lay missionaries: 2,560

Micronesia Region: Oceania Oldest diocese: Caroline (1993) Land mass: 784 km² Primary language(s): English Primary religion(s): Catholic, Protestant	Population: 117,000 Fertility rate: 4.6 Infant mortality per 1,000 births: 34.0 Life expectancy: 68 Literacy rate: 84.78 (1980 est.) GNI per capita (PPP): $ na
Catholics; %: 62,000; 53% Dioceses; all territories: 1; 1 Parishes; pastoral centers: 23; 30 Catholics/parish; /priest: 2,696; 2,696	Baptisms; % infants: 1,920; 89% % infants baptized Catholic (est.): 35% Confirmations: 613 Marriages; % both Catholic: 454; 83%
Hospitals: 0 Orphanages: 0 Homes for elderly, disabled: 0 Other charitable institutions: 0 Primary schools: 4 Secondary schools: 4 Colleges and universities: 0 Seminaries: 0	Permanent deacons: 39 Seminarians; % diocesan: 8; 62% Diocesan priests: 11 Religious priests; brothers: 12; 1 Women religious: 47 Catechists: 113 Lay missionaries: 11

Moldova Region: Eastern Europe Oldest diocese: Tiraspol (1848) Land mass: 33,700 km² Primary language(s): Moldovan Primary religion(s): Orthodox	Population: 4,340,000 Fertility rate: 1.4 Infant mortality per 1,000 births: 43.5 Life expectancy: 64 Literacy rate: 96.73 (1989 est.) GNI per capita (PPP): $ 2,100
Catholics; %: 20,000; <1% Dioceses; all territories: 2; 2 Parishes; pastoral centers: 11; 11 Catholics/parish; /priest: 1,818; 1,333	Baptisms; % infants: 98; 67% % infants baptized Catholic (est.): <1% Confirmations: 35 Marriages; % both Catholic: 82; 44%
Hospitals: 0 Orphanages: 0 Homes for elderly, disabled: 2 Other charitable institutions: 3 Primary schools: 0 Secondary schools: 0 Colleges and universities: 0 Seminaries: 0	Permanent deacons: 1 Seminarians; % diocesan: 12; 67% Diocesan priests: 8 Religious priests; brothers: 7; 2 Women religious: 26 Catechists: 0 Lay missionaries: 0

Monaco Region: Northwestern Europe Oldest diocese: Monaco (1868) Land mass: 1 km² Primary language(s): French Primary religion(s): Catholic	Population: 32,000 Fertility rate: na Infant mortality per 1,000 births: 6.0 Life expectancy: 79 Literacy rate: 99 (na est.) GNI per capita (PPP): $ na
Catholics; %: 29,000; 91% Dioceses; all territories: 1; 1 Parishes; pastoral centers: 6; 8 Catholics/parish; /priest: 4,833; 1,318	Baptisms; % infants: 162; 96% % infants baptized Catholic (est.): 95% Confirmations: 220 Marriages; % both Catholic: 82; 88%
Hospitals: 0 Orphanages: 0 Homes for elderly, disabled: 0 Other charitable institutions: 0 Primary schools: 3 Secondary schools: 1 Colleges and universities: 0 Seminaries: 0	Permanent deacons: 1 Seminarians; % diocesan: 2; 100% Diocesan priests: 14 Religious priests; brothers: 8; 0 Women religious: 18 Catechists: 0 Lay missionaries: 0

Mongolia Region: East Asia Oldest diocese: na (na) Land mass: 1,565,000 km² Primary language(s): Khalkha Mongol Primary religion(s): Buddhism	Population: 2,530,000 Fertility rate: 2.2 Infant mortality per 1,000 births: 56.7 Life expectancy: 64 Literacy rate: 97.02 (1989 est.) GNI per capita (PPP): $ 1,610
Catholics; %: 100; <1% Dioceses; all territories: 0; 1 Parishes; pastoral centers: 1; 1 Catholics/parish; /priest: 100; 14	Baptisms; % infants: 8; 12% % infants baptized Catholic (est.): <1% Confirmations: 0 Marriages; % both Catholic: 0; na
Hospitals: 0 Orphanages: 0 Homes for elderly, disabled: 1 Other charitable institutions: 0 Primary schools: 4 Secondary schools: 0 Colleges and universities: 0 Seminaries: 0	Permanent deacons: 0 Seminarians; % diocesan: 3; 0% Diocesan priests: 2 Religious priests; brothers: 5; 1 Women religious: 14 Catechists: 0 Lay missionaries: 0

Montserrat (United Kingdom) Region: Caribbean Oldest diocese: na (na) Land mass: 98 km² Primary language(s): English Primary religion(s): Protestant	Population: 4,000 Fertility rate: na Infant mortality per 1,000 births: 8.7 Life expectancy: 78 Literacy rate: 96.6 (1970 est.) GNI per capita (PPP): $ na
Catholics; %: 1,400; 13% Dioceses; all territories: 0; 0 Parishes; pastoral centers: 1; 1 Catholics/parish; /priest: 0; 0	Baptisms; % infants: 20; 100% % infants baptized Catholic (est.): 5% Confirmations: 4 Marriages; % both Catholic: 3; 67%
Hospitals: 1 Orphanages: 0 Homes for elderly, disabled: 0 Other charitable institutions: 1 Primary schools: 1 Secondary schools: 0 Colleges and universities: 0 Seminaries: 0	Permanent deacons: 0 Seminarians; % diocesan: 0; na Diocesan priests: 0 Religious priests; brothers: 1; 0 Women religious: 0 Catechists: 4 Lay missionaries: 0

Morocco Region: North Africa Oldest diocese: Tanger (1630) Land mass: 446,550 km² Primary language(s): Arabic, French Primary religion(s): Islam	Population: 28,710,000 Fertility rate: 3.4 Infant mortality per 1,000 births: 51.6 Life expectancy: 69 Literacy rate: 49.5 (1990 est.) GNI per capita (PPP): $ 3,320
Catholics; %: 24,000; <1% Dioceses; all territories: 2; 2 Parishes; pastoral centers: 35; 41 Catholics/parish; /priest: 686; 387	Baptisms; % infants: 49; 84% % infants baptized Catholic (est.): <1% Confirmations: 24 Marriages; % both Catholic: 18; 89%
Hospitals: 1 Orphanages: 1 Homes for elderly, disabled: 2 Other charitable institutions: 29 Primary schools: 27 Secondary schools: 22 Colleges and universities: 0 Seminaries: 0	Permanent deacons: 1 Seminarians; % diocesan: 0; na Diocesan priests: 19 Religious priests; brothers: 43; 16 Women religious: 270 Catechists: 11 Lay missionaries: 8

Mozambique
Region: Southern Africa
Oldest diocese: Maputo (1940)
Land mass: 801,590 km²
Primary language(s): Portuguese
Primary religion(s): Protestant,
Indigenous religions

Population: 17,690,000
Fertility rate: 5.6
Infant mortality per 1,000 births: 140.4
Life expectancy: 39
Literacy rate: 32.9 (1990 est.)
GNI per capita (PPP): $ 810

Catholics; %: 3,737,000; 21%
Dioceses; all territories: 12; 12
Parishes; pastoral centers: 271; 3,085
Catholics/parish; /priest: 13,790; 8,360

Baptisms; % infants: 131,957; 48%
% infants baptized Catholic (est.): 6%
Confirmations: 42,406
Marriages; % both Catholic: 22,216; 98%

Hospitals: 16
Orphanages: 21
Homes for elderly, disabled: 13
Other charitable institutions: 285
Primary schools: 281
Secondary schools: 32
Colleges and universities: 0
Seminaries: 4

Permanent deacons: 0
Seminarians; % diocesan: 312; 70%
Diocesan priests: 139
Religious priests; brothers: 308; 84
Women religious: 988
Catechists: 64,269
Lay missionaries: 64

Myanmar
Region: Southeast Asia
Oldest diocese: Mandalay (1866)
Land mass: 676,552 km²
Primary language(s): Burmese
Primary religion(s): Buddhism

Population: 47,750,000
Fertility rate: 3.3
Infant mortality per 1,000 births: 77.0
Life expectancy: 55
Literacy rate: 80.6 (1990 est.)
GNI per capita (PPP): $ na

Catholics; %: 600,000; 1%
Dioceses; all territories: 12; 12
Parishes; pastoral centers: 272; 306
Catholics/parish; /priest: 2,206; 1,242

Baptisms; % infants: 22,518; 70%
% infants baptized Catholic (est.): 1%
Confirmations: 14,214
Marriages; % both Catholic: 5,338; 86%

Hospitals: 0
Orphanages: 148
Homes for elderly, disabled: 8
Other charitable institutions: 263
Primary schools: 94
Secondary schools: 4
Colleges and universities: 0
Seminaries: 3

Permanent deacons: 0
Seminarians; % diocesan: 302; 95%
Diocesan priests: 461
Religious priests; brothers: 22; 100
Women religious: 1,294
Catechists: 2,840
Lay missionaries: 0

Namibia **Region: Southern Africa** Oldest diocese: **Windhoek (1892)** Land mass: **824,292 km²** Primary language(s): **English, Afrikaans** Primary religion(s): **Lutheran**	Population: 1,820,000 Fertility rate: 5 Infant mortality per 1,000 births: 69.6 Life expectancy: 44 Literacy rate: 38.4 (1960 est.) GNI per capita (PPP): $ 5,580
Catholics; %: 307,000; 17% Dioceses; all territories: 2; 3 Parishes; pastoral centers: 92; 182 Catholics/parish; /priest: 3,337; 3,987	Baptisms; % infants: 5,494; 82% % infants baptized Catholic (est.): <1% Confirmations: 3,294 Marriages; % both Catholic: 723; 50%
Hospitals: 7 Orphanages: 2 Homes for elderly, disabled: 2 Other charitable institutions: 23 Primary schools: 19 Secondary schools: 7 Colleges and universities: 0 Seminaries: 1	Permanent deacons: 42 Seminarians; % diocesan: 26; 54% Diocesan priests: 17 Religious priests; brothers: 60; 25 Women religious: 266 Catechists: 1,251 Lay missionaries: 6

Nauru **Region: Oceania** Oldest diocese: **Tarawa and Nauru (1982)** Land mass: **21 km²** Primary language(s): **Nauruan, English** Primary religion(s): **Protestant**	Population: 8,000 Fertility rate: 3.7 Infant mortality per 1,000 births: 11.1 Life expectancy: 60 Literacy rate: 38 (1960 est.) GNI per capita (PPP): $ na
Catholics; %: 3,000; 38% Dioceses; all territories: 1; 0 Parishes; pastoral centers: 1; 1 Catholics/parish; /priest: 3,000; 3,000	Baptisms; % infants: 95; 85% % Infants baptized Catholic (est.): 28% Confirmations: 0 Marriages; % both Catholic: 38; 26%
Hospitals: 0 Orphanages: 0 Homes for elderly, disabled: 0 Other charitable institutions: 0 Primary schools: 1 Secondary schools: 1 Colleges and universities: 0 Seminaries: 0	Permanent deacons: 2 Seminarians; % diocesan: 0; na Diocesan priests: 0 Religious priests; brothers: 1; 0 Women religious: 3 Catechists: 0 Lay missionaries: 0

Nepal	Population: 22,900,000
Region: South Asia	Fertility rate: 4.8
Oldest diocese: na (na)	Infant mortality per 1,000 births: 77.8
Land mass: 140,797 km²	Life expectancy: 57
Primary language(s): Nepali	Literacy rate: 38.16 (1993 est.)
Primary religion(s): Hinduism	GNI per capita (PPP): $ 1,280
Catholics; %: 6,000; <1%	Baptisms; % infants: 143; 31%
Dioceses; all territories: 0; 1	% infants baptized Catholic (est.): <1%
Parishes; pastoral centers: 35; 35	Confirmations: 101
Catholics/parish; /priest: 171; 118	Marriages; % both Catholic: 29; 66%
Hospitals: 0	Permanent deacons: 0
Orphanages: 0	Seminarians; % diocesan: 31; 16%
Homes for elderly, disabled: 7	Diocesan priests: 11
Other charitable institutions: 10	Religious priests; brothers: 40; 1
Primary schools: 13	Women religious: 104
Secondary schools: 6	Catechists: 14
Colleges and universities: 0	Lay missionaries: 0
Seminaries: 0	

Netherlands	Population: 15,860,000
Region: Northwestern Europe	Fertility rate: 1.7
Oldest diocese: Utrecht (1559)	Infant mortality per 1,000 births: 4.5
Land mass: 40,844 km²	Life expectancy: 78
Primary language(s): Dutch	Literacy rate: 99 (1979 est.)
Primary religion(s): Catholic, Protestant	GNI per capita (PPP): $ 24,410
Catholics; %: 5,365,000; 34%	Baptisms; % infants: 44,536; 98%
Dioceses; all territories: 7; 8	% infants baptized Catholic (est.): 24%
Parishes; pastoral centers: 1,492; 1,543	Confirmations: 33,943
Catholics/parish; /priest: 3,596; 1,384	Marriages; % both Catholic: 11,695; 98%
Hospitals: 0	Permanent deacons: 214
Orphanages: 0	Seminarians; % diocesan: 205; 61%
Homes for elderly, disabled: 0	Diocesan priests: 1,588
Other charitable institutions: 0	Religious priests; brothers: 2,288; 1,464
Primary schools: 500	Women religious: 11,350
Secondary schools: 60	Catechists: 178
Colleges and universities: 2	Lay missionaries: 0
Seminaries: 4	

Netherlands Antilles (Netherlands) Region: Caribbean Oldest diocese: Willemstad (1842) Land mass: 800 km² Primary language(s): Dutch Primary religion(s): Catholic, Protestant	Population: 197,000 Fertility rate: 2.1 Infant mortality per 1,000 births: 12.2 Life expectancy: 74 Literacy rate: 93.8 (1981 est.) GNI per capita (PPP): $ na
Catholics; %: 152,000; 77% Dioceses; all territories: 1; 1 Parishes; pastoral centers: 28; 28 Catholics/parish; /priest: 5,429; 5,067	Baptisms; % infants: 1,496; 94% % infants baptized Catholic (est.): 105% Confirmations: 976 Marriages; % both Catholic: 219; 95%
Hospitals: 2 Orphanages: 3 Homes for elderly, disabled: 7 Other charitable institutions: 4 Primary schools: 58 Secondary schools: 27 Colleges and universities: 0 Seminaries: 0	Permanent deacons: 1 Seminarians; % diocesan: 2; 50% Diocesan priests: 13 Religious priests; brothers: 17; 8 Women religious: 55 Catechists: 13 Lay missionaries: 0

New Caledonia (France) Region: Oceania Oldest diocese: Noumea (1966) Land mass: 19,079 km² Primary language(s): French Primary religion(s): Catholic, Protestant	Population: 200,000 Fertility rate: 2.6 Infant mortality per 1,000 births: 8.8 Life expectancy: 72 Literacy rate: 91.47 (1976 est.) GNI per capita (PPP): $ 21,130
Catholics; %: 110,000; 55% Dioceses; all territories: 1; 1 Parishes; pastoral centers: 27; 158 Catholics/parish; /priest: 4,074; 1,930	Baptisms; % infants: 2,046; 97% % infants baptized Catholic (est.): 52% Confirmations: 1,061 Marriages; % both Catholic: 317; 100%
Hospitals: 0 Orphanages: 0 Homes for elderly, disabled: 1 Other charitable institutions: 1 Primary schools: 36 Secondary schools: 22 Colleges and universities: 0 Seminaries: 0	Permanent deacons: 3 Seminarians; % diocesan: 5; 60% Diocesan priests: 12 Religious priests; brothers: 45; 31 Women religious: 117 Catechists: 150 Lay missionaries: 0

New Zealand
Region: Oceania
Oldest diocese: Wellington (1848)
Land mass: 268,676 km²
Primary language(s): English
Primary religion(s): Anglican, Protestant

Population: 3,816,000
Fertility rate: 2
Infant mortality per 1,000 births: 6.4
Life expectancy: 78
Literacy rate: 99 (1980 est.)
GNI per capita (PPP): $ 17,630

Catholics; %: 457,000; 12%
Dioceses; all territories: 6; 7
Parishes; pastoral centers: 272; 283
Catholics/parish; /priest: 1,680; 825

Baptisms; % infants: 7,671; 87%
% infants baptized Catholic (est.): 12%
Confirmations: 5,577
Marriages; % both Catholic: 1,400; 36%

Hospitals: 16
Orphanages: 1
Homes for elderly, disabled: 22
Other charitable institutions: 29
Primary schools: 195
Secondary schools: 47
Colleges and universities: 0
Seminaries: 2

Permanent deacons: 2
Seminarians; % diocesan: 29; 72%
Diocesan priests: 339
Religious priests; brothers: 215; 184
Women religious: 1,096
Catechists: 472
Lay missionaries: 0

Nicaragua
Region: Mesoamerica
Oldest diocese: León (1534)
Land mass: 130,000 km²
Primary language(s): Spanish
Primary religion(s): Catholic

Population: 5,070,000
Fertility rate: 4.3
Infant mortality per 1,000 births: 35.9
Life expectancy: 68
Literacy rate: 57.37 (1971 est.)
GNI per capita (PPP): $ 2,060

Catholics; %: 4,518,000; 89%
Dioceses; all territories: 7; 8
Parishes; pastoral centers: 243; 742
Catholics/parish; /priest: 18,593; 10,809

Baptisms; % infants: 81,221; 94%
% infants baptized Catholic (est.): 40%
Confirmations: 29,963
Marriages; % both Catholic: 9,053; 99%

Hospitals: 6
Orphanages: 11
Homes for elderly, disabled: 10
Other charitable institutions: 128
Primary schools: 525
Secondary schools: 111
Colleges and universities: 1
Seminaries: 4

Permanent deacons: 30
Seminarians; % diocesan: 263; 89%
Diocesan priests: 247
Religious priests; brothers: 171; 99
Women religious: 977
Catechists: 11,625
Lay missionaries: 11

Niger **Region: West Africa** Oldest diocese: Niamey (1942) Land mass: 1,267,000 km² Primary language(s): French Primary religion(s): Islam	Population: 10,830,000 Fertility rate: 7.5 Infant mortality per 1,000 births: 126.2 Life expectancy: 41 Literacy rate: 28.4 (1990 est.) GNI per capita (PPP): $ 740
Catholics; %: 20,000; <1% Dioceses; all territories: 2; 2 Parishes; pastoral centers: 22; 22 Catholics/parish; /priest: 909; 417	Baptisms; % infants: 344; 54% % infants baptized Catholic (est.): <1% Confirmations: 232 Marriages; % both Catholic: 41; 76%
Hospitals: 0 Orphanages: 1 Homes for elderly, disabled: 0 Other charitable institutions: 13 Primary schools: 9 Secondary schools: 3 Colleges and universities: 0 Seminaries: 1	Permanent deacons: 0 Seminarians; % diocesan: 18; 78% Diocesan priests: 7 Religious priests; brothers: 41; 6 Women religious: 92 Catechists: 340 Lay missionaries: 6

Nigeria **Region: West Africa** Oldest diocese: Lagos (1860) Land mass: 923,768 km² Primary language(s): English, Hausa, Yoraba, Ibo Primary religion(s): Protestant, Islam	Population: 115,220,000 Fertility rate: 5.8 Infant mortality per 1,000 births: 74.9 Life expectancy: 52 Literacy rate: 50.7 (1990 est.) GNI per capita (PPP): $ 770
Catholics; %: 16,579,000; 14% Dioceses; all territories: 45; 48 Parishes; pastoral centers: 1,752; 12,202 Catholics/parish; /priest: 9,463; 4,609	Baptisms; % infants: 566,324; 67% % infants baptized Catholic (est.): 6% Confirmations: 203,629 Marriages; % both Catholic: 59,259; 95%
Hospitals: 153 Orphanages: 22 Homes for elderly, disabled: 28 Other charitable institutions: 1,046 Primary schools: 2,744 Secondary schools: 271 Colleges and universities: 0 Seminaries: 18	Permanent deacons: 5 Seminarians; % diocesan: 4,281; 81% Diocesan priests: 2,995 Religious priests; brothers: 602; 501 Women religious: 3,464 Catechists: 26,560 Lay missionaries: 267

Niue (New Zealand) Region: Oceania	Population: 2,000
Oldest diocese: na (na)	Fertility rate: na
Land mass: 260 km²	Infant mortality per 1,000 births: 5.9
Primary language(s): Polynesian, English	Life expectancy: 75
Primary religion(s): Protestant	Literacy rate: 95 (na est.)
	GNI per capita (PPP): $ na

Catholics; %: 100; 5%	Baptisms; % infants: 8; 25%
Dioceses; all territories: 0; 0	% infants baptized Catholic (est.): <1%
Parishes; pastoral centers: 3; 3	Confirmations: 10
Catholics/parish; /priest: 33; 100	Marriages; % both Catholic: 1; 100%

Hospitals: 0	Permanent deacons: 0
Orphanages: 0	Seminarians; % diocesan: 0; na
Homes for elderly, disabled: 0	Diocesan priests: 1
Other charitable institutions: 0	Religious priests; brothers: 0; 0
Primary schools: 0	Women religious: 1
Secondary schools: 0	Catechists: 3
Colleges and universities: 0	Lay missionaries: 0
Seminaries: 0	

North Korea Region: East Asia	Population: 22,270,000
Oldest diocese: na (na)	Fertility rate: 2.3
Land mass: 120,538 km²	Infant mortality per 1,000 births: 25.5
Primary language(s): Korean	Life expectancy: 70
Primary religion(s): Buddhism	Literacy rate: 99.9 (1979 est.)
	GNI per capita (PPP): $ na

Catholics; %: 55,000; <1%	Baptisms; % infants: na; na
Dioceses; all territories: 0; 0	% infants baptized Catholic (est.): na%
Parishes; pastoral centers: 0; 0	Confirmations: na
Catholics/parish; /priest: na; na	Marriages; % both Catholic: na; na

Hospitals: 0	Permanent deacons: na
Orphanages: 0	Seminarians; % diocesan: na; na
Homes for elderly, disabled: 0	Diocesan priests: na
Other charitable institutions: 0	Religious priests; brothers: na; na
Primary schools: 0	Women religious: na
Secondary schools: 0	Catechists: na
Colleges and universities: 0	Lay missionaries: na
Seminaries: 0	

Northern Mariana Islands (United States) Region: Oceania Oldest diocese: Chalan Kanoa (1984) Land mass: 476 km² Primary language(s): English, Chamorro, Carolinian Primary religion(s): Catholic	Population: 67,000 Fertility rate: na Infant mortality per 1,000 births: na Life expectancy: na Literacy rate: 97 (1980 est.) GNI per capita (PPP): $ na
Catholics; %: 53,000; 79% Dioceses; all territories: 1; 1 Parishes; pastoral centers: 11; 13 Catholics/parish; /priest: 4,818; 3,118	Baptisms; % infants: 1,134; 97% % infants baptized Catholic (est.): 37% Confirmations: 429 Marriages; % both Catholic: 53; 94%
Hospitals: 0 Orphanages: 0 Homes for elderly, disabled: 0 Other charitable institutions: 1 Primary schools: 3 Secondary schools: 1 Colleges and universities: 0 Seminaries: 0	Permanent deacons: 2 Seminarians; % diocesan: 4; 100% Diocesan priests: 11 Religious priests; brothers: 6; 0 Women religious: 34 Catechists: 106 Lay missionaries: 0

Norway Region: Northwestern Europe Oldest diocese: Oslo (1869) Land mass: 323,895 km' Primary language(s): Norwegian Primary religion(s): Lutheran	Population: 4,490,000 Fertility rate: 1.8 Infant mortality per 1,000 births: 4.0 Life expectancy: 79 Literacy rate: 99 (1976 est.) GNI per capita (PPP): $ 28,140
Catholics; %: 53,000; 1% Dioceses; all territories: 1; 3 Parishes; pastoral centers: 32; 35 Catholics/parish; /priest: 1,656; 768	Baptisms; % infants: 709; 96% % infants baptized Catholic (est.): 1% Confirmations: 392 Marriages; % both Catholic: 147; 51%
Hospitals: 0 Orphanages: 2 Homes for elderly, disabled: 2 Other charitable institutions: 0 Primary schools: 3 Secondary schools: 2 Colleges and universities: 0 Seminaries: 0	Permanent deacons: 3 Seminarians; % diocesan: 8; 50% Diocesan priests: 31 Religious priests; brothers: 38; 3 Women religious: 184 Catechists: 73 Lay missionaries: 2

Oman	Population: 2,540,000
Region: Western Asia	Fertility rate: 6.1
Oldest diocese: na (na)	Infant mortality per 1,000 births: 24.2
Land mass: 212,457 km²	Life expectancy: 71
Primary language(s): Arabic, English	Literacy rate: 80 (na est.)
Primary religion(s): Islam	GNI per capita (PPP): $ na

Catholics; %: 66,000; 3%	Baptisms; % infants: 198; 93%
Dioceses; all territories: 0; 0	% infants baptized Catholic (est.): <1%
Parishes; pastoral centers: 4; 30	Confirmations: 172
Catholics/parish; /priest: 16,500; 8,250	Marriages; % both Catholic: 15; 53%

Hospitals: 0	Permanent deacons: 0
Orphanages: 0	Seminarians; % diocesan: 0; na
Homes for elderly, disabled: 0	Diocesan priests: 1
Other charitable institutions: 0	Religious priests; brothers: 7; 0
Primary schools: 0	Women religious: 0
Secondary schools: 0	Catechists: 0
Colleges and universities: 0	Lay missionaries: 0
Seminaries: 0	

Pakistan	Population: 137,500,000
Region: South Asia	Fertility rate: 5.6
Oldest diocese: Lahore (1886)	Infant mortality per 1,000 births: 84.6
Land mass: 796,095 km²	Life expectancy: 61
Primary language(s): Punjabi, English	Literacy rate: 34.8 (1990 est.)
Primary religion(s): Islam	GNI per capita (PPP): $ 1,860

Catholics; %: 1,237,000; 1%	Baptisms; % infants: 19,679; 87%
Dioceses; all territories: 6; 7	% infants baptized Catholic (est.): <1%
Parishes; pastoral centers: 112; 276	Confirmations: 8,413
Catholics/parish; /priest: 11,045; 4,650	Marriages; % both Catholic: 5,173; 60%

Hospitals: 11	Permanent deacons: 3
Orphanages: 36	Seminarians; % diocesan: 150; 47%
Homes for elderly, disabled: 10	Diocesan priests: 136
Other charitable institutions: 73	Religious priests; brothers: 130; 51
Primary schools: 200	Women religious: 711
Secondary schools: 153	Catechists: 522
Colleges and universities: 0	Lay missionaries: 7
Seminaries: 6	

Palau	Population: 19,000
Region: Oceania	Fertility rate: 2.5
Oldest diocese: na (na)	Infant mortality per 1,000 births: 17.7
Land mass: 459 km²	Life expectancy: 68
Primary language(s): **English, Palauan**	Literacy rate: 85.9 (1980 est.)
Primary religion(s): **Protestant**	GNI per capita (PPP): $ na
Catholics; %: 8,000; 42%	Baptisms; % infants: 191; 46%
Dioceses; all territories: 0; 0	% infants baptized Catholic (est.): 34%
Parishes; pastoral centers: 3; 7	Confirmations: 44
Catholics/parish; /priest: 2,667; 1,600	Marriages; % both Catholic: 2; 0%
Hospitals: 0	Permanent deacons: 2
Orphanages: 0	Seminarians; % diocesan: 0; na
Homes for elderly, disabled: 0	Diocesan priests: 2
Other charitable institutions: 0	Religious priests; brothers: 3; 1
Primary schools: 1	Women religious: 6
Secondary schools: 1	Catechists: 1
Colleges and universities: 0	Lay missionaries: 0
Seminaries: 0	

Panama	Population: 2,860,000
Region: Mesoamerica	Fertility rate: 2.6
Oldest diocese: **Panama (1513)**	Infant mortality per 1,000 births: 21.6
Land mass: 77,082 km²	Life expectancy: 75
Primary language(s): **Spanish**	Literacy rate: 88.7 (1990 est.)
Primary religion(s): **Catholic**	GNI per capita (PPP): $ 5,450
Catholics; %: 2,434,000; 85%	Baptisms; % infants: 28,241; 91%
Dioceses; all territories: 6; 8	% infants baptized Catholic (est.): 43%
Parishes; pastoral centers: 176; 269	Confirmations: 12,212
Catholics/parish; /priest: 13,830; 6,209	Marriages; % both Catholic: 2,027; 99%
Hospitals: 1	Permanent deacons: 66
Orphanages: 71	Seminarians; % diocesan: 135; 87%
Homes for elderly, disabled: 6	Diocesan priests: 181
Other charitable institutions: 110	Religious priests; brothers: 211; 53
Primary schools: 38	Women religious: 566
Secondary schools: 40	Catechists: 2,130
Colleges and universities: 1	Lay missionaries: 516
Seminaries: 0	

Papua New Guinea Region: Oceania Oldest diocese: Port Moresby (1889) Land mass: 462,840 km² Primary language(s): English Primary religion(s): Catholic	Population: 4,810,000 Fertility rate: 4.8 Infant mortality per 1,000 births: 61.8 Life expectancy: 63 Literacy rate: 49.66 (1990 est.) GNI per capita (PPP): $ 2,260
Catholics; %: 1,630,000; 34% Dioceses; all territories: 18; 18 Parishes; pastoral centers: 342; 1,189 Catholics/parish; /priest: 4,766; 2,980	Baptisms; % infants: 34,542; 84% % infants baptized Catholic (est.): 27% Confirmations: 22,021 Marriages; % both Catholic: 4,664; 90%
Hospitals: 91 Orphanages: 1 Homes for elderly, disabled: 7 Other charitable institutions: 344 Primary schools: 1,029 Secondary schools: 84 Colleges and universities: 0 Seminaries: 5	Permanent deacons: 8 Seminarians; % diocesan: 348; 72% Diocesan priests: 175 Religious priests; brothers: 372; 254 Women religious: 851 Catechists: 2,970 Lay missionaries: 70

Paraguay Region: South America Oldest diocese: Asunción (1547) Land mass: 406,752 km² Primary language(s): Spanish Primary religion(s): Catholic	Population: 5,500,000 Fertility rate: 4.3 Infant mortality per 1,000 births: 32.0 Life expectancy: 73 Literacy rate: 90.1 (1990 est.) GNI per capita (PPP): $ 4,380
Catholics; %: 4,708,000; 86% Dioceses; all territories: 12; 15 Parishes; pastoral centers: 358; 1,154 Catholics/parish; /priest: 13,151; 6,013	Baptisms; % infants: 88,927; 93% % infants baptized Catholic (est.): 61% Confirmations: 55,917 Marriages; % both Catholic: 15,467; 99%
Hospitals: 4 Orphanages: 12 Homes for elderly, disabled: 13 Other charitable institutions: 175 Primary schools: 199 Secondary schools: 121 Colleges and universities: 1 Seminaries: 7	Permanent deacons: 120 Seminarians; % diocesan: 363; 40% Diocesan priests: 355 Religious priests; brothers: 428; 118 Women religious: 2,132 Catechists: 54,359 Lay missionaries: 13

Peru **Region: South America** Oldest diocese: Cuzco (1536) Land mass: 1,285,216 km² Primary language(s): Spanish Primary religion(s): Catholic	Population: 25,660,000 Fertility rate: 2.9 Infant mortality per 1,000 births: 42.0 Life expectancy: 70 Literacy rate: 85.1 (1990 est.) GNI per capita (PPP): $ 4,480
Catholics; %: 23,020,000; 90% Dioceses; all territories: 25; 45 Parishes; pastoral centers: 1,426; 4,435 Catholics/parish; /priest: 16,143; 8,251	Baptisms; % infants: 351,904; 74% % infants baptized Catholic (est.): 38% Confirmations: 196,134 Marriages; % both Catholic: 47,391; 99%
Hospitals: 89 Orphanages: 181 Homes for elderly, disabled: 55 Other charitable institutions: 1,611 Primary schools: 839 Secondary schools: 635 Colleges and universities: 1 Seminaries: 49	Permanent deacons: 51 Seminarians; % diocesan: 1,700; 72% Diocesan priests: 1,401 Religious priests; brothers: 1,389; 639 Women religious: 5,537 Catechists: 42,489 Lay missionaries: 2,983

Philippines **Region: Southeast Asia** Oldest diocese: Manila (1579) Land mass: 300,000 km² Primary language(s): Tagalog, English Primary religion(s): Catholic	Population: 76,320,000 Fertility rate: 3.5 Infant mortality per 1,000 births: 30.6 Life expectancy: 67 Literacy rate: 93.54 (1990 est.) GNI per capita (PPP): $ 3,990
Catholics; %: 63,025,000; 83% Dioceses; all territories: 66; 80 Parishes; pastoral centers: 2,795; 5,478 Catholics/parish; /priest: 22,549; 8,380	Baptisms; % infants: 1,642,371; 94% % infants baptized Catholic (est.): 73% Confirmations: 636,490 Marriages; % both Catholic: 406,221; 98%
Hospitals: 58 Orphanages: 90 Homes for elderly, disabled: 46 Other charitable institutions: 649 Primary schools: 599 Secondary schools: 1,043 Colleges and universities: 14 Seminaries: 109	Permanent deacons: 17 Seminarians; % diocesan: 6,211; 64% Diocesan priests: 5,013 Religious priests; brothers: 2,508; 664 Women religious: 10,798 Catechists: 95,566 Lay missionaries: 308

Poland	Population: 38,610,000
Region: Eastern Europe	Fertility rate: 1.4
Oldest diocese: Wloclawek (996)	Infant mortality per 1,000 births: 9.7
Land mass: 312,677 km²	Life expectancy: 73
Primary language(s): Polish	Literacy rate: 98.35 (1978 est.)
Primary religion(s): Catholic	GNI per capita (PPP): $ 8,390

Catholics; %: 37,002,000; 96%	Baptisms; % infants: 379,371; 99%
Dioceses; all territories: 41; 43	% infants baptized Catholic (est.): 104%
Parishes; pastoral centers: 9,966; 10,779	Confirmations: 500,241
Catholics/parish; /priest: 3,713; 1,348	Marriages; % both Catholic: 175,044; 99%

Hospitals: 32	Permanent deacons: 13
Orphanages: 315	Seminarians; % diocesan: 6,789; 70%
Homes for elderly, disabled: 275	Diocesan priests: 21,280
Other charitable institutions: 3,269	Religious priests; brothers: 6,178; 1,297
Primary schools: 83	Women religious: 23,945
Secondary schools: 192	Catechists: 14,776
Colleges and universities: 4	Lay missionaries: 0
Seminaries: 83	

Polynesia (France)	Population: 238,000
Region: Oceania	Fertility rate: 2.6
Oldest diocese: na (na)	Infant mortality per 1,000 births: 9.5
Land mass: 4,000 km²	Life expectancy: 75
Primary language(s): French, Tahitian	Literacy rate: 97.8 (1977 est.)
Primary religion(s): Catholic, Protestant	GNI per capita (PPP): $ 22,200

Catholics; %: 91,000; 38%	Baptisms; % infants: 1,293; 86%
Dioceses; all territories: 2; 2	% infants baptized Catholic (est.): 21%
Parishes; pastoral centers: 91; 114	Confirmations: 1,275
Catholics/parish; /priest: 1,000; 2,459	Marriages; % both Catholic: 230; 78%

Hospitals: 0	Permanent deacons: 23
Orphanages: 2	Seminarians; % diocesan: 17; 71%
Homes for elderly, disabled: 0	Diocesan priests: 15
Other charitable institutions: 12	Religious priests; brothers: 22; 35
Primary schools: 11	Women religious: 57
Secondary schools: 11	Catechists: 527
Colleges and universities: 0	Lay missionaries: 0
Seminaries: 1	

Portugal Region: Southwestern Europe Oldest diocese: Viseu (572) Land mass: 92,389 km² Primary language(s): Portuguese Primary religion(s): Catholic	Population: 10,010,000 Fertility rate: 1.5 Infant mortality per 1,000 births: 6.2 Life expectancy: 75 Literacy rate: 84.73 (1991 est.) GNI per capita (PPP): $ 15,860
Catholics; %: 9,404,000; 94% Dioceses; all territories: 20; 21 Parishes; pastoral centers: 4,362; 6,721 Catholics/parish; /priest: 2,156; 2,219	Baptisms; % infants: 98,139; 94% % infants baptized Catholic (est.): 89% Confirmations: 55,263 Marriages; % both Catholic: 50,513; 98%
Hospitals: 29 Orphanages: 130 Homes for elderly, disabled: 652 Other charitable institutions: 912 Primary schools: 190 Secondary schools: 96 Colleges and universities: 1 Seminaries: 27	Permanent deacons: 125 Seminarians; % diocesan: 547; 68% Diocesan priests: 3,159 Religious priests; brothers: 1,078; 341 Women religious: 6,446 Catechists: 54,327 Lay missionaries: 0

Puerto Rico (United States) Region: Caribbean Oldest diocese: San Juan (1511) Land mass: 8,897 km² Primary language(s): English, Spanish Primary religion(s): Catholic	Population: 3,880,000 Fertility rate: 1.9 Infant mortality per 1,000 births: 10.0 Life expectancy: 75 Literacy rate: 89.1 (1980 est.) GNI per capita (PPP): $ na
Catholics; %: 3,045,000; 78% Dioceses; all territories: 5; 5 Parishes; pastoral centers: 354; 912 Catholics/parish; /priest: 8,602; 4,001	Baptisms; % infants: 34,516; 93% % infants baptized Catholic (est.): 54% Confirmations: 20,053 Marriages; % both Catholic: 5,170; 93%
Hospitals: 3 Orphanages: 6 Homes for elderly, disabled: 15 Other charitable institutions: 67 Primary schools: 129 Secondary schools: 106 Colleges and universities: 2 Seminaries: 10	Permanent deacons: 418 Seminarians; % diocesan: 96; 56% Diocesan priests: 374 Religious priests; brothers: 387; 69 Women religious: 1,152 Catechists: 9,944 Lay missionaries: 164

Qatar **Region: Western Asia** Oldest diocese: na (na) Land mass: 11,000 km² Primary language(s): Arabic, English Primary religion(s): Islam	Population: 550,000 Fertility rate: 3.9 Infant mortality per 1,000 births: 23.0 Life expectancy: 72 Literacy rate: 75.7 (1986 est.) GNI per capita (PPP): $ na
Catholics; %: 65,000; 12% Dioceses; all territories: 0; 0 Parishes; pastoral centers: 1; 7 Catholics/parish; /priest: 65,000; 65,000	Baptisms; % infants: 119; 100% % infants baptized Catholic (est.): 1% Confirmations: 77 Marriages; % both Catholic: 8; 88%
Hospitals: 0 Orphanages: 0 Homes for elderly, disabled: 0 Other charitable institutions: 0 Primary schools: 0 Secondary schools: 0 Colleges and universities: 0 Seminaries: 0	Permanent deacons: 2 Seminarians; % diocesan: 0; na Diocesan priests: 1 Religious priests; brothers: 0; 0 Women religious: 0 Catechists: 0 Lay missionaries: 0

Réunion (France) **Region: Indian Ocean** Oldest diocese: na (na) Land mass: 2,510 km² Primary language(s): French Primary religion(s): Catholic	Population: 645,000 Fertility rate: 2.3 Infant mortality per 1,000 births: 8.9 Life expectancy: 72 Literacy rate: 70.31 (1982 est.) GNI per capita (PPP): $ na
Catholics; %: 595,000; 92% Dioceses; all territories: 1; 1 Parishes; pastoral centers: 75; 135 Catholics/parish; /priest: 7,933; 5,509	Baptisms; % infants: 11,157; 98% % infants baptized Catholic (est.): 69% Confirmations: 9,587 Marriages; % both Catholic: 2,246; 98%
Hospitals: 1 Orphanages: 1 Homes for elderly, disabled: 3 Other charitable institutions: 6 Primary schools: 24 Secondary schools: 16 Colleges and universities: 0 Seminaries: 1	Permanent deacons: 13 Seminarians; % diocesan: 19; 68% Diocesan priests: 56 Religious priests; brothers: 52; 28 Women religious: 505 Catechists: 500 Lay missionaries: 0

Romania	Population: 22,440,000
Region: Eastern Europe	Fertility rate: 1.3
Oldest diocese: Alba Iulia (1009)	Infant mortality per 1,000 births: 20.3
Land mass: 237,500 km²	Life expectancy: 70
Primary language(s): Romanian,	Literacy rate: 96.44 (1992 est.)
Hungarian, German	GNI per capita (PPP): $ 5,970
Primary religion(s): Orthodox	

Catholics; %: 2,032,000; 9%	Baptisms; % infants: 12,816; 96%
Dioceses; all territories: 11; 12	% infants baptized Catholic (est.): 5%
Parishes; pastoral centers: 1,770; 1,785	Confirmations: 12,986
Catholics/parish; /priest: 1,148; 1,205	Marriages; % both Catholic: 6,602; 71%

Hospitals: 13	Permanent deacons: 3
Orphanages: 11	Seminarians; % diocesan: 1,039; 85%
Homes for elderly, disabled: 18	Diocesan priests: 1,475
Other charitable institutions: 87	Religious priests; brothers: 211; 84
Primary schools: 8	Women religious: 1,232
Secondary schools: 20	Catechists: 512
Colleges and universities: 0	Lay missionaries: 0
Seminaries: 7	

Russia	Population: 105,012,000
Region: Eastern Europe	Fertility rate: 1.2
Oldest diocese: na (na)	Infant mortality per 1,000 births: 20.6
Land mass: 3,912,785 km²	Life expectancy: 67
Primary language(s): Russian	Literacy rate: 98.11 (1989 est.)
Primary religion(s): Russian Orthodox	GNI per capita (PPP): $ 6,990

Catholics; %: 255,000; <1%	Baptisms; % infants: 906; 50%
Dioceses; all territories: 0; 3	% infants baptized Catholic (est.): <1%
Parishes; pastoral centers: 109; 133	Confirmations: 346
Catholics/parish; /priest: 2,339; 1,197	Marriages; % both Catholic: 227; 52%

Hospitals: 0	Permanent deacons: 2
Orphanages: 2	Seminarians; % diocesan: 95; 29%
Homes for elderly, disabled: 1	Diocesan priests: 63
Other charitable institutions: 28	Religious priests; brothers: 150; 12
Primary schools: 0	Women religious: 166
Secondary schools: 0	Catechists: 10
Colleges and universities: 0	Lay missionaries: 18
Seminaries: 1	

Russian Federation (in Asia) Region: East Asia Oldest diocese: Vladivostok (1921) Land mass: 13,290,000 km² Primary language(s): na Primary religion(s): na	Population: 40,478,000 Fertility rate: na Infant mortality per 1,000 births: 120.1 Life expectancy: 39 Literacy rate: 98.11 (1989 est.) GNI per capita (PPP): $ na
Catholics; %: 1,049,000; 3% Dioceses; all territories: 1; 3 Parishes; pastoral centers: 197; 257 Catholics/parish; /priest: 5,325; 10,927	Baptisms; % infants: 662; 42% % infants baptized Catholic (est.): <1% Confirmations: 311 Marriages; % both Catholic: 114; 78%
Hospitals: 0 Orphanages: 2 Homes for elderly, disabled: 4 Other charitable institutions: 62 Primary schools: 1 Secondary schools: 1 Colleges and universities: 0 Seminaries: 0	Permanent deacons: 1 Seminarians; % diocesan: 14; 64% Diocesan priests: 59 Religious priests; brothers: 37; 3 Women religious: 116 Catechists: 68 Lay missionaries: 2

Rwanda Region: Central Africa Oldest diocese: Kabgayi (1922) Land mass: 26,338 km² Primary language(s): French Primary religion(s): Catholic	Population: 7,610,000 Fertility rate: 5.8 Infant mortality per 1,000 births: 136.7 Life expectancy: 49 Literacy rate: 50.2 (1990 est.) GNI per capita (PPP): $ 880
Catholics; %: 3,628,000; 48% Dioceses; all territories: 9; 9 Parishes; pastoral centers: 132; 187 Catholics/parish; /priest: 27,485; 7,480	Baptisms; % infants: 162,241; 59% % infants baptized Catholic (est.): 19% Confirmations: 99,508 Marriages; % both Catholic: 23,228; 98%
Hospitals: 11 Orphanages: 25 Homes for elderly, disabled: 19 Other charitable institutions: 227 Primary schools: 1,073 Secondary schools: 108 Colleges and universities: 0 Seminaries: 2	Permanent deacons: 2 Seminarians; % diocesan: 347; 85% Diocesan priests: 366 Religious priests; brothers: 119; 134 Women religious: 1,217 Catechists: 3,455 Lay missionaries: 20

Sahara (Morocco) Region: North Africa Oldest diocese: na (na) Land mass: 266,000 km² Primary language(s): Arabic Primary religion(s): Islam	Population: 350,000 Fertility rate: 6.8 Infant mortality per 1,000 births: 24.3 Life expectancy: 77 Literacy rate: na (na est.) GNI per capita (PPP): $ na
Catholics; %: 200; <1% Dioceses; all territories: 0; 1 Parishes; pastoral centers: 2; 2 Catholics/parish; /priest: 100; 67	Baptisms; % infants: 0; na % infants baptized Catholic (est.): na% Confirmations: 0 Marriages; % both Catholic: 0; na
Hospitals: 0 Orphanages: 0 Homes for elderly, disabled: 0 Other charitable institutions: 0 Primary schools: 0 Secondary schools: 0 Colleges and universities: 0 Seminaries: 0	Permanent deacons: 0 Seminarians; % diocesan: 0; na Diocesan priests: 0 Religious priests; brothers: 3; 0 Women religious: 0 Catechists: 0 Lay missionaries: 0

Saint Helena (United Kingdom) Region: Southern Africa Oldest diocese: na (na) Land mass: 314 km² Primary language(s): English Primary religion(s): Anglican	Population: 6,000 Fertility rate: na Infant mortality per 1,000 births: 18.7 Life expectancy: 70 Literacy rate: 97.3 (1987 est.) GNI per capita (PPP): $ na
Catholics; %: 100; 2% Dioceses; all territories: 0; 1 Parishes; pastoral centers: 1; 1 Catholics/parish; /priest: 100; 100	Baptisms; % infants: 1; 100% % infants baptized Catholic (est.): 3% Confirmations: 0 Marriages; % both Catholic: 1; 0%
Hospitals: 0 Orphanages: 0 Homes for elderly, disabled: 0 Other charitable institutions: 0 Primary schools: 0 Secondary schools: 0 Colleges and universities: 0 Seminaries: 0	Permanent deacons: 0 Seminarians; % diocesan: 0; na Diocesan priests: 0 Religious priests; brothers: 1; 0 Women religious: 0 Catechists: 0 Lay missionaries: 0

Saint Kitts and Nevis Region: Caribbean Oldest diocese: na (na) Land mass: 261 km² Primary language(s): English Primary religion(s): Anglican	Population: 46,000 Fertility rate: 2.5 Infant mortality per 1,000 births: 16.1 Life expectancy: 72 Literacy rate: 97.6 (1970 est.) GNI per capita (PPP): $ 10,400
Catholics; %: 5,000; 11% Dioceses; all territories: 0; 0 Parishes; pastoral centers: 3; 3 Catholics/parish; /priest: 1,667; 1,250	Baptisms; % infants: 63; 100% % infants baptized Catholic (est.): 5% Confirmations: 38 Marriages; % both Catholic: 14; 43%
Hospitals: 1 Orphanages: 0 Homes for elderly, disabled: 0 Other charitable institutions: 1 Primary schools: 2 Secondary schools: 1 Colleges and universities: 0 Seminaries: 0	Permanent deacons: 0 Seminarians; % diocesan: 0; na Diocesan priests: 1 Religious priests; brothers: 3; 0 Women religious: 6 Catechists: 24 Lay missionaries: 0

Saint Lucia Region: Caribbean Oldest diocese: Castries (1956) Land mass: 622 km² Primary language(s): English, French Primary religion(s): Catholic	Population: 147,000 Fertility rate: 2.1 Infant mortality per 1,000 births: 33.9 Life expectancy: 69 Literacy rate: 66.66 (1980 est.) GNI per capita (PPP): $ 5,200
Catholics; %: 116,000; 79% Dioceses; all territories: 1; 1 Parishes; pastoral centers: 22; 23 Catholics/parish; /priest: 5,273; 4,000	Baptisms; % infants: 1,862; 100% % infants baptized Catholic (est.): 69% Confirmations: 1,057 Marriages; % both Catholic: 278; 94%
Hospitals: 1 Orphanages: 1 Homes for elderly, disabled: 2 Other charitable institutions: 3 Primary schools: 36 Secondary schools: 3 Colleges and universities: 0 Seminaries: 0	Permanent deacons: 8 Seminarians; % diocesan: 2; 100% Diocesan priests: 16 Religious priests; brothers: 13; 6 Women religious: 42 Catechists: 400 Lay missionaries: 0

Saint Pierre and Miquelon (France) Region: North America Oldest diocese: na (na) Land mass: 242 km² Primary language(s): French Primary religion(s): Catholic	Population: 6,000 Fertility rate: na Infant mortality per 1,000 births: 8.9 Life expectancy: 77 Literacy rate: 99.3 (1982 est.) GNI per capita (PPP): $ na
Catholics; %: 6,000; 100% Dioceses; all territories: 0; 1 Parishes; pastoral centers: 2; 3 Catholics/parish; /priest: 3,000; 3,000	Baptisms; % infants: 64; 91% % infants baptized Catholic (est.): 61% Confirmations: 58 Marriages; % both Catholic: 14; 100%
Hospitals: 0 Orphanages: 0 Homes for elderly, disabled: 0 Other charitable institutions: 0 Primary schools: 2 Secondary schools: 2 Colleges and universities: 0 Seminaries: 0	Permanent deacons: 0 Seminarians; % diocesan: 0; na Diocesan priests: 0 Religious priests; brothers: 2; 0 Women religious: 7 Catechists: 0 Lay missionaries: 0

Saint Vincent and the Grenadines Region: Caribbean Oldest diocese: na (na) Land mass: 388 km² Primary language(s): English, French Primary religion(s): Anglican	Population: 107,000 Fertility rate: 2.2 Infant mortality per 1,000 births: 17.7 Life expectancy: 72 Literacy rate: 95.6 (1970 est.) GNI per capita (PPP): $ 4,990
Catholics; %: 10,000; 9% Dioceses; all territories: 1; 1 Parishes; pastoral centers: 6; 6 Catholics/parish; /priest: 1,667; 1,667	Baptisms; % infants: 149; 93% % infants baptized Catholic (est.): 6% Confirmations: 57 Marriages; % both Catholic: 32; 38%
Hospitals: 1 Orphanages: 0 Homes for elderly, disabled: 0 Other charitable institutions: 1 Primary schools: 2 Secondary schools: 3 Colleges and universities: 0 Seminaries: 0	Permanent deacons: 0 Seminarians; % diocesan: 0; na Diocesan priests: 3 Religious priests; brothers: 3; 0 Women religious: 14 Catechists: 62 Lay missionaries: 4

Samoa Region: Oceania Oldest diocese: Samoa-Apia (1850) Land mass: 2,831 km² Primary language(s): English Primary religion(s): Protestant	Population: 183,000 Fertility rate: 6.8 Infant mortality per 1,000 births: 10.6 Life expectancy: 75 Literacy rate: 98.33 (1971 est.) GNI per capita (PPP): $ 4,070
Catholics; %: 30,000; 16% Dioceses; all territories: 1; 1 Parishes; pastoral centers: 29; 31 Catholics/parish; /priest: 1,034; 600	Baptisms; % infants: 1,469; 73% % infants baptized Catholic (est.): 21% Confirmations: 463 Marriages; % both Catholic: 218; 82%
Hospitals: 0 Orphanages: 0 Homes for elderly, disabled: 1 Other charitable institutions: 3 Primary schools: 7 Secondary schools: 9 Colleges and universities: 0 Seminaries: 0	Permanent deacons: 24 Seminarians; % diocesan: 22; 50% Diocesan priests: 29 Religious priests; brothers: 21; 20 Women religious: 71 Catechists: 133 Lay missionaries: 0

San Marino Region: Southwestern Europe Oldest diocese: na (na) Land mass: 61 km² Primary language(s): Italian Primary religion(s): Catholic	Population: 26,000 Fertility rate: 1.3 Infant mortality per 1,000 births: 52.0 Life expectancy: 65 Literacy rate: 96 (1976 est.) GNI per capita (PPP): $ na
Catholics; %: 26,000; 100% Dioceses; all territories: 0; 0 Parishes; pastoral centers: 12; 25 Catholics/parish; /priest: 2,167; 839	Baptisms; % infants: 275; 99% % infants baptized Catholic (est.): 92% Confirmations: 248 Marriages; % both Catholic: 92; 98%
Hospitals: 0 Orphanages: 3 Homes for elderly, disabled: 0 Other charitable institutions: 1 Primary schools: 0 Secondary schools: 0 Colleges and universities: 0 Seminaries: 0	Permanent deacons: 1 Seminarians; % diocesan: 0; na Diocesan priests: 12 Religious priests; brothers: 19; 1 Women religious: 20 Catechists: 113 Lay missionaries: 0

São Tomé and Principe Region: West Africa Oldest diocese: Sao Tomé and Príncipe (1534) Land mass: 964 km² Primary language(s): Portuguese Primary religion(s): Protestant	Population: 131,000 Fertility rate: 6.2 Infant mortality per 1,000 births: 54.8 Life expectancy: 67 Literacy rate: 57.4 (1981 est.) GNI per capita (PPP): $ na
Catholics; %: 109,000; 83% Dioceses; all territories: 1; 1 Parishes; pastoral centers: 12; 13 Catholics/parish; /priest: 9,083; 9,083	Baptisms; % infants: 2,153; 78% % infants baptized Catholic (est.): 31% Confirmations: 194 Marriages; % both Catholic: 75; 99%
Hospitals: 0 Orphanages: 1 Homes for elderly, disabled: 1 Other charitable institutions: 8 Primary schools: 0 Secondary schools: 1 Colleges and universities: 0 Seminaries: 0	Permanent deacons: 0 Seminarians; % diocesan: 12; 42% Diocesan priests: 2 Religious priests; brothers: 10; 2 Women religious: 44 Catechists: 438 Lay missionaries: 4

Saudi Arabia Region: Western Asia Oldest diocese: na (na) Land mass: 2,149,690 km² Primary language(s): Arabic Primary religion(s): Islam	Population: 20,350,000 Fertility rate: 5.7 Infant mortality per 1,000 births: 59.5 Life expectancy: 62 Literacy rate: 62.4 (1990 est.) GNI per capita (PPP): $ 11,050
Catholics; %: 625,875; 3% Dioceses; all territories: 0; 0 Parishes; pastoral centers: 4; 4 Catholics/parish; /priest: 225,000; 180,000	Baptisms; % infants: 504; 99% % infants baptized Catholic (est.): <1% Confirmations: 104 Marriages; % both Catholic: 1; 100%
Hospitals: 0 Orphanages: 0 Homes for elderly, disabled: 0 Other charitable institutions: 0 Primary schools: 0 Secondary schools: 0 Colleges and universities: 0 Seminaries: 0	Permanent deacons: 1 Seminarians; % diocesan: 0; na Diocesan priests: 1 Religious priests; brothers: 4; 0 Women religious: 15 Catechists: 0 Lay missionaries: 0

Senegal Region: West Africa Oldest diocese: Saint-Louis du Sénégal (1763) Land mass: 196,722 km² Primary language(s): French, Wolof Primary religion(s): Islam	Population: 9,520,000 Fertility rate: 5.7 Infant mortality per 1,000 births: 22.9 Life expectancy: 71 Literacy rate: 38.3 (1990 est.) GNI per capita (PPP): $ 1,400
Catholics; %: 483,000; 5% Dioceses; all territories: 7; 7 Parishes; pastoral centers: 98; 409 Catholics/parish; /priest: 4,929; 1,220	Baptisms; % infants: 9,231; 75% % infants baptized Catholic (est.): 2% Confirmations: 7,633 Marriages; % both Catholic: 941; 92%
Hospitals: 13 Orphanages: 41 Homes for elderly, disabled: 2 Other charitable institutions: 322 Primary schools: 154 Secondary schools: 37 Colleges and universities: 0 Seminaries: 3	Permanent deacons: 1 Seminarians; % diocesan: 133; 75% Diocesan priests: 254 Religious priests; brothers: 142; 181 Women religious: 714 Catechists: 2,435 Lay missionaries: 1

Seychelles Region: Indian Ocean Oldest diocese: Port Victoria o Seychelles (1892) Land mass: 358 km² Primary language(s): English, French Primary religion(s): Catholic	Population: 81,000 Fertility rate: 2 Infant mortality per 1,000 births: 18.2 Life expectancy: 70 Literacy rate: 57.7 (1971 est.) GNI per capita (PPP): $ na
Catholics; %: 69,000; 85% Dioceses; all territories: 1; 1 Parishes; pastoral centers: 17; 17 Catholics/parish; /priest: 4,059; 4,600	Baptisms; % infants: 1,245; 100% % infants baptized Catholic (est.): 64% Confirmations: 1,422 Marriages; % both Catholic: 125; 92%
Hospitals: 0 Orphanages: 3 Homes for elderly, disabled: 3 Other charitable institutions: 7 Primary schools: 0 Secondary schools: 0 Colleges and universities: 0 Seminaries: 0	Permanent deacons: 1 Seminarians; % diocesan: 4; 100% Diocesan priests: 9 Religious priests; brothers: 6; 0 Women religious: 58 Catechists: 365 Lay missionaries: 0

Sierra Leone **Region: West Africa** Oldest diocese: Freetown and Bo (1858) Land mass: 71,740 km² Primary language(s): English Primary religion(s): Islam	Population: 4,523,000 Fertility rate: 6.3 Infant mortality per 1,000 births: 150.8 Life expectancy: 45 Literacy rate: 20.7 (1990 est.) GNI per capita (PPP): $ 440
Catholics; %: 72,000; 2% Dioceses; all territories: 3; 3 Parishes; pastoral centers: 38; 671 Catholics/parish; /priest: 1,895; 595	Baptisms; % infants: 3,365; 65% % infants baptized Catholic (est.): 1% Confirmations: 677 Marriages; % both Catholic: 115; 71%
Hospitals: 4 Orphanages: 12 Homes for elderly, disabled: 2 Other charitable institutions: 24 Primary schools: 218 Secondary schools: 29 Colleges and universities: 0 Seminaries: 1	Permanent deacons: 3 Seminarians; % diocesan: 48; 96% Diocesan priests: 44 Religious priests; brothers: 77; 31 Women religious: 15 Catechists: 334 Lay missionaries: 3

Singapore **Region: Southeast Asia** Oldest diocese: Singapore (1558) Land mass: 618 km² Primary language(s): Chinese, Malay, Tamil, English Primary religion(s): Islam, Buddhism	Population: 4,020,000 Fertility rate: 1.6 Infant mortality per 1,000 births: 3.7 Life expectancy: 80 Literacy rate: 90.13 (1990 est.) GNI per capita (PPP): $ 22,640
Catholics; %: 152,000; 4% Dioceses; all territories: 1; 1 Parishes; pastoral centers: 30; 30 Catholics/parish; /priest: 5,067; 1,160	Baptisms; % infants: 4,234; 51% % infants baptized Catholic (est.): 4% Confirmations: 2,851 Marriages; % both Catholic: 1,110; 43%
Hospitals: 1 Orphanages: 0 Homes for elderly, disabled: 5 Other charitable institutions: 4 Primary schools: 20 Secondary schools: 15 Colleges and universities: 0 Seminaries: 0	Permanent deacons: 0 Seminarians; % diocesan: 16; 56% Diocesan priests: 69 Religious priests; brothers: 62; 49 Women religious: 221 Catechists: 1,375 Lay missionaries: 0

Slovakia Region: Eastern Europe Oldest diocese: Nitra (880) Land mass: 49,450 km² Primary language(s): Slovak Primary religion(s): Catholic	Population: 5,400,000 Fertility rate: 1.3 Infant mortality per 1,000 births: 9.5 Life expectancy: 73 Literacy rate: na (na est.) GNI per capita (PPP): $ 10,430
Catholics; %: 3,659,000; 68% Dioceses; all territories: 7; 8 Parishes; pastoral centers: 1,480; 1,525 Catholics/parish; /priest: 2,472; 1,459	Baptisms; % infants: 45,508; 92% % infants baptized Catholic (est.): 82% Confirmations: 42,004 Marriages; % both Catholic: 16,965; 90%
Hospitals: 2 Orphanages: 8 Homes for elderly, disabled: 30 Other charitable institutions: 49 Primary schools: 86 Secondary schools: 46 Colleges and universities: 0 Seminaries: 20	Permanent deacons: 21 Seminarians; % diocesan: 933; 74% Diocesan priests: 1,893 Religious priests; brothers: 615; 226 Women religious: 2,895 Catechists: 1,793 Lay missionaries: 0

Slovenia Region: Eastern Europe Oldest diocese: na (na) Land mass: 20,248 km² Primary language(s): Slovenian Primary religion(s): Catholic	Population: 1,990,000 Fertility rate: 1.2 Infant mortality per 1,000 births: 4.6 Life expectancy: 75 Literacy rate: 99 (na est.) GNI per capita (PPP): $ 16,050
Catholics; %: 1,622,000; 82% Dioceses; all territories: 3; 3 Parishes; pastoral centers: 805; 817 Catholics/parish; /priest: 2,015; 1,410	Baptisms; % infants: 14,169; 96% % infants baptized Catholic (est.): 86% Confirmations: 16,207 Marriages; % both Catholic: 4,364; 95%
Hospitals: 0 Orphanages: 0 Homes for elderly, disabled: 12 Other charitable institutions: 10 Primary schools: 0 Secondary schools: 4 Colleges and universities: 0 Seminaries: 2	Permanent deacons: 9 Seminarians; % diocesan: 142; 65% Diocesan priests: 855 Religious priests; brothers: 295; 40 Women religious: 787 Catechists: 509 Lay missionaries: 0

Solomon Islands Region: Oceania Oldest diocese: Gizo (1959) Land mass: 28,896 km² Primary language(s): Melanesian pidgin, English Primary religion(s): Anglican	Population: 440,000 Fertility rate: 5.7 Infant mortality per 1,000 births: 26.2 Life expectancy: 71 Literacy rate: na (na est.) GNI per capita (PPP): $ 2,050
Catholics; %: 83,000; 19% Dioceses; all territories: 3; 3 Parishes; pastoral centers: 27; 68 Catholics/parish; /priest: 3,074; 1,660	Baptisms; % infants: 2,884; 88% % infants baptized Catholic (est.): 16% Confirmations: 2,097 Marriages; % both Catholic: 582; 76%
Hospitals: 1 Orphanages: 0 Homes for elderly, disabled: 0 Other charitable institutions: 48 Primary schools: 4 Secondary schools: 4 Colleges and universities: 0 Seminaries: 2	Permanent deacons: 0 Seminarians; % diocesan: 46; 76% Diocesan priests: 23 Religious priests; brothers: 27; 20 Women religious: 88 Catechists: 1,068 Lay missionaries: 1

Somalia Region: East Africa Oldest diocese: Mogadishu (1904) Land mass: 637,657 km² Primary language(s): Arabic, Somali Primary religion(s): Islam	Population: 8,780,000 Fertility rate: 7.3 Infant mortality per 1,000 births: 125.8 Life expectancy: 46 Literacy rate: 24.1 (1990 est.) GNI per capita (PPP): $ na
Catholics; %: 100; 0% Dioceses; all territories: 1; 1 Parishes; pastoral centers: 1; 1 Catholics/parish; /priest: 100; 25	Baptisms; % infants: 0; na % infants baptized Catholic (est.): na% Confirmations: 0 Marriages; % both Catholic: 0; na
Hospitals: 0 Orphanages: 0 Homes for elderly, disabled: 0 Other charitable institutions: 0 Primary schools: 0 Secondary schools: 0 Colleges and universities: 0 Seminaries: 0	Permanent deacons: 0 Seminarians; % diocesan: 0; na Diocesan priests: 1 Religious priests; brothers: 3; 1 Women religious: 3 Catechists: 2 Lay missionaries: 0

South Africa Region: Southern Africa Oldest diocese: Port Elizabeth (1818) Land mass: 1,221,037 km² Primary language(s): English, Afrikaans Primary religion(s): Protestant	Population: 43,690,000 Fertility rate: 2.9 Infant mortality per 1,000 births: 57.1 Life expectancy: 53 Literacy rate: 60.46 (1980 est.) GNI per capita (PPP): $ 8,710
Catholics; %: 3,081,000; 7% Dioceses; all territories: 25; 27 Parishes; pastoral centers: 729; 3,318 Catholics/parish; /priest: 4,226; 2,861	Baptisms; % infants: 54,536; 65% % infants baptized Catholic (est.): 3% Confirmations: 25,674 Marriages; % both Catholic: 6,079; 44%
Hospitals: 16 Orphanages: 172 Homes for elderly, disabled: 77 Other charitable institutions: 429 Primary schools: 266 Secondary schools: 115 Colleges and universities: 0 Seminaries: 6	Permanent deacons: 217 Seminarians; % diocesan: 584; 43% Diocesan priests: 401 Religious priests; brothers: 676; 189 Women religious: 2,658 Catechists: 12,101 Lay missionaries: 9

South Korea Region: East Asia Oldest diocese: Seoul (1831) Land mass: 99,016 km² Primary language(s): Korean Primary religion(s): Protestant, Buddhism	Population: 47,270,000 Fertility rate: 1.5 Infant mortality per 1,000 births: 8.0 Life expectancy: 74 Literacy rate: 97.96 (1995 est.) GNI per capita (PPP): $ 15,530
Catholics; %: 4,047,000; 9% Dioceses; all territories: 14; 15 Parishes; pastoral centers: 1,152; 1,748 Catholics/parish; /priest: 3,513; 1,482	Baptisms; % infants: 170,397; 20% % infants baptized Catholic (est.): 5% Confirmations: 72,521 Marriages; % both Catholic: 21,853; 35%
Hospitals: 34 Orphanages: 60 Homes for elderly, disabled: 185 Other charitable institutions: 196 Primary schools: 10 Secondary schools: 60 Colleges and universities: 3 Seminaries: 8	Permanent deacons: 0 Seminarians; % diocesan: 1,803; 84% Diocesan priests: 2,299 Religious priests; brothers: 432; 616 Women religious: 7,938 Catechists: 12,067 Lay missionaries: 42

Spain Region: Southwestern Europe Oldest diocese: Huesca (533) Land mass: 504,782 km² Primary language(s): Spanish Primary religion(s): Catholic	Population: 39,470,000 Fertility rate: 1.2 Infant mortality per 1,000 births: 5.1 Life expectancy: 79 Literacy rate: 94.78 (1991 est.) GNI per capita (PPP): $ 17,850
Catholics; %: 37,152,000; 94% Dioceses; all territories: 67; 68 Parishes; pastoral centers: 22,618; 26,464 Catholics/parish; /priest: 1,643; 1,362	Baptisms; % infants: 309,996; 98% % infants baptized Catholic (est.): 79% Confirmations: 146,487 Marriages; % both Catholic: 165,704; 99%
Hospitals: 103 Orphanages: 278 Homes for elderly, disabled: 918 Other charitable institutions: 2,166 Primary schools: 2,445 Secondary schools: 2,133 Colleges and universities: 5 Seminaries: 91	Permanent deacons: 231 Seminarians; % diocesan: 2,728; 61% Diocesan priests: 18,439 Religious priests; brothers: 8,842; 5,073 Women religious: 60,525 Catechists: 101,995 Lay missionaries: 100

Sri Lanka Region: South Asia Oldest diocese: Colombo (1834) Land mass: 65,610 km² Primary language(s): Sinhala, Tamil Primary religion(s): Buddhism	Population: 19,360,000 Fertility rate: 2.1 Infant mortality per 1,000 births: 17.0 Life expectancy: 72 Literacy rate: 88.4 (1990 est.) GNI per capita (PPP): $ 3,230
Catholics; %: 1,300,000; 7% Dioceses; all territories: 11; 11 Parishes; pastoral centers: 376; 1,296 Catholics/parish; /priest: 3,457; 1,382	Baptisms; % infants: 28,737; 84% % infants baptized Catholic (est.): 6% Confirmations: 18,626 Marriages; % both Catholic: 11,093; 72%
Hospitals: 6 Orphanages: 93 Homes for elderly, disabled: 44 Other charitable institutions: 310 Primary schools: 41 Secondary schools: 49 Colleges and universities: 0 Seminaries: 7	Permanent deacons: 2 Seminarians; % diocesan: 463; 63% Diocesan priests: 604 Religious priests; brothers: 337; 246 Women religious: 2,232 Catechists: 9,257 Lay missionaries: 0

Sudan	Population: 31,100,000
Region: East Africa	Fertility rate: 4.9
Oldest diocese: Khartoum (1846)	Infant mortality per 1,000 births: 71.8
Land mass: 2,505,813 km²	Life expectancy: 56
Primary language(s): Arabic	Literacy rate: 27.1 (1990 est.)
Primary religion(s): Islam	GNI per capita (PPP): $ na

Catholics; %: 3,810,000; 12%	Baptisms; % infants: 52,305; 59%
Dioceses; all territories: 9; 10	% infants baptized Catholic (est.): 2%
Parishes; pastoral centers: 164; 690	Confirmations: 23,619
Catholics/parish; /priest: 23,232; 11,796	Marriages; % both Catholic: 1,714; 96%

Hospitals: 16	Permanent deacons: 4
Orphanages: 3	Seminarians; % diocesan: 253; 95%
Homes for elderly, disabled: 11	Diocesan priests: 205
Other charitable institutions: 249	Religious priests; brothers: 118; 74
Primary schools: 324	Women religious: 326
Secondary schools: 24	Catechists: 3,945
Colleges and universities: 0	Lay missionaries: 9
Seminaries: 2	

Suriname	Population: 436,000
Region: South America	Fertility rate: 3
Oldest diocese: Paramaribo (1817)	Infant mortality per 1,000 births: 26.0
Land mass: 163,265 km²	Life expectancy: 71
Primary language(s): Dutch	Literacy rate: 94.9 (1990 est.)
Primary religion(s): Hinduism, Protestant	GNI per capita (PPP): $ 3,780

Catholics; %: 100,000; 23%	Baptisms; % infants: 2,138; 76%
Dioceses; all territories: 1; 1	% infants baptized Catholic (est.): 17%
Parishes; pastoral centers: 31; 118	Confirmations: 1,149
Catholics/parish; /priest: 3,226; 5,000	Marriages; % both Catholic: 132; 62%

Hospitals: 1	Permanent deacons: 0
Orphanages: 5	Seminarians; % diocesan: 0; na
Homes for elderly, disabled: 2	Diocesan priests: 6
Other charitable institutions: 0	Religious priests; brothers: 14; 7
Primary schools: 59	Women religious: 18
Secondary schools: 11	Catechists: 122
Colleges and universities: 0	Lay missionaries: 2
Seminaries: 0	

Svalbard and Jan Mayen Islands (Norway) Region: Northwestern Europe Oldest diocese: na (na) Land mass: 62,422 km² Primary language(s): Russian, Norwegian Primary religion(s): Protestant	Population: 3,700 Fertility rate: na Infant mortality per 1,000 births: na Life expectancy: na Literacy rate: na (na est.) GNI per capita (PPP): $ na
Catholics; %: na; na Dioceses; all territories: 0; 0 Parishes; pastoral centers: 0; 0 Catholics/parish; /priest: na; na	Baptisms; % infants: 0; na % infants baptized Catholic (est.): na% Confirmations: 0 Marriages; % both Catholic: 0; na
Hospitals: 0 Orphanages: 0 Homes for elderly, disabled: 0 Other charitable institutions: 0 Primary schools: 0 Secondary schools: 0 Colleges and universities: 0 Seminaries: 0	Permanent deacons: 0 Seminarians; % diocesan: 0; na Diocesan priests: 0 Religious priests; brothers: 0; 0 Women religious: 0 Catechists: 0 Lay missionaries: 0

Swaziland Region: Southern Africa Oldest diocese: Manzini (1923) Land mass: 17,364 km² Primary language(s): English, siSwati Primary religion(s): Protestant, Indigenous religions	Population: 990,000 Fertility rate: 5.9 Infant mortality per 1,000 births: 108.3 Life expectancy: 42 Literacy rate: 70.41 (1986 est.) GNI per capita (PPP): $ 4,380
Catholics; %: 53,000; 5% Dioceses; all territories: 1; 1 Parishes; pastoral centers: 15; 165 Catholics/parish; /priest: 3,533; 1,325	Baptisms; % infants: 468; 84% % infants baptized Catholic (est.): 1% Confirmations: 179 Marriages; % both Catholic: 80; 46%
Hospitals: 1 Orphanages: 4 Homes for elderly, disabled: 3 Other charitable institutions: 18 Primary schools: 45 Secondary schools: 15 Colleges and universities: 0 Seminaries: 0	Permanent deacons: 0 Seminarians; % diocesan: 6; 100% Diocesan priests: 9 Religious priests; brothers: 31; 6 Women religious: 57 Catechists: 182 Lay missionaries: 0

Sweden
Region: Northwestern Europe
Oldest diocese: Stockholm (1783)
Land mass: 440,945 km²
Primary language(s): Swedish
Primary religion(s): Lutheran

Population: 8,870,000
Fertility rate: 1.5
Infant mortality per 1,000 births: 3.5
Life expectancy: 79
Literacy rate: 99 (1979 est.)
GNI per capita (PPP): $ 22,150

Catholics; %: 97,000; 1%
Dioceses; all territories: 1; 1
Parishes; pastoral centers: 40; 40
Catholics/parish; /priest: 2,425; 660

Baptisms; % infants: 1,152; 97%
% infants baptized Catholic (est.): 1%
Confirmations: 813
Marriages; % both Catholic: 284; 36%

Hospitals: 1
Orphanages: 0
Homes for elderly, disabled: 5
Other charitable institutions: 4
Primary schools: 3
Secondary schools: 0
Colleges and universities: 0
Seminaries: 2

Permanent deacons: 17
Seminarians; % diocesan: 18; 44%
Diocesan priests: 71
Religious priests; brothers: 76; 12
Women religious: 236
Catechists: 455
Lay missionaries: 0

Switzerland
Region: Northwestern Europe
Oldest diocese: Basel, Bâle, Basilea
(740)
Land mass: 41,293 km²
Primary language(s): German, French
Primary religion(s): Catholic, Protestant

Population: 7,170,000
Fertility rate: 1.5
Infant mortality per 1,000 births: 4.6
Life expectancy: 79
Literacy rate: 99 (1980 est.)
GNI per capita (PPP): $ 28,760

Catholics; %: 3,169,000; 44%
Dioceses; all territories: 6; 8
Parishes; pastoral centers: 1,695; 2,011
Catholics/parish; /priest: 1,870; 1,014

Baptisms; % infants: 31,800; 99%
% infants baptized Catholic (est.): 40%
Confirmations: 24,868
Marriages; % both Catholic: 11,498; 85%

Hospitals: 13
Orphanages: 46
Homes for elderly, disabled: 43
Other charitable institutions: 231
Primary schools: 33
Secondary schools: 47
Colleges and universities: 1
Seminaries: 7

Permanent deacons: 139
Seminarians; % diocesan: 216; 54%
Diocesan priests: 1,882
Religious priests; brothers: 1,244; 454
Women religious: 5,924
Catechists: 1,842
Lay missionaries: 0

Syria Region: Western Asia Oldest diocese: Damascus - Maronite Church (1527) Land mass: 185,180 km² Primary language(s): Arabic Primary religion(s): Islam	Population: 16,320,000 Fertility rate: 4.1 Infant mortality per 1,000 births: 36.1 Life expectancy: 68 Literacy rate: 64 (1990 est.) GNI per capita (PPP): $ 3,450
Catholics; %: 335,000; 2% Dioceses; all territories: 16; 18 Parishes; pastoral centers: 203; 229 Catholics/parish; /priest: 1,650; 1,324	Baptisms; % infants: 2,906; 86% % infants baptized Catholic (est.): <1% Confirmations: 2,401 Marriages; % both Catholic: 1,257; 66%
Hospitals: 3 Orphanages: 13 Homes for elderly, disabled: 16 Other charitable institutions: 150 Primary schools: 23 Secondary schools: 6 Colleges and universities: 0 Seminaries: 0	Permanent deacons: 12 Seminarians; % diocesan: 80; 91% Diocesan priests: 178 Religious priests; brothers: 75; 9 Women religious: 371 Catechists: 1,698 Lay missionaries: 12

Tajikistan Region: Western Asia Oldest diocese: na (na) Land mass: 143,100 km² Primary language(s): Tajik, Russian Primary religion(s): Islam	Population: 6,170,000 Fertility rate: 2.4 Infant mortality per 1,000 births: 114.8 Life expectancy: 64 Literacy rate: 98 (1989 est.) GNI per capita (PPP): $ na
Catholics; %: 200; <1% Dioceses; all territories: 0; 1 Parishes; pastoral centers: 2; 5 Catholics/parish; /priest: 100; 50	Baptisms; % infants: 65; 18% % infants baptized Catholic (est.): <1% Confirmations: 39 Marriages; % both Catholic: 1; 100%
Hospitals: 0 Orphanages: 0 Homes for elderly, disabled: 0 Other charitable institutions: 0 Primary schools: 0 Secondary schools: 0 Colleges and universities: 0 Seminaries: 0	Permanent deacons: 0 Seminarians; % diocesan: 0; na Diocesan priests: 1 Religious priests; brothers: 3; 0 Women religious: 4 Catechists: 2 Lay missionaries: 0

Tanzania Region: East Africa Oldest diocese: Tabora (1880) Land mass: 945,087 km² Primary language(s): Swahili, English Primary religion(s): Protestant, Islam	Population: 35,120,000 Fertility rate: 5.6 Infant mortality per 1,000 births: 82.5 Life expectancy: 53 Literacy rate: 52 (1988 est.) GNI per capita (PPP): $ 500
Catholics; %: 9,470,000; 27% Dioceses; all territories: 30; 30 Parishes; pastoral centers: 792; 5,292 Catholics/parish; /priest: 11,957; 4,582	Baptisms; % infants: 303,975; 69% % infants baptized Catholic (est.): 13% Confirmations: 120,599 Marriages; % both Catholic: 36,942; 89%
Hospitals: 51 Orphanages: 40 Homes for elderly, disabled: 22 Other charitable institutions: 663 Primary schools: 21 Secondary schools: 213 Colleges and universities: 0 Seminaries: 9	Permanent deacons: 1 Seminarians; % diocesan: 1,073; 63% Diocesan priests: 1,359 Religious priests; brothers: 708; 630 Women religious: 7,128 Catechists: 12,044 Lay missionaries: 107

Thailand Region: Southeast Asia Oldest diocese: Ratchaburi (1930) Land mass: 513,115 km² Primary language(s): Thai, English Primary religion(s): Buddhism	Population: 62,320,000 Fertility rate: 1.8 Infant mortality per 1,000 births: 32.6 Life expectancy: 68 Literacy rate: 93 (1990 est.) GNI per capita (PPP): $ 5,950
Catholics; %: 273,000; <1% Dioceses; all territories: 10; 10 Parishes; pastoral centers: 350; 783 Catholics/parish; /priest: 780; 425	Baptisms; % infants: 7,254; 60% % infants baptized Catholic (est.): <1% Confirmations: 4,686 Marriages; % both Catholic: 2,603; 35%
Hospitals: 4 Orphanages: 80 Homes for elderly, disabled: 24 Other charitable institutions: 88 Primary schools: 214 Secondary schools: 160 Colleges and universities: 2 Seminaries: 7	Permanent deacons: 1 Seminarians; % diocesan: 275; 52% Diocesan priests: 406 Religious priests; brothers: 236; 129 Women religious: 1,454 Catechists: 1,812 Lay missionaries: 43

Togo Region: West Africa Oldest diocese: Lomé (1892) Land mass: 56,785 km² Primary language(s): French Primary religion(s): Indigenous religions	Population: 4,530,000 Fertility rate: 5.8 Infant mortality per 1,000 births: 72.8 Life expectancy: 55 Literacy rate: 43 (1990 est.) GNI per capita (PPP): $ 1,380
Catholics; %: 1,259,000; 28% Dioceses; all territories: 7; 7 Parishes; pastoral centers: 133; 1,864 Catholics/parish; /priest: 9,466; 3,340	Baptisms; % infants: 36,239; 53% % infants baptized Catholic (est.): 7% Confirmations: 16,584 Marriages; % both Catholic: 2,346; 89%
Hospitals: 7 Orphanages: 9 Homes for elderly, disabled: 4 Other charitable institutions: 201 Primary schools: 506 Secondary schools: 35 Colleges and universities: 0 Seminaries: 1	Permanent deacons: 0 Seminarians; % diocesan: 265; 80% Diocesan priests: 259 Religious priests; brothers: 118; 168 Women religious: 625 Catechists: 4,606 Lay missionaries: 25

Tokelau (New Zealand) Region: Oceania Oldest diocese: na (na) Land mass: 12 km² Primary language(s): Tokelauan, English Primary religion(s): Protestant	Population: 2,000 Fertility rate: na Infant mortality per 1,000 births: na Life expectancy: na Literacy rate: na (na est.) GNI per capita (PPP): $ na
Catholics; %: 1,000; 50% Dioceses; all territories: 0; 1 Parishes; pastoral centers: 2; 2 Catholics/parish; /priest: 500; 1,000	Baptisms; % infants: 15; 80% % infants baptized Catholic (est.): na% Confirmations: 110 Marriages; % both Catholic: 3; 100%
Hospitals: 0 Orphanages: 0 Homes for elderly, disabled: 0 Other charitable institutions: 0 Primary schools: 0 Secondary schools: 0 Colleges and universities: 0 Seminaries: 0	Permanent deacons: 1 Seminarians; % diocesan: 2; 100% Diocesan priests: 1 Religious priests; brothers: 0; 0 Women religious: 3 Catechists: 3 Lay missionaries: 0

Tonga Region: Oceania Oldest diocese: Tonga (1842) Land mass: 750 km² Primary language(s): Tongan, English Primary religion(s): Protestant	Population: 95,000 Fertility rate: 4.2 Infant mortality per 1,000 births: 14.9 Life expectancy: 68 Literacy rate: 47 (1976 est.) GNI per capita (PPP): $ na
Catholics; %: 15,000; 16% Dioceses; all territories: 1; 1 Parishes; pastoral centers: 10; 10 Catholics/parish; /priest: 1,500; 714	Baptisms; % infants: 516; 94% % infants baptized Catholic (est.): 20% Confirmations: 427 Marriages; % both Catholic: 64; 52%
Hospitals: 0 Orphanages: 0 Homes for elderly, disabled: 0 Other charitable institutions: 3 Primary schools: 0 Secondary schools: 7 Colleges and universities: 0 Seminaries: 0	Permanent deacons: 0 Seminarians; % diocesan: 41; 76% Diocesan priests: 12 Religious priests; brothers: 9; 8 Women religious: 47 Catechists: 119 Lay missionaries: 0

Trinidad and Tobago Region: Caribbean Oldest diocese: Port of Spain (1850) Land mass: 5,130 km² Primary language(s): English Primary religion(s): Catholic, Hinduism	Population: 1,278,000 Fertility rate: 1.7 Infant mortality per 1,000 births: 26.7 Life expectancy: 68 Literacy rate: 95 (1980 est.) GNI per capita (PPP): $ 7,690
Catholics; %: 383,000; 30% Dioceses; all territories: 1; 1 Parishes; pastoral centers: 61; 61 Catholics/parish; /priest: 6,279; 3,482	Baptisms; % infants: 4,639; 85% % infants baptized Catholic (est.): 26% Confirmations: 2,209 Marriages; % both Catholic: 833; 70%
Hospitals: 0 Orphanages: 3 Homes for elderly, disabled: 24 Other charitable institutions: 21 Primary schools: 129 Secondary schools: 24 Colleges and universities: 0 Seminaries: 0	Permanent deacons: 0 Seminarians; % diocesan: 18; 33% Diocesan priests: 44 Religious priests; brothers: 66; 8 Women religious: 175 Catechists: 211 Lay missionaries: 0

Tunisia **Region: North Africa** Oldest diocese: Tunis (1884) Land mass: 163,610 km² Primary language(s): Arabic Primary religion(s): Islam	Population: 9,560,000 Fertility rate: 2.3 Infant mortality per 1,000 births: 31.4 Life expectancy: 73 Literacy rate: 65 (1990 est.) GNI per capita (PPP): $ 5,700
Catholics; %: 22,000; <1% Dioceses; all territories: 1; 1 Parishes; pastoral centers: 12; 12 Catholics/parish; /priest: 1,833; 667	Baptisms; % infants: 28; 54% % infants baptized Catholic (est.): <1% Confirmations: 14 Marriages; % both Catholic: 3; 100%
Hospitals: 1 Orphanages: 0 Homes for elderly, disabled: 0 Other charitable institutions: 0 Primary schools: 7 Secondary schools: 4 Colleges and universities: 0 Seminaries: 0	Permanent deacons: 0 Seminarians; % diocesan: 2; 100% Diocesan priests: 12 Religious priests; brothers: 21; 7 Women religious: 165 Catechists: 0 Lay missionaries: 0

Turkey **Region: Western Asia** Oldest diocese: Izmir (1322) Land mass: 780,576 km² Primary language(s): Turkish Primary religion(s): Islam	Population: 67,380,000 Fertility rate: 2.5 Infant mortality per 1,000 births: 50.7 Life expectancy: 71 Literacy rate: 81 (1990 est.) GNI per capita (PPP): $ 6,440
Catholics; %: 32,000; <1% Dioceses; all territories: 3; 7 Parishes; pastoral centers: 52; 58 Catholics/parish; /priest: 615; 542	Baptisms; % infants: 97; 77% % infants baptized Catholic (est.): <1% Confirmations: 104 Marriages; % both Catholic: 66; 52%
Hospitals: 4 Orphanages: 1 Homes for elderly, disabled: 5 Other charitable institutions: 6 Primary schools: 9 Secondary schools: 12 Colleges and universities: 0 Seminaries: 0	Permanent deacons: 4 Seminarians; % diocesan: 13; 15% Diocesan priests: 15 Religious priests; brothers: 44; 12 Women religious: 114 Catechists: 29 Lay missionaries: 12

Turkmenistan Region: Western Asia Oldest diocese: na (na) Land mass: 488,100 km² Primary language(s): Turkmen, Russian Primary religion(s): Islam	Population: 4,740,000 Fertility rate: 2.2 Infant mortality per 1,000 births: 73.1 Life expectancy: 61 Literacy rate: 98 (1989 est.) GNI per capita (PPP): $ 3,340
Catholics; %: 1,000; <1% Dioceses; all territories: 0; 1 Parishes; pastoral centers: 1; 1 Catholics/parish; /priest: 1,000; 333	Baptisms; % infants: 10; 30% % infants baptized Catholic (est.): <1% Confirmations: 7 Marriages; % both Catholic: 1; 100%
Hospitals: 0 Orphanages: 0 Homes for elderly, disabled: 0 Other charitable institutions: 0 Primary schools: 0 Secondary schools: 0 Colleges and universities: 0 Seminaries: 0	Permanent deacons: 0 Seminarians; % diocesan: 0; na Diocesan priests: 0 Religious priests; brothers: 3; 0 Women religious: 0 Catechists: 0 Lay missionaries: 0

Turks and Caicos Islands (United Kingdom) Region: Caribbean Oldest diocese: na (na) Land mass: 430 km² Primary language(s): English Primary religion(s): Baptist	Population: 20,000 Fertility rate: na Infant mortality per 1,000 births: 19.4 Life expectancy: 73 Literacy rate: 98 (1970 est.) GNI per capita (PPP): $ na
Catholics; %: 6,000; 30% Dioceses; all territories: 0; 1 Parishes; pastoral centers: 2; 2 Catholics/parish; /priest: 3,000; 2,000	Baptisms; % infants: 39; 97% % infants baptized Catholic (est.): na% Confirmations: 0 Marriages; % both Catholic: 5; 80%
Hospitals: 0 Orphanages: 0 Homes for elderly, disabled: 0 Other charitable institutions: 0 Primary schools: 0 Secondary schools: 0 Colleges and universities: 0 Seminaries: 0	Permanent deacons: 0 Seminarians; % diocesan: 0; na Diocesan priests: 3 Religious priests; brothers: 0; 0 Women religious: 0 Catechists: 6 Lay missionaries: 0

Tuvalu **Region: Oceania** Oldest diocese: na (na) Land mass: 26 km² Primary language(s): **Tuvaluan, English** Primary religion(s): **Protestant**	Population: 10,000 Fertility rate: 3.1 Infant mortality per 1,000 births: 24.0 Life expectancy: 66 Literacy rate: na (na est.) GNI per capita (PPP): $ na
Catholics; %: 100; 1% Dioceses; all territories: 0; 1 Parishes; pastoral centers: 1; 1 Catholics/parish; /priest: 100; 100	Baptisms; % infants: 7; 71% % infants baptized Catholic (est.): <1% Confirmations: 11 Marriages; % both Catholic: 1; 100%
Hospitals: 0 Orphanages: 0 Homes for elderly, disabled: 0 Other charitable institutions: 0 Primary schools: 0 Secondary schools: 0 Colleges and universities: 0 Seminaries: 0	Permanent deacons: 0 Seminarians; % diocesan: 0; na Diocesan priests: 0 Religious priests; brothers: 1; 0 Women religious: 0 Catechists: 0 Lay missionaries: 0

Uganda **Region: East Africa** Oldest diocese: **Kampala (1894)** Land mass: 235,880 km² Primary language(s): **English** Primary religion(s): **Catholic, Protestant**	Population: 22,210,000 Fertility rate: 6.9 Infant mortality per 1,000 births: 95.2 Life expectancy: 42 Literacy rate: 54 (1991 est.) GNI per capita (PPP): $ 1,160
Catholics; %: 10,057,000; 45% Dioceses; all territories: 19; 20 Parishes; pastoral centers: 424; 6,569 Catholics/parish; /priest: 23,719; 6,325	Baptisms; % infants: 320,451; 86% % infants baptized Catholic (est.): 22% Confirmations: 103,939 Marriages; % both Catholic: 18,803; 94%
Hospitals: 30 Orphanages: 23 Homes for elderly, disabled: 17 Other charitable institutions: 501 Primary schools: 3,266 Secondary schools: 667 Colleges and universities: 1 Seminaries: 7	Permanent deacons: 1 Seminarians; % diocesan: 900; 81% Diocesan priests: 1,263 Religious priests; brothers: 327; 475 Women religious: 2,711 Catechists: 12,021 Lay missionaries: 24

Ukraine	Population: 49,570,000
Region: Eastern Europe	Fertility rate: 1.1
Oldest diocese: Kyiv-Zhytomyr (1321)	Infant mortality per 1,000 births: 21.7
Land mass: 603,700 km²	Life expectancy: 66
Primary language(s): Ukrainian, Russian	Literacy rate: 100 (1979 est.)
Primary religion(s): Orthodox	GNI per capita (PPP): $ 3,360

Catholics; %: 4,611,000; 9%	Baptisms; % infants: 28,658; 98%
Dioceses; all territories: 15; 17	% infants baptized Catholic (est.): 6%
Parishes; pastoral centers: 3,676; 4,075	Confirmations: 27,038
Catholics/parish; /priest: 1,254; 1,828	Marriages; % both Catholic: 17,975; 91%

Hospitals: 22	Permanent deacons: 14
Orphanages: 14	Seminarians; % diocesan: 1,236; 82%
Homes for elderly, disabled: 10	Diocesan priests: 2,140
Other charitable institutions: 22	Religious priests; brothers: 382; 124
Primary schools: 2	Women religious: 970
Secondary schools: 4	Catechists: 869
Colleges and universities: 0	Lay missionaries: 0
Seminaries: 9	

United Arab Emirates	Population: 2,610,000
Region: Western Asia	Fertility rate: 3.5
Oldest diocese: na (na)	Infant mortality per 1,000 births: 17.8
Land mass: 83,600 km²	Life expectancy: 74
Primary language(s): Arabic	Literacy rate: 68 (1980 est.)
Primary religion(s): Islam	GNI per capita (PPP): $ na

Catholics; %: 336,000; 13%	Baptisms; % infants: 1,325; 94%
Dioceses; all territories: 0; 1	% infants baptized Catholic (est.): 3%
Parishes; pastoral centers: 5; 17	Confirmations: 505
Catholics/parish; /priest: 67,200; 19,765	Marriages; % both Catholic: 233; 75%

Hospitals: 0	Permanent deacons: 0
Orphanages: 0	Seminarians; % diocesan: 0; na
Homes for elderly, disabled: 0	Diocesan priests: 3
Other charitable institutions: 0	Religious priests; brothers: 14; 0
Primary schools: 5	Women religious: 32
Secondary schools: 5	Catechists: 0
Colleges and universities: 0	Lay missionaries: 0
Seminaries: 0	

United Kingdom of Great Britain and Northern Ireland Region: Northwestern Europe Oldest diocese: Hexham and Newcastle (1850) Land mass: 230,762 km² Primary language(s): English Primary religion(s): Anglican	Population: 57,168,000 Fertility rate: 1.7 Infant mortality per 1,000 births: 5.8 Life expectancy: 77 Literacy rate: 99 (1978 est.) GNI per capita (PPP): $ 22,220
Catholics; %: 5,293,000; 9% Dioceses; all territories: 30; 32 Parishes; pastoral centers: 3,157; 3,421 Catholics/parish; /priest: 1,677; 870	Baptisms; % infants: 80,156; 89% % infants baptized Catholic (est.): 11% Confirmations: 49,553 Marriages; % both Catholic: 16,112; 38%
Hospitals: 18 Orphanages: 40 Homes for elderly, disabled: 211 Other charitable institutions: 233 Primary schools: 2,101 Secondary schools: 512 Colleges and universities: 1 Seminaries: 8	Permanent deacons: 533 Seminarians; % diocesan: 512; 53% Diocesan priests: 4,244 Religious priests; brothers: 1,837; 512 Women religious: 8,029 Catechists: 20,595 Lay missionaries: 30

United States Region: North America Oldest diocese: Baltimore (1789) Land mass: 9,372,614 km² Primary language(s): English Primary religion(s): Protestant	Population: 281,420,000 Fertility rate: 2.1 Infant mortality per 1,000 births: 6.9 Life expectancy: 77 Literacy rate: 97 (1980 est.) GNI per capita (PPP): $ 31,910
Catholics; %: 63,347,000; 23% Dioceses; all territories: 191; 193 Parishes; pastoral centers: 19,356; 20,897 Catholics/parish; /priest: 3,273; 1,312	Baptisms; % infants: 1,097,290; 92% % infants baptized Catholic (est.): 26% Confirmations: 631,421 Marriages; % both Catholic: 260,565; 71%
Hospitals: 585 Orphanages: 664 Homes for elderly, disabled: 1,134 Other charitable institutions: 4,149 Primary schools: 6,793 Secondary schools: 1,297 Colleges and universities: 221 Seminaries: 97	Permanent deacons: 12,971 Seminarians; % diocesan: 5,109; 68% Diocesan priests: 31,201 Religious priests; brothers: 17,087; 5,609 Women religious: 79,630 Catechists: 365,592 Lay missionaries: 587

Uruguay Region: South America Oldest diocese: Montevideo (1878) Land mass: 177,414 km² Primary language(s): Spanish Primary religion(s): Catholic	Population: 3,330,000 Fertility rate: 2.3 Infant mortality per 1,000 births: 16.0 Life expectancy: 75 Literacy rate: 96 (1990 est.) GNI per capita (PPP): $ 8,750
Catholics; %: 2,507,000; 75% Dioceses; all territories: 10; 10 Parishes; pastoral centers: 229; 771 Catholics/parish; /priest: 10,948; 5,034	Baptisms; % infants: 31,372; 93% % infants baptized Catholic (est.): 57% Confirmations: 3,746 Marriages; % both Catholic: 4,532; 92%
Hospitals: 7 Orphanages: 20 Homes for elderly, disabled: 23 Other charitable institutions: 239 Primary schools: 170 Secondary schools: 82 Colleges and universities: 1 Seminaries: 5	Permanent deacons: 63 Seminarians; % diocesan: 86; 48% Diocesan priests: 221 Religious priests; brothers: 277; 96 Women religious: 1,281 Catechists: 3,320 Lay missionaries: 4

Uzbekistan Region: Western Asia Oldest diocese: na (na) Land mass: 447,000 km² Primary language(s): Uzbek, Russian Primary religion(s): Islam	Population: 24,750,000 Fertility rate: 2.7 Infant mortality per 1,000 births: 71.6 Life expectancy: 64 Literacy rate: 99 (na est.) GNI per capita (PPP): $ 2,230
Catholics; %: 3,000; <1% Dioceses; all territories: 0; 1 Parishes; pastoral centers: 3; 6 Catholics/parish; /priest: 1,000; 333	Baptisms; % infants: 24; 8% % infants baptized Catholic (est.): <1% Confirmations: 0 Marriages; % both Catholic: 4; 75%
Hospitals: 0 Orphanages: 0 Homes for elderly, disabled: 0 Other charitable institutions: 1 Primary schools: 0 Secondary schools: 0 Colleges and universities: 0 Seminaries: 0	Permanent deacons: 0 Seminarians; % diocesan: 0; na Diocesan priests: 2 Religious priests; brothers: 7; 2 Women religious: 8 Catechists: 0 Lay missionaries: 0

Vanuatu Region: Oceania Oldest diocese: Port-Vila (1966) Land mass: 12,189 km² Primary language(s): English, French Primary religion(s): Presbyterian	Population: 190,000 Fertility rate: 4.6 Infant mortality per 1,000 births: 64.1 Life expectancy: 60 Literacy rate: 55 (1979 est.) GNI per capita (PPP): $ 2,880
Catholics; %: 29,000; 15% Dioceses; all territories: 1; 1 Parishes; pastoral centers: 18; 18 Catholics/parish; /priest: 1,611; 1,000	Baptisms; % infants: 620; 58% % infants baptized Catholic (est.): 6% Confirmations: 560 Marriages; % both Catholic: 132; 88%
Hospitals: 0 Orphanages: 0 Homes for elderly, disabled: 2 Other charitable institutions: 8 Primary schools: 50 Secondary schools: 8 Colleges and universities: 0 Seminaries: 0	Permanent deacons: 1 Seminarians; % diocesan: 9; 56% Diocesan priests: 16 Religious priests; brothers: 13; 23 Women religious: 63 Catechists: 144 Lay missionaries: 1

Venezuela Region: South America Oldest diocese: Coro (1531) Land mass: 912,050 km² Primary language(s): Spanish Primary religion(s): Catholic	Population: 24,170,000 Fertility rate: 2.9 Infant mortality per 1,000 births: 27.1 Life expectancy: 73 Literacy rate: 91 (1990 est.) GNI per capita (PPP): $ 5,420
Catholics; %: 21,414,000; 89% Dioceses; all territories: 31; 38 Parishes; pastoral centers: 1,185; 2,981 Catholics/parish; /priest: 18,071; 9,230	Baptisms; % infants: 436,695; 90% % infants baptized Catholic (est.): 66% Confirmations: 123,300 Marriages; % both Catholic: 22,085; 99%
Hospitals: 10 Orphanages: 67 Homes for elderly, disabled: 77 Other charitable institutions: 913 Primary schools: 498 Secondary schools: 375 Colleges and universities: 1 Seminaries: 22	Permanent deacons: 104 Seminarians; % diocesan: 1,128; 71% Diocesan priests: 1,364 Religious priests; brothers: 956; 284 Women religious: 3,812 Catechists: 21,442 Lay missionaries: 9,329

Vietnam Region: Southeast Asia Oldest diocese: Hanoi (1678) Land mass: 329,556 km² Primary language(s): Vietnamese Primary religion(s): Catholic, Buddhism	Population: 77,690,000 Fertility rate: 2.3 Infant mortality per 1,000 births: 32.2 Life expectancy: 69 Literacy rate: 94 (1995 est.) GNI per capita (PPP): $ 1,860
Catholics; %: 5,301,000; 7% Dioceses; all territories: 25; 25 Parishes; pastoral centers: 2,570; 4,066 Catholics/parish; /priest: 2,063; 2,170	Baptisms; % infants: 157,127; 77% % infants baptized Catholic (est.): 8% Confirmations: 138,277 Marriages; % both Catholic: 52,153; 90%
Hospitals: 1 Orphanages: 27 Homes for elderly, disabled: 34 Other charitable institutions: 255 Primary schools: 84 Secondary schools: 4 Colleges and universities: 0 Seminaries: 12	Permanent deacons: 11 Seminarians; % diocesan: 1,832; 77% Diocesan priests: 1,993 Religious priests; brothers: 450; 1,455 Women religious: 9,672 Catechists: 37,859 Lay missionaries: 10

Virgin Islands (United Kingdom) Region: Caribbean Oldest diocese: na (na) Land mass: 153 km² Primary language(s): English Primary religion(s): Baptist, Anglican	Population: 11,000 Fertility rate: na Infant mortality per 1,000 births: 22.0 Life expectancy: 75 Literacy rate: 98 (1970 est.) GNI per capita (PPP): $ na
Catholics; %: 1,000; 9% Dioceses; all territories: 0; 0 Parishes; pastoral centers: 3; 3 Catholics/parish; /priest: 333; 333	Baptisms; % infants: 19; 53% % infants baptized Catholic (est.): na% Confirmations: 19 Marriages; % both Catholic: 21; 81%
Hospitals: 0 Orphanages: 0 Homes for elderly, disabled: 0 Other charitable institutions: 0 Primary schools: 0 Secondary schools: 0 Colleges and universities: 0 Seminaries: 0	Permanent deacons: 0 Seminarians; % diocesan: 0; na Diocesan priests: 1 Religious priests; brothers: 2; 0 Women religious: 1 Catechists: 18 Lay missionaries: 0

Virgin Islands (United States) Region: Caribbean Oldest diocese: St. Thomas (1982) Land mass: 342 km² Primary language(s): English Primary religion(s): Baptist, Catholic	Population: 102,000 Fertility rate: na Infant mortality per 1,000 births: 9.9 Life expectancy: 78 Literacy rate: na (na est.) GNI per capita (PPP): $ na
Catholics; %: 30,000; 29% Dioceses; all territories: 1; 1 Parishes; pastoral centers: 8; 9 Catholics/parish; /priest: 3,750; 1,875	Baptisms; % infants: 336; 91% % infants baptized Catholic (est.): 20% Confirmations: 195 Marriages; % both Catholic: 95; 63%
Hospitals: 0 Orphanages: 0 Homes for elderly, disabled: 0 Other charitable institutions: 5 Primary schools: 3 Secondary schools: 2 Colleges and universities: 0 Seminaries: 0	Permanent deacons: 18 Seminarians; % diocesan: 11; 36% Diocesan priests: 9 Religious priests; brothers: 7; 11 Women religious: 17 Catechists: 206 Lay missionaries: 0

Wallis and Futuna Islands (France) Region: Oceania Oldest diocese: Wallis and Futuna (1966) Land mass: 200 km² Primary language(s): French, Wallisian Primary religion(s): Catholic	Population: 15,000 Fertility rate: na Infant mortality per 1,000 births: 19.6 Life expectancy: 74 Literacy rate: 50 (1969 est.) GNI per capita (PPP): $ na
Catholics; %: 14,000; 93% Dioceses; all territories: 1; 1 Parishes; pastoral centers: 5; 8 Catholics/parish; /priest: 2,800; 1,400	Baptisms; % infants: 311; 100% % infants baptized Catholic (est.): na% Confirmations: 310 Marriages; % both Catholic: 102; 100%
Hospitals: 0 Orphanages: 0 Homes for elderly, disabled: 0 Other charitable institutions: 0 Primary schools: 14 Secondary schools: 2 Colleges and universities: 0 Seminaries: 0	Permanent deacons: 0 Seminarians; % diocesan: 15; 47% Diocesan priests: 7 Religious priests; brothers: 3; 5 Women religious: 38 Catechists: 37 Lay missionaries: 0

Yemen Region: Western Asia Oldest diocese: na (na) Land mass: 527,968 km² Primary language(s): Arabic Primary religion(s): Islam	Population: 18,300,000 Fertility rate: 7.2 Infant mortality per 1,000 births: 72.2 Life expectancy: 59 Literacy rate: 38 (1990 est.) GNI per capita (PPP): $ 730
Catholics; %: 4,000; <1% Dioceses; all territories: 0; 0 Parishes; pastoral centers: 4; 8 Catholics/parish; /priest: 1,000; 1,000	Baptisms; % infants: 19; 100% % infants baptized Catholic (est.): <1% Confirmations: 6 Marriages; % both Catholic: 0; na
Hospitals: 0 Orphanages: 1 Homes for elderly, disabled: 4 Other charitable institutions: 3 Primary schools: 0 Secondary schools: 0 Colleges and universities: 0 Seminaries: 0	Permanent deacons: 0 Seminarians; % diocesan: 0; na Diocesan priests: 0 Religious priests; brothers: 4; 0 Women religious: 27 Catechists: 0 Lay missionaries: 0

Yugoslavia Region: Eastern Europe Oldest diocese: Bar (1034) Land mass: 81,376 km² Primary language(s): Serbian Primary religion(s): Orthodox	Population: 10,640,000 Fertility rate: 1.6 Infant mortality per 1,000 births: na Life expectancy: na Literacy rate: na (na est.) GNI per capita (PPP): $ na
Catholics; %: 553,000; 5% Dioceses; all territories: 5; 6 Parishes; pastoral centers: 287; 294 Catholics/parish; /priest: 1,927; 2,041	Baptisms; % infants: 4,957; 90% % infants baptized Catholic (est.): 2% Confirmations: 5,179 Marriages; % both Catholic: 1,651; 90%
Hospitals: 14 Orphanages: 0 Homes for elderly, disabled: 4 Other charitable institutions: 3 Primary schools: 0 Secondary schools: 0 Colleges and universities: 0 Seminaries: 0	Permanent deacons: 7 Seminarians; % diocesan: 51; 90% Diocesan priests: 227 Religious priests; brothers: 44; 6 Women religious: 356 Catechists: 102 Lay missionaries: 0

Zambia Region: East Africa Oldest diocese: Kasama (1913) Land mass: 752,614 km² Primary language(s): English Primary religion(s): Protestant, Islam	Population: 10,720,000 Fertility rate: 6.1 Infant mortality per 1,000 births: 93.7 Life expectancy: 37 Literacy rate: 73 (1990 est.) GNI per capita (PPP): $ 720
Catholics; %: 3,012,000; 28% Dioceses; all territories: 10; 10 Parishes; pastoral centers: 256; 2,362 Catholics/parish; /priest: 11,766; 5,238	Baptisms; % infants: 88,678; 58% % infants baptized Catholic (est.): 7% Confirmations: 18,430 Marriages; % both Catholic: 9,135; 73%
Hospitals: 33 Orphanages: 18 Homes for elderly, disabled: 12 Other charitable institutions: 87 Primary schools: 41 Secondary schools: 47 Colleges and universities: 0 Seminaries: 4	Permanent deacons: 3 Seminarians; % diocesan: 381; 67% Diocesan priests: 240 Religious priests; brothers: 335; 167 Women religious: 1,475 Catechists: 20,170 Lay missionaries: 39

Zimbabwe Region: Southern Africa Oldest diocese: Harare (1927) Land mass: 390,580 km² Primary language(s): English Primary religion(s): Protestant, Indigenous religions	Population: 12,630,000 Fertility rate: 4 Infant mortality per 1,000 births: 61.4 Life expectancy: 39 Literacy rate: 80 (1992 est.) GNI per capita (PPP): $ 2,690
Catholics; %: 1,172,000; 9% Dioceses; all territories: 8; 8 Parishes; pastoral centers: 152; 2,511 Catholics/parish; /priest: 7,711; 2,831	Baptisms; % infants: 38,292; 36% % infants baptized Catholic (est.): 4% Confirmations: 16,611 Marriages; % both Catholic: 4,485; 75%
Hospitals: 42 Orphanages: 8 Homes for elderly, disabled: 13 Other charitable institutions: 114 Primary schools: 72 Secondary schools: 59 Colleges and universities: 0 Seminaries: 3	Permanent deacons: 12 Seminarians; % diocesan: 314; 60% Diocesan priests: 166 Religious priests; brothers: 248; 114 Women religious: 1,095 Catechists: 5,008 Lay missionaries: 10

Bibliography

Books and Articles

Anderson, Charles S. 1967. *Augsburg Historical Atlas of Christianity in the Middle Ages and Reformation.* Minneapolis: Augsburg Publishing House.

Attwater, Donald., ed. 1938. *Orbis Catholicus.* London: Burns, Oates and Washbourne Ltd.

Bamat, Thomas and Jean-Paul Wiest, eds. 1999. *Popular Catholicism in a World Church.* Maryknoll, NY: Orbis Books.

Barrett, David B. 2001. *World Christian Encyclopedia.* New York: Oxford University Press.

Barrett, David B. and Todd M. Johnson. 2001. "Annual Statistical Table on Global Mission: 2001." *International Bulletin of Missionary Research.* Vol. 25, No. 1.

Bendyna, Mary E., RSM and Paul Perl. 2000. *Young Adult Catholics in the Context of Other Catholic Generations: Living with Diversity, Seeking Service, Waiting to be Welcomed.* Washington, DC: Center for Applied Research in the Apostolate.

Bibby, Reginald W. 1995. *The Bibby Report: Social Trends Canadian Style.* Toronto: Stoddart Publishing Company.

Bibby, Reginald W. 1995. *There's Got to Be More! Connecting Churches and Canadians.* Winfield: Wood Lake Books.

Bouma, Gary D., ed. 1996. *Many Religions, All Australian: Religious Settlement, Identity and Cultural Diversity.* Adelaide, South Australia: Open Book Publishers.

Brierley, Peter. 1995. *A Century of British Christianity: Historical Statistics, 1900-1985.* London: MARC Europe.

Bruce, Steven. 1995. *Religion in Modern Britain.* Oxford: Oxford University Press.

Bühlman, Walbert. 1977. *The Coming of the Third Church: An Analysis of the Present and Future of the Church.* Maryknoll, NY: Orbis Books.

Carroll, Bret E. 2000. *The Routledge Historical Atlas of Religion in America.* Routledge: New York.

de Carvalho Azevedo, Marcello, SJ. 1982. "Inculturation and the Challenges of Modernity." In Amy A. Roest Crollius, SJ, *Working Papers on Living Faith and Cultures.* Rome: Pontifical Gregorian University Centre.

Castello-Cortes, Ian, ed. 1996. *World Reference Atlas.* New York: Dorling Kindersley Publishing.

Cook, Guillermo, ed. 1994. *New Face of the Church in Latin America.* Maryknoll, NY: Orbis Books.

Coriden, James A., Thomas J. Green, and Donald E. Heintschel, eds. 1985. *The Code of Canon Law: A Text and Commentary.* New York: Paulist Press.

Davie, Grace. 2000. *Religion in Modern Europe: A Memory Mutates.* New York and Oxford: Oxford University Press.

Delaney, Joan, MM. 2000. "My Pilgrimage in Mission." *International Bulletin of Missionary Research.* Vol. 25, No. 1.

Dixon, Robert E. 1996. *The Catholics in Australia.* Canberra: Australian Government Publishing Service.

Dries, Angelyn, OSF. 1998. *The Missionary Movement in American Catholic History.* Maryknoll, NY: Orbis Books.

Dussel, Enrique, ed. 1992. *The Church in Latin America, 1492-1992.* Maryknoll, NY: Orbis Books.

Finch, Andrew J. 2000. "A Persecuted Church: Roman Catholicism in Early Nineteenth-Century Korea." *Journal of Ecclesiastical History.* Vol. 51, No. 3.

Fletcher, Richard. 1997. *The Barbarian Conversion: From Paganism to Christianity.* Berkeley and Los Angeles: University of California Press.

Froehle, Bryan and Mary Gautier. 2000. *Catholicism USA: A Portrait of the Catholic Church in the United States.* Maryknoll, NY: Orbis Books.

Gannon, Thomas M., SJ, ed. *World Catholicism in Transition*, New York and London: Macmillan Publishing Co., 1988.

Gareffa, Peter M. et al., 2001. *The New Catholic Encyclopedia: Jubilee Volume, The Wojtyla Years.* Washington, DC: Gale Group.

Garrard-Burnett, Virginia and David Stoll. 1993. *Rethinking Protestantism in Latin America.* Philadelphia: Temple University Press.

Gill, Anthony. 1998. *Rendering unto Caesar: The Catholic Church and the State in Latin America.* Chicago and London: The University of Chicago Press.

Hanson, Eric O. 1987. *The Catholic Church in World Politics.* Princeton, NJ: Princeton University Press.

Harris, Joseph Claude. 2002. "The Future Church." *America.* Vol. 186, No. 9.

Hastings, Adrian, ed. 1959. *The Church and the Nations: A Study of Minority Catholicism in England, India, Norway, America, Lebanon, Australia, Wales, Japan, the Netherlands, Vietnam, Brazil, Egypt, Southern Africa and among the Lele of the Congo.* New York and London: Sheed and Ward.

Haub, Carl. 1995, "How Many People Have Ever Lived on Earth?" *Population Today.* February, p. 5.

Haupt, Arthur and Thomas T. Kane. 1998. *Population Handbook.* Washington, DC: Population Reference Bureau.

Hezel, Francis X., SJ. 1991. Culture in Crisis: Trends in the Church and Society in the Pacific. Diocese of Caroline Islands Home Page. http://www.diocesecarolines.org/culture.html (viewed February 7, 2002).

Hsia, R. Po-Chia. 1998. *The World of Catholic Renewal 1540-1770.* Cambridge: Cambridge University Press.

Hughes, Philip J. 1997. *Religion in Australia: Facts and Figures.* Kew: The Christian Research Association.

Hughes, Philip, Gary D. Bouma, Rohan Pryor, and Craig Thompson. 1997. *Believe It or Not: Australian Spirituality and the Churches in the 90s.* Kew: The Christian Research Association.

Hughes, Philip J. and 'Tricia Blombery. 1990. *Patterns of Faith in Australian Churches.* Hawthorn: The Christian Research Association.

Hupchick, Dennis P. and Harold E. Cox. 2001. *The Palgrave Concise Historical Atlas of the Balkans*. New York: Palgrave.

Hupchick, Dennis P. and Harold E. Cox. 2001. *The Palgrave Concise Historical Atlas of Eastern Europe*. New York: Palgrave.

Ireland, Rowan. 1991. *Kingdoms Come: Religion and Politics in Brazil*. Pittsburgh: University of Pittsburgh Press.

Jenkins, Philip. 2002. *The Next Christendom: The Coming of Global Christianity*. New York and Oxford: Oxford University Press.

Kaldor, Peter, et al. 1994. *Winds of Change: The Experience of Church in a Changing Australia*. Australia: Anzea Publishers.

Kaldor, Peter, et al. 1995. *Mission under the Microscope: Keys to Effective and Sustainable Mission*. Adelaide, Australia: Openbook Publishers.

Kaldor, Peter, et al. 1997. *Shaping a Future: Characteristics of Vital Congregations*. Adelaide, Australia: Openbook Publishers.

Kaldor, Peter, et al. 1999. *Taking Stock: A Profile of Australian Church Attenders*. Adelaide, Australia: Openbook Publishers.

Kerhofs, Jan, ed. 1995. *Europe without Priests*. London: SCM Press.

Kosmin, Barry A. 1998. "A Religious Question in the British Census?" *Patterns of Prejudice*. Vol. 32, No. 2: 39-46.

Kroeger, James H. 2001. "A Continuing Pentecost: Appreciating 'Ecclesia in Asia'." *Review for Religious*. Vol. 60, No. 1.

Lacko, Michael, SJ. 1963. *Atlas Hierarchicus Ecclesiae Catholicae Orientalis*. Second edition. Rome: Pontificum Institutum Orientalorum Studiorum.

van Leeuwen, Arend. 1964. *Christianity in the World*. New York: Charles Scribner's Sons.

Levine, Daniel H., ed. 1980. *Churches and Politics in Latin America*. Beverly Hills and London: Sage Publications.

Littell, Franklin H. 2001. *Historical Atlas of Christianity*. New York: Continuum Publishing Group.

Llobera, Joseph P. 1994. *The God of Modernity: The Development of Nationalism in Western Europe*. Oxford and Providence: Berg.

Lye, Keith. 1997. *The Portable World Factbook*. New York: Avon Books.

McBrien, Richard P. 1995. *The Harper Collins Encyclopedia of Catholicism*. New York: Harper San Francisco.

McEvedy, Colin and Richard Jones. 1978. *Atlas of World Population History*. New York: Facts on File, Inc.

Miller, Donald E. 2001. "Emergent Patterns of Christian Leadership: Lessons from the Developing World." Unpublished paper, University of Southern California.

Misztal, Bronislaw and Anson Shupe, eds. 1992. *Religion and Politics in Comparative Perspective: Revival of Religious Fundamentalism in East and West*. Westport, CT and London: Praeger.

Monsma, Stephen V. and J. Christopher Soper. 1997. *The Challenge of Pluralism: Church and State in Five Democracies*. Lanham and New York: Rowman & Littlefield Publishers, Inc.

New Zealand Catholic Bishops' Conference. 1998. *Federation of Catholic Bishops' Conferences of Oceania: Directory 1998.* Wellington: New Zealand Catholic Bishops' Conference.

O' Brien, Joanne and Martin Palmer. 1993. *The State of Religion Atlas.* New York and London: Simon & Schuster.

Parker, Geoffrey. 1997. *Compact Atlas of World History.* New York: Random House.

Population Reference Bureau. 1998. *Population Handbook. Fourth edition.* New York: Population Reference Bureau.

Putnam, Robert D. 2000. *Bowling Alone: The Collapse and Revival of American Community.* New York and London: Simon & Schuster.

Reid, T.R. 2001. "Hollow Halls in Europe's Churches." *The Washington Post.* Vol. 124, No. 152.

Roberson, Ronald, CSP. 1999. *The Eastern Christian Churches.* Rome: Edizioni Orientalia Christiana.

Roof, Wade Clark, Jackson W. Carroll, and David A. Roozen, eds. 1995. *The Post-War Generation and Establishment Religion: Cross-Cultural Perspectives.* Boulder: Westview Press.

Secretaria Status. 1716 to present (annual series). *Annuario Pontificio.* Vatican City: Libreria Editrice Vaticana.

Secretaria Status. 1970 to present (annual series). *Annuarium Statisticum Ecclesiae* (Statistical Yearbook of the Church). Vatican City: Typis Polyglottis Vaticanis.

Secretaria Status. 1969. *Tabularum Statisticarum Collectio.* Vatican City: Typis Polyglottis Vaticanis.

Smith, Christian and Joshua Prokopy, eds. 1997. *Latin American Religion in Motion.* New York and London: Routledge.

Smith, Dan. 1997. *The State of War and Peace Atlas.* New York and London: Penguin Reference.

Smith, Dan. 1999. *The State of the World Atlas.* New York and London: Penguin Reference.

Society for the Propagation of the Faith. 1926. *Little Atlas of Catholic Missions.* Rome: Society for the Propagation of the Faith.

Stoll, David. 1990. *Is Latin America Turning Protestant? The Politics of Evangelical Growth.* Berkeley and Los Angeles: University of California Press.

Streit, F.C. 1929. *Catholic World Atlas: Containing a Geographic and Statistical Description with Maps of the Holy Roman Catholic Church, with Historical and Ethnographic Notices.* Second edition. Paderborn, Germany: St. Boniface Press.

Swatos, William H., Jr., ed. 1989. *Religious Politics in Global and Comparative Perspective.* New York and Westport, CT: Greenwood Press.

Swatos, William H., Jr., ed. 1994. *Politics and Religion in Central and Eastern Europe: Traditions and Transitions.* London and Westport, CT: Praeger.

Tipografia Poliglotta Vaticana. 1969. *Raccolta Di Tavole Statistiche.* Vatican City: Tipografia Poliglotta Vaticana.

United Nations. 1973. *The Determinants and Consequences of Population Trends.* Population Studies. No. 50, p. 10.

United Nations Development Program. 1995. *Human Development Report 1995.* New York and Oxford: Oxford University Press.

United Nations Development Program. 2001. *Human Development Report 2001: Making New Technologies Work for Human Development.* New York and Oxford: Oxford University Press.

United States Department of Commerce, Bureau of the Census. 1994. *World Population Profile: 1994.* Washington: United States Government Printing Office.

Walton, Robert C. 1986. *Chronological and Background Charts of Church History.* Grand Rapids: The Zondervan Corporation.

The World Bank. 2000. *World Development Report 2000/2001: Attacking Poverty.* New York and Oxford: Oxford University Press.

Selected Websites

Adherents
www.adherents.org
Statistics on adherents to various religions worldwide.

Canada
www.catholicanada.com
Guide to the Church in Canada.

Holy See
www.vatican.va
The official website of the Vatican.

Ireland
www.catholiccommunciations.ie
The Catholic Communications Office for the Church in Ireland, with links to dioceses, liturgical calendar, statistics, and other sites pertaining to the Church in Ireland.

Ireland
www.irishcatholic.net
General guide to the Catholic Church in Ireland.

United States
www.catholic-usa.com
Comprehensive listing of Catholic institutions (dioceses, parishes, schools, religious orders) nationwide.

United States–Bishops' Conference
www.usccb.org
Contact information for bishops nationwide, as well as links to all dioceses whose bishops belong to the United States Conference of Catholic Bishops (USCCB).

United States–Catholic Colleges and Universities
www.accunet.org
The Association of Catholic Colleges and Universities in the United States.

United States–Catholic Education
www.ncea.org
National Catholic Educational Association. Provides information on Catholic educational institutions and programs in the United States.

World–Catholic Dioceses
www.catholicgoldmine.com
Links to dioceses worldwide (in native language), as well as resources on liturgy, prayer, music.

World–Catholic Hierarchy
www.catholic-hierarchy.org
Current and historical information about dioceses and Church personnel worldwide.

World–Catholic Information
www.fides.org
Agenzia Fides is a collection of Catholic news services based in Rome. Available in English, Spanish, French, Italian, German, Portuguese, and Chinese.

World–Catholic Universities
www.fiuc.org
Provided by the International Federation of Catholic Universities (IFCU). Contains statistics, lists of members, and other information on Catholic higher education worldwide.

World–Country Information
www.state.gov
Provides country background notes, as well as lists of State Department and international organization programs and missions overseas.

World–Country Information
www.cia.gov/cia/publications/factbook/index.html
The United States Central Intelligence Agency's World Factbook for 2001 lists country and territory histories and statistics for the year 2000.

World–Demographics
www.prb.org
The Population Reference Bureau provides statistics on world demography, printed resources, and websites on the subject.

World–Demographics
"World Population from Year 0 to Stabilization"
http://www.flash.net/~hoselton/worldpop/worldpop.htm

World–Demographics
www.census.gov/ipc/www/worldpop.html
The total midyear population for the world: 1950-2000, data updated in 1996 as maintained by the United States Bureau of the Census.

INDEX

abbeys, 110

Africa: baptisms in, 8, 46; confirmations in, 8; French mission and, 108; growth of the number of nations in, 3; institutions in, 20, 22, 47–49; Latin America compared with, 70–71; marriage in, 9, 47; overview of regions of, 50–51; pastoral centers in, 17; percentage of population that is Catholic in, 6; personnel in, 49–50; population of, 2, 4, 8, 45–46; priests in, 32, 34, 35, 36, 89; relation of number of Catholics to number of parishes in, 22; seminarians in, 34, 35–36, 136; summary of the Church in, 127–28; women religious in, 42–43. *See also* Central Africa; East Africa; Indian Ocean islands; North Africa; Southern Africa; West Africa

African Americans, 78

AIDS, 58, 63–64, 127–28

Algeria, 53

Americas, the: baptisms in, 8; Catholic population in, 71–72; Catholics per bishop in, 30; charitable institutions in, 19; comparison of the proportion of world Catholic population in Europe and, 6; deacons in, 40; dioceses in, 23; educational institutions in, 17–18; eparchies in, 15; future of Catholic population in, 8; institutions in, 25, 72–73; men religious in, 41; number of Catholics per school in, 23; overview of Catholicism in, 67–71; overview of regions of, 74–75; percentage of countries in which Catholics are a majority in, 7; percentage of population that is Catholic in, 6; personnel in, 73–74; priests in, 36, 37–38, 89; proportion of world Catholic population in, 5–6; relation of number of Catholics to number of parishes in, 23; theological schools in, 18; women

religious in, 42, 43. *See also* Caribbean, the; Mesoamerica; North America; South America

Angola, 60

apostolic movements, 20-21

archbishops, 30

archdioceses, 15, 29–30

Argentina, 83

Armenia, 92

Asia: Catholic population in, 4, 5, 8, 86–87; charitable institutions in, 19-20; Church personnel in, 88–89; diocesan priests per diocesan seminarians in, 36; eparchies in, 15; French mission and, 108; institutions in, 24–25, 87–88; mixed marriages in, 9; overview of Catholicism in, 85–86, 128; overview of regions of, 89–90; pastoral centers in, 17; percentage of population that is Catholic in, 6; population growth in, 2–3; priests in, 34–35, 36; seminarians in, 35–36, 136; women religious in, 42, 43, 119. *See also* Northeast Asia; South Asia; Southeast Asia; Western Asia

atheism, 112, 113

Augustine, St., 52

Augustinian Recollects, 126

Australia, 117, 118, 119, 120, 122–23

Austria, 107

auxiliary bishops, 30

Baltimore, 77

baptisms: in Africa, 46; in the Americas, 71–72; in Asia, 86, 87; in Brazil and Mexico, 84; in the Congo, 57; current number of, in relation to births worldwide, 7–8; in Europe, 37, 102; in Kenya, 63; in Latin America, 69; number of, on various continents, 8; in Oceania, 117; trends in ordinations and, 36–37

Barrett, David, 69

Belgium, 107, 108
Belize, 80
bishops: dioceses and, 13; educational and charitable institutions' relation to, 14; overview of distribution of, 29–30; parishes and, 13
Brazil, 69, 84, 110
brothers. *See* men religious
Buddhism, 96

Canada, 76–77
Cape Verde, 54
cardinals, 30
Caribbean, the, 78–80, 128
Carroll, John, 77
catechists: in Angola, 60; in Australia, 122; in the Dominican Republic, 79; in France, 108; in Japan, 97; in Kenya, 63; in Mexico, 81; in South Korea, 96–97; in Sri Lanka, 93; in Wallis and Futuna, 125
Central Africa: Catholic institutions in, 23–24; Catholic population in, 51; overall statistics on the Church in, 56–58; priests in, 33
Central America. *See* Mesoamerica
Chad, 132
charitable institutions: in Africa, 49; in the Americas, 25; in Asia, 26; in the Congo, 58; dioceses' relation to, 14; in Europe, 26, 103; in Kenya, 63; in Nigeria, 55; in North America, 76; in Oceania, 118; overview of types of, 18–19; relative installed capacity of, 22. *See also specific institutions*
Chile, 83
China, 86–87, 98
colonialism, 52, 56–57, 62
communism, 101, 102, 112–13
confirmations, 8
Congo, the. *See* Democratic Republic of the Congo
Constantine, 109
Coptic Catholic Church, the, 53
Cortes, Hernando, 80
councils, ecumenical, 29–30

countries: growth of the number of, 3
Cursillos de Cristiandad, 21
Czech Republic, the, 113

deacons: in Asia, 89; comparison of, in poor and rich nations, 131; in Europe, 105; in Oceania, 119; in Southern Africa, 58–59; in the United States, 105; Vatican II and, 28; worldwide distribution of, 38–41
Democratic Republic of the Congo, 57-58
diocesan priests: in Africa, 32, 50; in the Americas, 73; in Asia, 88–89; comparison of, in poor and rich nations, 131; in the Dominican Republic, 79; in East Africa, 62; in Europe, 104; in Guatemala, 81; in Italy, 111; in Mexico, 80; need for caution on data related to, 28; in Nigeria, 55; in North America, 75; in Northwestern Europe, 107; number of diocesan seminarians in relation to, 36; numbers of, since 1950, 31; in Oceania, 118–19; religious priests compared with, 31; in Rome, 111; in South America, 82; in Southeast Asia, 95; in Southern Africa, 58; in Sri Lanka, 93; in West Africa, 54
dioceses: in Africa, 45, 46, 47; in the Americas, 25, 72; in Asia, 87; in Australia, 123; in Brazil, 84, 110; in the Dominican Republic, 79; in East Africa, 62; ecclesiastical territories and, 15; in England, 107; in France, 108; future distribution of bishops and, 29–30; in Italy, 103, 110; as the key institution in Catholic life worldwide, 13; in Madagascar, 61; in New Zealand, 123; in North Africa, 52; in Oceania, 116, 117; in the Philippines, 95; relation to various apostolic structures, 15; in Scandinavia, 15, 107–8; in South Africa, 59; South American, compared with European, 82; in the United States, 110; in West Africa, 53

Divine Word missionaries, 121, 124

Dominican Republic, the, 79

East Africa: Catholic institutions in, 23–24; Catholic population in, 51; overall statistics on the Church in, 61–64

Eastern Churches: in Asia, 87; the diaconate in, 39; growth patterns in, 15; institutional structures and, 15; in the United States, 78

Eastern Europe, 26, 106, 111–13

Eastern Rites, 15

East Timor, 94, 96

ecclesiastical territories: in Africa, 23, 47; in Asia, 24–25, 87; in Australia, 123; in Brazil, 84, 110; composite portrait of, in the Americas, 25; in East Africa, 62; growth of, 14–15; in Italy, 110; in North Africa, 52; in Oceania, 116, 117; South American, compared with European, 82. *See also specific types of territories*

educational institutions: in Africa, 23, 48; in the Americas, 25, 72–73; in Asia, 26; dioceses' relation to, 14; in Europe, 26; in Oceania, 26; worldwide distribution of, 17–18. *See also specific types of institutions*

Egypt, 53

elementary/primary schools: in Africa, 48; in Australia, 122; in Canada, 77; in the Congo, 58; in Europe, 103; in Kenya, 63; in Nigeria, 55; in Oceania, 117; in Wallis and Futuna, 125. *See also* educational institutions; schools

eparchies: geographical distribution, 15; in North America, 78; in Oceania, 117

Eritrea, 62–63

Ethiopia, 62

Europe: African population growth compared with that in, 2; Asian dioceses compared with those in, 87; baptisms in, 8, 37; Catholic population growth in, 4; Church personnel in, 104–5; comparison of the proportion of world Catholic population in the Americas and, 6; confirmations in, 8; deacons in, 40; decline in its share of world population, 3; eparchies in, 15; institutions in, 17–18, 19, 20, 26, 103–4; men religious in, 41; number of Catholics per school in, 23; ordinations in, 36–37; overview of Catholicism in, 101–2; overview of regions of, 105–7; percentage of countries in which Catholics are a majority, 7; percentage of population that is Catholic in, 6; pluralism and, 132–33; priests in, 31, 32, 36, 37–38, 89; proportion of world Catholic population in, 4–5; relation of number of Catholics to number of parishes in, 23; seminarians in, 37, 38; sizes of dioceses in, 23; South America compared with, 81–82; summary of the Church in, 129; women religious in, 42, 43. *See also* Eastern Europe; Northwestern Europe; Southwestern Europe

evangelical Christianity, 69–70, 80, 96, 128–29

fertility rates, 101

Fiji, 118

France, 107, 108

Franciscans, 77

French Polynesia, 119

French Revolution, the, 108

Futuna, 125

Germany, 101

Greenland, 74–75

Guam, 125–26

Guatemala, 80, 81

Henry VIII, King, 107

homes for the elderly, 49, 58, 103

homes for the handicapped, 49, 103

Hong Kong, 98–99

hospitals: in Africa, 49; in Central Asia, 92; in the Congo, 58; in Europe, 103; in Kenya, 63; in Nigeria, 55

India, 19, 93–94
Indian Ocean islands, 60–61
installed capacity, 21–23, 131
institutions, Catholic: in Africa, 47–49; in the Americas, 72–73; in Asia, 87–88; composite regional portraits of, 23–25; in the Congo, 58; contrasting relative installed capacity of, 21–23; in Europe, 103–4; in Italy, 110; in Oceania, 117–18; overview of distribution and growth of, 13–22; in Rome, 111; in West Africa, 54. *See also* charitable institutions; educational institutions; elementary/ primary schools; hospitals; orphanages; schools; secondary schools
Ireland, 107, 108–9
Islam: in Africa, 52, 128; in Asia, 128; in Central Asia, 92; and Christianity in the Middle East, 87; in East Africa, 62; in the Indian Ocean islands, 61; in Nigeria, 55; in the Sudan, 63
Islamic Republic of the Comorros, 61
Israel, 91
Italy, 101, 103, 109–10

Japan, 97–98
Jesuits, 77, 93, 98, 126
John Paul II, Pope, 30
Josephites, 122

Kazakhstan, 92
Kenya, 63
Kiribati, 121

laity, the, 28–29. See also deacons; lay brothers
land mass, 2–3
Latin America: Africa compared with, 70–71; mixed populations in, 68; Protestantism in, 69–70; seminarians in, 136; summary of the Church in, 128–29; women religious in, 43. *See also* Americas, the
Latin Rite, the, 15
lay brothers, 41

Lebanon, 53, 92
Legion of Mary, the, 21
Lesser Antilles, the, 79–80
Libya, 53
Liechtenstein, 107
Louisiana, 77
Luxembourg, 107

Macau, 98–99
Madagascar, 61
Malawi, 63
Mao Zedong, 98
Marianas, the, 126
Marist missionaries, 121
Maronite Church, the, 87, 92
marriage: in Africa, 47; in the Americas, 71; in Asia, 87; in Europe, 102; mixed, 8–9; in Nigeria, 55–56; in Oceania, 117; and the worldwide distribution of Catholics, 9
Mass attendance: in Australia, 122; in Canada, 77; in France, 108; in Ireland, 109; in New Zealand, 123; in North America, 78; in Spain, 111
men religious: in Africa, 46; in China, 98; comparison of, in poor and rich nations, 131; in Europe, 104; in France, 108; in India, 94; in the Indian Ocean islands, 60; in Japan, 97; in South Korea, 96; the Spanish Civil War and, 111; in Wallis and Futuna, 125; worldwide distribution of, 41
Mesoamerica, 80–81, 128. *See also specific nations and regions*
Mexico, 80–81, 84
Micronesia, 119
Middle East, the. *See* Western Asia
mission: in Africa, 24, 47; in East Africa, 62; France and, 108; growth and deterioration of, 16–17; history of institutions related to, 16; in the Indian Ocean islands, 60–61; Ireland and, 109; in North America, 77; in Oceania, 121; in Papua New Guinea, 124; resident priests and, 16
Missionaries of Charity, 19, 94

mixed marriages, 8–9
Monaco, 107
Mongolia, 97
Morocco, 53

native peoples, 77
Netherlands, the, 108
New Caledonia, 118
New Orleans, 76
New Zealand, 117, 118, 122, 123–24
Nigeria, 54
North Africa, 52–53
North America: composite portrait of institutions in, 25; deacons in, 40–41; overview of Catholicism in, 75–78; women religious in, 43. *See also specific nations and regions*
Northeast Asia, 96–99
Northern Ireland, 108–9
North Korea, 98
Northwestern Europe, 26, 40–41, 106, 107–9

Oceania: baptism and marriage in, 117; Catholic population of, 116–17; Catholics per bishop in, 30; eparchies in, 15; French mission and, 108; institutions in, 26, 117–18; number of Catholics per school in, 23; number of priests in, 32, 36; overview of Catholicism in, 115–16, 129; overview of regions of, 120–21; percentage of population that is Catholic in, 6–7; women religious in, 42, 43
ordinations: in Africa, 50; in the Americas, 73; in Asia, 88–89; in Europe, 38; in France, 108; in Oceania, 119; in Poland, 112; relative to distribution of priests, 36; in West Africa, 53–54; worldwide trends in, 36–38
orphanages, 49, 58, 103
Orthodox Christianity, 106, 107

Palestinian Territory, the, 91
Panama, 80
Papua New Guinea, 117-18, 121, 124-25

parishes: in Africa, 23, 24, 46, 47–48; in the Americas, 25, 72; in Asia, 87; in Brazil, 84; comparison of distribution of Catholics in, 23; deacons and, 40–41; defined, 13, 17; in the Dominican Republic, 79; in Europe, 26, 102; in Latin America, 128; in Madagascar, 61; in Mexico, 81; in New Zealand, 123; in Nigeria, 55; in North Africa, 52; in North America, 76; in Poland, 112; relative installed capacity of, 22–23; relative sizes of, 24-25; in South Africa, 59; South American, compared with European, 82
pastoral centers, 17
patriarchates, 15
permanent deacons. *See* deacons
personnel, Church: in Africa, 49–50; in the Americas, 73–74; in Asia, 88–89; bishops as, 29–30; comparison of, in poor and rich nations, 131; composite global portrait of, 43–44; in Europe, 104–5; men religious as, 41; in Oceania, 118–20; permanent deacons as, 38–41; priests as, 31–35; recent patterns of change in, 27–29; seminarians as, 35–38; women religious as, 42–43
Philippines, the, 94, 95–96
Pius IX, Pope, 109
pluralism, 131–33
Poland, 111–12, 113
population, Catholic: African, 45–46; in the Americas, 68–69, 71–72; Asian, 86–87; Brazilian and Mexican, 84; Central African, 56; Chinese, 98; current dynamics within, 7–9; in the Dominican Republic, 79; East African, 61; European, 101–3; global portrait of the distribution of, 9–11; on the Indian Ocean islands, 60; Nigerian, 55; North African, 52; North American, 75; Oceania's, 116–17; patterns of worldwide growth of, 1–7; South African, 59; South American, 81; South Asian, 93; Southern Afri-

can, 58; Ugandan, 63; West African, 53; Western Asian, 91
Portugal, 109, 111
poverty, 129–31
prefectures, 14
prelatures, 14
priests: in Africa, 49–50; in the Americas, 73; in Angola, 60; in Asia, 88, 89; in Asian Russia, 97; in Australia, 122; in China, 98; in the Congo, 58; in the Dominican Republic, 79; in East Africa, 61–62; in East Timor, 96; in Ethiopia, 62; in Europe, 104; examples of care needed regarding data about, 28; in France, 108; in Guam, 126; in Guatemala, 81; in India, 94; in the Indian Ocean islands, 60; in Italy, 111; in Japan, 97; in Kenya, 63; in Madagascar, 61; in Mexico, 80; in the Middle East, 92; in Nigeria, 55; in North Africa, 52–53; in North America, 75, 76; in Northwestern Europe, 107; number of seminarians and ordinations in relation to, 35–38; in Oceania, 118–19; patterns of distribution of ordination and, 36–38; in Poland, 112; in Rome, 111; in South Africa, 59; South American, compared with European, 82; in Southeast Asia, 95; in Southern Africa, 58; in South Korea, 96; in Sri Lanka, 93; in Wallis and Futuna, 125; in West Africa, 53–54; worldwide growth and distribution of, 31–35, 133
primary schools. *See* elementary/primary schools
Propaganda Fide, 14
Protestantism, 59–60, 69, 85, 95, 96

Qatar, 92
Quebec, 76, 77

Reformation, the, 108
religious institutes, 19–20. *See also* *specific institutes*
religious priests: in Africa, 32, 50; diocesan priests compared with, 31; in Oceania, 119; need for caution on data related to, 28; numbers of, since 1950, 31. *See also* priests
renewal movements, 21
Reunion (island), 60, 61
Rome, 111
Russia, 97

Sacred Heart missionaries, 121
Samoa, 119, 122
Scandinavia, 14–15, 107–8
schools: in Africa, 48; in Australia, 123; in Ethiopia, 62; in New Zealand, 123; in North America, 76; in Oceania, 26, 117; relation of number of Catholics to number of, 22-23. *See also* educational institutions; elementary/primary schools; secondary schools; universities
secondary schools: in Canada, 77; in the Congo, 58; in Europe, 103; in Kenya, 63; in Nigeria, 55; in Oceania, 117; in Wallis and Futuna, 125
secular institutes, 21
seminarians: in Africa, 34, 50, 136; in the Americas, 73; in Asia, 34–35, 88, 136; in East Africa, 62; in Europe, 37, 38; in Latin America, 136; in Nigeria, 55; in Oceania, 118, 119; overview of worldwide distribution of, 35–36
Seychelles island chain, 60
sisters. *See* women religious
Sisters of Mercy, 122
Sisters of St. Joseph, 122
South Africa, 58–59
South America: composite portrait of institutions in, 25-26; overview of Catholicism in, 81–84; parishes in, 128; priests in, 49. *See also specific nations and regions*
South Asia, 93–94
Southeast Asia, 94–96
Southern Africa, 33, 58–60
Southern Cone of South America, the, 83–84

Southern Europe, 40
South Korea, 96–97
Southwestern Europe, 106, 109–11
Spain, 109, 111
Spanish Civil War, the, 111
Sri Lanka, 93
Sudan, 63
Switzerland, 107, 108
Syro-Malabar Church, the, 87

Tanzania, 63
territorial abbacies, 16
theological schools, 18. *See also* seminarians; universities, Catholic
Theresa, Mother, 19, 94
Tobago, 80
Trinidad, 80
Tunisia, 53

Uganda, 63–64
United Arab Emirates, 92
United Kingdom, the, 107
United Nations, the, 3
United States, the: dioceses in, 110; Eastern Catholic Churches in, 78; history of Catholicism in, 77; non-European influences on the Church in, 78; pluralism and, 132; theological schools in, 18; women religious in, 88. *See also* Americas, the; North America
universities, Catholic: in Europe, 17-18; in Oceania, 118; patterns of creation of, 18-19; in Rome, 111. *See also* seminarians
Uruguay, 83, 84

Vanuatu, 118
Vatican City, 109–10
Vatican II, 27, 28, 29
vicariates, 14
vocations, 55

Wallis, 125
wealth, 129–31
West Africa, 53–56
Western Africa, 33, 34
Western Asia, 90–92
women religious: in Africa, 46, 49; in the Americas, 73–74; in Asia, 88; in Australia, 122, 125; in China, 98; comparison of, in poor and rich nations, 131; in the Congo, 58; in the Dominican Republic, 79; in Europe, 104; in France, 108; in India, 94; in the Indian Ocean islands, 60; in Italy, 111; in Japan, 97–98; in Kenya, 63; in Madagascar, 61; in North America, 76; in Oceania, 119; in South Africa, 59; South American, compared with European, 82; in Southern Africa, 58; in South Korea, 96; the Spanish Civil War and, 111; in Wallis and Futuna, 125; in West Africa, 53, 54; worldwide distribution of, 42–43

Yugoslavia, 102

Zambia, 63